Carrying Existence Forward is a milestone in the array of books aimed at practical, research-based, and depth-oriented existential-humanistic practice. Drawing on the person-centered, experiential, and existential-humanistic literature, along with very convincing data regarding the necessity of therapists' comfort level with the deeper questions about life, Vanhooren has gifted us with a volume that is of great value to clinicians, researchers, and trainees. In sum, by lucidly exploring the primal anxieties of living, Vanhooren methodically illustrates how an *existential-experiential approach* to therapy is necessary for many clients not merely to cope, but to attain an awe-informed experience of life. This is life-changing therapy at its best, and it is high time that it be prioritized—not only for the welfare of individuals but for the society upon which all of us inter-depend.

Kirk J. Schneider, PhD, President,
Existential-Humanistic Institute, USA

This is a lovely book—wise, heartfelt, and moving, refreshingly down-to-earth and free of obscure philosophy and jargon. Vanhooren makes a convincing case for an experiential-existential psychotherapy within the family of person-centered-experiential psychotherapies, providing clear connections to person-centered, focusing-oriented, and emotion-focused therapies, all of which I believe to be completely compatible with the author's approach. This approach is illustrated with a series of well-chosen, unusual, and fascinating case studies, including clients in prison, grappling with mortality and meaninglessness, and in spiritual crisis. I was particularly taken by the emphasis on the spiritual aspects of the author's existential approach as well as his familiarity with wider issues, such as attachment theory, evidence-based practice, emotion regulation, endings in therapy, and the role of inspiration in humanistic-experiential psychotherapies. I found *Carrying Existence Forward* to be an inspiring and useful read!

Prof. Dr. Robert Elliott, University of Strathclyde, Scotland, UK

Siebrecht Vanhooren is one of the most innovative, creative, and exciting new voices in the field of psychotherapy. In *Carrying Existence Forward,* he shows how existential insights and practices can be integrated into a deeply relational and healing therapeutic encounter. Illustrated throughout with vivid and engaging case examples, this book will be invaluable reading for person-centered and experiential psychotherapists and counselors seeking to expand and deepen their practice, as well as for integrative and pluralistic therapists who wish to support clients wrestling with fundamental questions of being.

Prof. Dr. Mick Cooper, Professor of Counseling Psychology, University of Roehampton, London, UK

I love this clear, thorough, well-written explanation of existential theory and psychotherapy. It is an important addition to the literature and will stimulate hours of contemplation about living, death, and meaning. I most highly recommend it for people at every level who want to immerse themselves in deep introspection to help them live more authentically.

Prof. Dr. Clara Hill, Professor of Counseling Psychology and Psychotherapy Research, University of Maryland, USA

Carrying Existence Forward is a beautifully written, deeply human book and the first Introductory text describing the *experiential-existential approach* to psychotherapy. With warmth, clarity, and depth, Vanhooren offers not theory at a distance but wisdom forged in the consulting room—where meaning, suffering, and growth are encountered bodily, moment by moment. Rich in clinical detail and experiential insight, this quietly powerful book does not simply describe an approach—it embodies one. An essential guide for therapists and students who value working at the level where "evidence" is based upon life as it is actually being lived.

Dr. Greg Madison, Psychologist and Focusing-Oriented and Experiential-Existential Psychotherapy Trainer, London Focusing Institute, UK

For those who wish to meet their clients on a deep existential level and to remain grounded in what emerges within that encounter, this book is a *must*-read and a rich source of knowledge. It will resonate both with experienced practitioners and with those who are new to humanistic and existential approaches. In these turbulent times, when many therapeutic modalities increasingly engage with the existential dimensions of life, the material thoughtfully presented by the author invites the reader to immerse themselves in both the theory and the lived practice of experiential-existential therapy.

Yana Gololob, Psychologist and Person-Centered Psychotherapy Trainer at the Ukrainian Psychotherapy University, Kiev, Ukraine, and Board Member of PCE World Association for Person-Centered and Experiential Psychotherapy

I was utterly mesmerized by Dr. Vanhooren's work. It is a rare gift to find a writer who can translate difficult and abstract existential concepts into such a humane and accessible narrative. Reading this work felt like a true re-awakening—as if I were discovering these profound truths for the first time. The professional community will be significantly enriched by this contribution, and I fully intend to make it a foundational text for my students. A vital, masterful, and deeply moving work.

Dr. Katerina Zymnis, Existential Psychotherapy Trainer at Gignesthai, the Hellenic Association for Existential Psychology and at the American College of Greece, Athens, Greece

Carrying Existence Forward:

Introducing
Experiential–Existential Psychotherapy

Siebrecht Vanhooren

Colorado Springs, CO
www.universityprofessorspress.com

Carrying Existence Forward: Introducing Experiential–Existential Psychotherapy
By Siebrecht Vanhooren

First published in 2026, University Professors Press.

Hardcover ISBN: 978-1-955737-71-5
Paperback ISBN: 978-1-955737-72-2
ebook ISBN: 978-1-955737-73-9

University Professors Press
Colorado Springs, CO
www.universityprofessorspress.com

Cover Design by Laura Ross
Cover Image by Siebrecht Vanhooren

Translated from *Op de bodem: Existentiële thema's in psychotherapie en begeleiding* by Siebrecht Vanhooren. Translated by the author. Original Belgium version published by Pelckmans in 2023. Translated and published with permission from Pelckmans.

Table of Contents

Introduction: There is Nothing Beyond Existence i

Chapter 1. Existential Awareness 1

Chapter 2. Existential Concerns, Processes, and Dynamics 19
- Death and Life 24
- Meaninglessness and Meaning 42
- Isolation and Connectedness 59
- Freedom, Choice, and Responsibility 75

Chapter 3. On Existential Suffering and Growing 96
- Relating to Existence 99
- Existential Transdiagnostic Suffering 102
- Getting Stuck at the Bottom of Living 106
- Growth and Basic Trust 117

Chapter 4. A Therapeutic Process 123
- Not Our First Journey Ever 128
- First Stage: Searching for Authentic Contact 135
- Second Stage: Death, Meaninglessness, and Responsibility 154
- Third Stage: Living the Full Life 170
- Saying Goodbye, Over and Over Again 188

Chapter 5. Some Encouragement from a Fellow Traveler 194

References 199
Index 219
Author Bio and Websites 223

Introduction:
There is Nothing Beyond Existence

"Therapy is of the essence of life, and is to be so understood"
(Rogers, 1951, p. x).

A while ago I was wondering if psychological suffering is not always a problem of living. After all, what else would we suffer from since everything we experience in this life is life itself? The same applies to our joys, of course. When we are enjoying the moment, no matter how basic or sophisticated, we are enjoying existence. When watching the sunset, the endless ocean, or the stars, we are savoring not only ourselves in that very moment but also something of this existence that goes beyond us. We might be filled with awe and wonder. Whether we are talking about the weather, sharing our deepest secrets, or enjoying a cup of coffee, we are always expressing our existence in some way. At the same time, while having that coffee, we ourselves are an expression of the existence that was before us and will be beyond us. It is existence from the kitchen table to the far ends of our galaxy that we are living. Each of us is a particular expression of life. There is nothing beyond existence, and yet we are only rarely aware of this. Despite its power and its clarity, this truth is hidden from us most of the time, as the medieval Jewish philosopher Maimonides already told us (Heschel, 2011b). Or as Rank puts it, we are not only masters in denying our mortality but also the very fact that we are living this existence right now (Kramer, 2019).

When we fear darkness, a spider, or climate change, we are essentially concerned about our *being*, the beingness of others, and about life as such. In our fear, we taste the fragility of our own existence and the fact that it will be over one day. This fear of *non-being* can also be sensed when we experience a loss of meaning, when we experience a rupture in our intimate or work relationships, or when we sense a loss of connection with ourselves (Tillich, 2000). Reversely, deep joy could be understood as a celebration of *being*. While celebrating and enjoying the moment, we might feel more connected to ourselves and others. We might have the feeling that life makes more sense and that we are part of a bigger whole. We might feel more grounded and integrated. We might feel better understood, loved, and accepted. For a moment, it might not matter anymore who we are or what we have accomplished.

No matter how small or how big our worries or our joys are, they are all expressions of our existence in this universe. This means, as May (1983) describes, that clients who come for help do not only bring their concrete problem but also their whole existence into our consultation rooms. Or as Rank (1932) might say, when we engage in counseling or therapy, the cosmic also takes a seat and encompasses whatever we say, feel, or think.

Within the realm of psychotherapy, counseling, or psychological interventions, there is probably no approach that would not claim being interested in taking care of their clients' lives (Vanhooren, 2022a, p. 1). However, not all therapeutic approaches state explicitly that they are willing to help their clients make sense of their existence beyond their daily struggles (Bugental, 1978). Unlike other schools of therapy, humanistic and existential therapies have made it precisely their mission to help their clients relate differently to their existential challenges. Decades of empirical research show that humanistic-experiential and existential psychotherapies are not only effective in dealing with the symptomatic sides of depression—anxiety, trauma, psychosis, eating disorders, addiction, and relational problems—but also in finding new ways of living (Elliott et al., 2021; Vos, 2023; Zegers & Vanhooren, 2026). Even when meaninglessness, guilt, or existential anxiety seem insurmountable, humanistic and existential approaches might find ways to help their clients develop *existential well-being* and *posttraumatic growth* (Leijssen, 2013; Vanhooren et al., 2018, 2022a, 2022b).

Although some schools of therapies might debate whether existential concerns are part of what needs to addressed in therapy, from a humanistic and existential point of view, it does not make much sense to differentiate between psychological and existential suffering. Indeed, we can understand our depression and anxiety as a specific, unique, and personal way of experiencing our *shared* existential challenges. In depression, for example, we meet our challenge to experience meaning or make sense of our existence. Instead, we might struggle with emptiness, meaninglessness, or nothingness (Vanhooren, 2019a). When we experience trauma, we might experience death anxiety, existential isolation, and sense how fragile we truly are as human beings (Arredondo & Caparrós, 2019). When we suffer from compulsive or obsessive thoughts, we might be trying to get control over life itself—without too much success.

It is precisely because our daily suffering and joys are rooted in our shared *human condition* that therapy works (Rogers, 1961). It is precisely there—where we feel the most fragile, afraid, lonely, or powerless—that we can also feel the most deeply understood, connected, and supported. It is through experiencing our existential struggle within an empathic therapeutic relationship that we can uncover the essence of our pain and experience a new way that moves us forward. It is because we share the same existential struggles as clients and therapists that the therapeutic relationship can turn into an existential encounter, leading to a different way of being with ourselves (Anderson & Cissna, 1997; May, 1983). It is not a coincidence that clients report leading a more authentic, open, connected, and meaningful life after having felt met at this deepest level in therapy (Elliott et al., 2021; Rogers, 1961, 1980).

However, psychologists, social workers, psychiatrists, therapists, counselors, and health care professionals don't always find it easy to connect with their clients existentially (Frediani et al., 2023, 2025). This book is written in the hope it helps therapists and counselors with all types of training encounter the existential layer of their clients' challenges more openly and learn to engage differently with their clients on an existential level.

The humanistic–existential approach we refer to in this book is called *experiential–existential psychotherapy* (Madison, 2010; Vanhooren, 2018). It is a relatively newer branch on the existential and humanistic psychology family tree, which spontaneously developed in Europe as a crossing among person-centered, focusing-oriented, and existential therapeutic approaches (Madison, 2010; Leijssen, 2007; Vanhooren, 2019a, 2019b). It could be identified as a carrying forward expression of the broader humanistic and experiential movement once initiated by Rank and Taft (Kramer, 2019), further developed by Rogers (1961, 1980), embodied by Gendlin (1962, 1970, 1973, 1996, 1997), studied by Elliott and colleagues (2004), and crossed with existential–humanistic therapies (Bugental, 1999; May, 1983; Schneider & Krug, 2026) and other existential resources (Madison, 2010).

As experiential–existential psychotherapy is strongly rooted in Rogers' person-centered therapy, some might understand experiential–existential psychotherapy as a kind of existentially informed person-centered therapy (Vanhooren & Cooper, 2024). Others might situate experiential–existential psychotherapy as a focusing-oriented existential therapy (Madison, 2014) because in its practice there is a lot of focusing and felt sensing of existence. American readers might discover many similarities with existential–humanistic therapy (Bugental, 1978; Schneider & Krug, 2026). Because experiential–existential psychotherapy is also practiced in populations that have suffered chronically and have been diagnosed with multiple psychiatric disorders (e.g. Verdegem et al., 2025), some readers might discover similarities between experiential–existential psychotherapy and Prouty's person-centered pre-therapy. Wherever experiential–existential psychotherapy could or should be situated, this book wants to be there for you and hopes to help your particular journey.

This book itself consists of five chapters. Step by step, the chapters will provide you with maps, a compass, and boots to help you explore this existential layer with your clients. The first chapter explains how existential challenges are a continuous part of our lives. We reflect on the concept of *existential awareness* and explain other concepts such as ontic and ontological aspects and the micro-, meso-, and macro-dimensions of our experience. These concepts will help us notice and understand the existential layer in our conversations with clients, other people, and ourselves.

Inspired by Yalom (1980), Gendlin (1970), Rank (1936), and Greening (1992), the second chapter covers an exploration of the four major *existential concerns and processes* that we can use to explore our *terra incognita*. These existential concerns are not synonymous with the existential layer as such. We can understand them as signposts to help us get a sense of which existential challenges our clients might be facing. We will successively explore death and life, meaninglessness and meaning, isolation and connection, and choice and responsibility. This chapter gives us more *language* to enter this existential space with others. It shows what these existential concerns might look like in clinical practice and also points at identifiable *processes* that we might encounter in therapy. It gives us a framework for recognizing blocked existential experiences and dynamics.

The third chapter is an important interlude in which we reflect upon what *existential suffering and growth* might mean. Both are often part of the same therapeutic process. We explain different forms of existential suffering such as ontological insecurity, lack of a sense of basic trust, and the right to exist. We also consider what existential growth might mean. In all these chapters, we will encounter the stories of different clients I have met during the various stages of my career. They all gave their consent to have their stories published under pseudonyms and read how their stories were portrayed in this book before publication. Their stories will help to bring difficult psychological and philosophical concepts to life and make them more understandable.

The fourth chapter takes a closer look at how existential struggles can unfold during a longer *therapeutic process*. This chapter explicitly shows how existence reveals itself not only in the content but also in the dynamics of therapy. We will further explore concepts such as *existential empathy* and methods such as focusing and chair dialogues. We will also address *inspiration* as a method that can facilitate and support growth. This chapter portrays three different stages of my therapy with Thomas. After Thomas gets the last word in this fourth section, we conclude this book with a short final chapter. Together with my colleagues and my clients, I hope that this book may inspire you and serve as an existential base camp from where you might feel encouraged to explore existence with your clients and many others.

Finally, I would like to thank everyone who contributed to this book in one way or another. In the spirit of Buber (2010), I dare to state that every person I have met has been a teacher to me, although I have not always been the best student. And I hope that everyone might feel fully acknowledged as being my teacher. The list of people I would like to thank is endlessly long, including my clients, who play an important role in this book. Their stories show how experiential–existential psychotherapy—besides easing psychological pains and suffering—can lead to unexpected growth, vitality, and the discovery of new ways of experiencing oneself, the other, and the mystery of life.

Chapter 1

Existential Awareness

The phenomenon of reflecting and worrying about existential questions is probably as old as humanity itself. Not coincidentally, our oldest stories often tell about our struggles with our search for meaning and how to be with our finitude (Schneider, 2013). In a 4,000-year-old epic, one of the earliest stories ever written, we see King Gilgamesh of Uruk struggling with mortality and the meaning of life. Bereaved by the sudden death of his best friend, Enkidu, we see Gilgamesh wandering alone over the plains with a heavy heart. Formerly known for his need to shine and to be praised for his exceptional bravery, Gilgamesh feels lost now and does not care for glitter and glory:

> Should my cheeks not be emaciated, my expression desolate? Should my heart not be wretched, my features not haggard? Should there not be sadness deep within me? [...] Should I not roam the wilderness?[...] Enkidu, my friend, whom I love deeply, who went through every hardship with me, the fate of mankind has overtaken him. Six days and seven nights I mourned over him and would not allow him to be buried until a maggot fell out of his nose. I began to fear death, and so I roam the wilderness [...]. Enkidu, my friend, has turned into clay! The tavern-keeper said to him, to Gilgamesh: The life you seek, you will certainly not find. When the gods created mankind, they gave death to men. [...]. So Gilgamesh, eat fat! Make fun, celebrate daily! Go dancing day and night, play music! [...] See the little one holding your hand? Let your wife rejoice in your fire! [...] Gilgamesh said to her, to the tavern-keeper: Why do you talk like this? I am grieved, my heart grieves for my friend. Tavern-keeper, why do you talk like this? I am sad, my heart grieves for Enkidu. (de Feyter, 2002, pp. 110–111).

The *pep talk* of Siduri, the tavern-keeper, makes no impression on Gilgamesh. Faced with death, he sets out in search for immortality. Gilgamesh travels to the edge of the world. When he meets his distant ancestor who survived the Flood, he gets the sobering answer that death cannot be escaped. To make matters worse, the consolation prize for his long search, a cosmetic plant that would make him look younger, is stolen by the serpent. Gilgamesh's journey did not lead anywhere. He cries and asks the ferryman: "For whom, Ushanabi, did I weary my arms? For whom does my blood flow in me? I am not even good for myself" (de Feyter, 2002, p. 129). A new quest, this time for meaning in life, commences.

Like the story of Gilgamesh, myths, religious writings, and fairy tales ponder the same questions (May, 1991; Vanhooren, 1997). Each is an expression of our struggle with mortality, our search for meaning and significance, our longing for deep connection, and the challenge of making choices over and over again. Although we no longer carve into clay tablets or write on papyrus and even hardly on paper, our main existential concerns have hardly changed over these centuries. In a way, the Gilgamesh story might as well have been written today. Similarly, our own life stories are attempts to make sense of our existence.

Like Gilgamesh, many of us only become fully aware of our existence when our lives take an unexpected turn and the routine of our daily lives is disrupted. As in Gilgamesh's story, the death of a loved one or some other kind of loss can make us more aware of the fragility of our existence. By the same token, extraordinary positive experiences such birth, marriage, unconditional acceptance, or peak experiences in nature can give us a taste of a dimension that deepens or expands our perspective. As in the film *The Matrix* by Lana and Lilly Wachowski (1999), we discover a different kind of reality that we pass by in "normal" circumstances. We can call it *existential awareness*: a sensing of another, existential layer that encompasses our daily living. As Gendlin (1970) explains, it is an embodied knowing rather than a conceptual knowing — a knowing that we, as human beings, are just dust and ashes and at the same time also the bearers of life (Rogers, 1980).

These unexpected turns, big or tiny, can open our minds and hearts to this deeper existential awareness. We also become more sensitive and more deeply aware of the human tragedy and maybe also of the miracle of existence. Anyone who has ever been present when a person is dying or being born can hardly remain insensitive to the existential doors that are suddenly opened. In those moments, our meaning as well as our futility, our existential isolation and our fundamental connectedness become palpable. It is an awareness that carries beyond an intellectual knowing or existential concepts (Gendlin, 1962). We are not just wondering about life. We are fully involved in the existential experience itself.

This existential awareness—or the absence of it—is an important touchstone when it comes to existential therapy. To what extent is the client fully *present* in their life (Bugental, 1978), and to what extent do they allow life to be fully present in themselves? The degree to which we can allow this existential awareness will influence our lives deeply. Sensing or avoiding this layer plays a role in psychological suffering and in the possible *growth process* that might follow (see Chapter 3). Therapy or counseling can help to raise this embodied existential awareness by exploring our concerns beyond the story that we have constructed about ourselves and the world. Psychotherapy can be understood as a condensed life process through which we gradually discover who we are and how we want to shape our existence. However, therapy is far from the only place where we can discover who we are. In essence, every moment carries the seeds of a broader and deeper awareness, though some moments invite us more openly than others.

Rituals and Sensitive Periods

While life circumstances vary significantly from person to person, there are predictable moments in life that might expand existential awareness. In many, if not all, cultures these moments have been ritualized. Rituals can help us seize transitional moments in life as moments of growth. Rituals offer symbols to mark these moments and—if we allow it—help us to weave them in our life story and internalize them. Traditionally, rituals around birth, coming of age, marriage, divorce, illness, healing, and death offer a language and a scenario to help us make sense of those moments that transcend our individual experiences. While traditional religious frameworks are crumbling in Western countries, people still turn to these rituals or look for alternatives to mark these events.

In addition, developmental psychology also points at sensitive periods when we are more open to change. These sensitive periods are characterized by our changing emotional, cognitive, and relational capacities, on the one hand, and the changing expectations set by our society, on the other hand (Verhofstadt-Denève et al., 1991). During these particular times, we are also more prone to be more aware of our existence (Andrews, 2016). Changing cognitive, emotional, and social capacities make us experience ourselves, the world, and life as such differently.

Verhofstadt-Denève (1994) indicates how even the youngest children experience some forms of existential awareness. Children acquire important building blocks that will help them later navigate existential challenges. One of these basic building blocks is the experience that objects or people keep existing, even when we do not see them. The learning of *object permanence* and *person permanence,* documented by Piaget, has significant emotional and existential consequences (Verhofstadt-Denève, 1994). Person permanence helps us know that our dearest friends are still there even when we are not in the same room. Imagine what a scary place life would be if we would not have acquired this knowledge. Realizing how this must feel might help us to empathize with babies who start crying when their mother or father leaves the room. Would they know that their parents were not disappearing into nothingness? Indeed, this early development in babies touches upon Tillich's (2000) notion of *being* and *non-being.* Who would still dare to think that babies or children would not have existential feelings or thoughts?

A related early learning is the difference between self and others (Verhofstadt-Denève, 1994). In the same first months, babies learn to distinguish between themselves and others and discover the association between their own name and themselves. This distinction between self and other, as well as the association with one's own name, contribute to a preliminary answer to the existential question of who we are. Along with this distinction between self and other grows the awareness that there are *many* others, which goes hand in hand with a growing attachment to our parent(s) or caregiver(s). The way we feel connected with or disconnected from significant people in our lives has important consequences for how we feel at home in and with ourselves. Research on attachment supports the idea that we also need a secure enough relationship with others to develop the capacity to experience a distinction between our own feelings and those of others (Demeulemeester et al., 2021). It also has repercussions for the way we explore the world: with confidence, with ambivalence, with too much or not enough fear. In addition to, but not separate from our basic attachment, is the need to experience the right to exist and experience basic trust. The latter indicates the need for a sufficiently secure relationship with life itself (Frankl, 1967). These basic experiences might help or impair our capacities to deal with life and its challenges (see Chapter 3).

Every parent might remember how eager children are to understand the world and to absorb language. Acquiring language and the ability to symbolize are essential existential building blocks to make *sense* of what we experience and to experience life as meaningful. Although we can imagine that we try to make sense of our experiences without words, the way we think about and try to grasp meaning runs dominantly through inner and interpersonal speech (Gendlin, 1997). Language enables us to understand ourselves and the situations we are part of. It enables us to build complex meaning structures like our life stories or stories as such. Children go through a stage where they explicitly ask "why" and "how" things work. It is a healthy expression of the need for meaning and *purpose*. Ultimately, Simopoulou (2019) indicates that children struggle with the same existential challenges as adults do. Within the range of their cognitive–affective capabilities, they try to find answers to how to relate to life and death, good and evil, isolation and connection, and hopelessness and meaning.

Another sensitive period is puberty and adolescence (Andrews, 2016; Renders, 2005). Physical, cognitive, emotional, and relational transformations are accompanied by a larger existential awareness, posing ultimate life questions, often very sharply (Erikson, 1962; Verhofstadt-Denève, 1994). One of the most noticeable expressions of this expanding awareness is the search for a unique identity. Interestingly, this identity-formation process is not only a matter of creating a distinct social identity (Zock, 1990). Erikson also speaks of the need to develop an existential identity, a kind of a sense of knowing who one is or can be within in the larger world and vast universe (Erikson, 1962; Zock 1990). This development is often accompanied by existential doubt, dread, and despair. Some young people become painfully aware of their finiteness and discover that the answers from their childhood no longer suffice. Dabrowski (2015) calls this *positive disintegration*: As our life experience and capacity to think and feel increase, former answers and meanings disintegrate and fall apart. Therefore, adolescence is also often experienced as an extended quest for meaning and purpose in a teenager's enlarged world.

At various times we are challenged to adjust our responses to the questions of life. The experience of brand-new parenthood often fosters an increased existential awareness. Steele Lebeau and Webster (2022) argue that in addition to a sense of wonder and amazement at the newborn life, new parents also experience enhanced dimensions of uncertainty and vulnerability. Recurring themes include having to build confidence in oneself as a parent and learning to live with a larger sense of not being in control over life, a newly perceived isolation in the face of the outside world, and a new fear of the unknown.

Yet another well-known sensitive period where we are often struck by existential questions is the so-called midlife crisis. We become painfully aware of the limited time that is left and question ourselves about what we made out of our lives so far. Not infrequently, this sensitive period leads to ruptures and changes. Relationship breakdowns, a change of jobs, or taking up new hobbies are common. There is sometimes a pressing need for expansion and *freedom*—be it in terms of spiritual deepening or the desire to break from one's routines. It is a rushed attempt to live the unlived life while it is still possible, prompted by existential guilt: I am not living the life I wanted to live; I am not the person I envisioned myself to be.

When the rhythm of our professional lives starts to slow down (Andrews, 2016) or when the children leave the nest, another existential challenge awaits us. Retirement and being suddenly an empty nester might come with a loss of meaning and loneliness. Again, life sends us on the road to find new meaning. And even in late adulthood, when we are increasingly confronted with our fragility, we are challenged to pause. Increasing loneliness, as well as the shrinking of our physical and cognitive abilities, can challenge us existentially (Dezutter & Dewitte, 2019; Sundström et al., 2018). How can I make sense of a life that runs on its last legs? What is there left for me to do? How do I look back on my life? Which lessons do I want to pass on to the next generation?

When Life Throws a Spanner in the Works

For some of us, existential awareness seems to fluctuate during our lifetime. At certain moments, we might be fully aware of our existential reality while at other moments our existential awareness seems to be dormant. According to Heschel (2011b), people differ in the extent to which they reside in this explicit existential space. For some of us, existential awareness is limited to those momentary experiences. There are also people who actively seek this existential space and want to live there. It becomes the residence from which they live their lives. However, even one encounter or a single moment in which we become aware of the existential contours of our lives can have a major impact on how we understand ourselves and the world (Kaufman, 2020;

Maslow, 1964). Whether our existential awareness deepens through growth spurts or through deliberate cultivation, our experience of *the whole* expands throughout our lives, shifting not only how we sense the world but also how we experience ourselves within our expanding realities (Gendlin, 1986).

However, not everybody feels the need to pay attention to this existential reality. Schnell (2010) speaks of *existential indifference.* People who display existential indifference do not seem to have more or less psychological complaints, but they do experience less meaning and life satisfaction. It also appears that people who are content with everyday pleasures seem to be more vulnerable when their lives are confronted with negative twists (Ryff, 2012). Adverse life events such as losses, illness, victimization, divorce, and traumatic experiences can throw us off track at any time.

This happened to 26-year-old Annabel, who came to me for therapy because of a traumatic experience (Vanhooren, 2016b, pp. 15–16). Annabel was living a fairly carefree life until she was on her way home after a night out. She was sexually assaulted by an unknown man in her neighborhood. Annabel managed to live as if nothing had happened during the first month after this traumatic experience. She dismissed the event as a *fait-divers*. She did drink more alcohol and made sure she always had something to do. However, as she crossed a square one evening, she was suddenly overwhelmed with a wave of fear that seemed to come out of nowhere. Since that moment, she became hyperalert to her surroundings, was afraid to go to sleep, and looked under her bed to see if anyone was hiding there. She constantly checked to see that her front door was properly locked. She could not fall asleep because she was listening to environmental sounds. She was so overwhelmed by anxiety that she decided to go back to living with her parents.

In addition to her anxiety, she no longer recognized herself. Her body was constantly restless. Whereas she usually felt full of energy before her traumatic experience, she now felt mostly tired and nauseated. Previously, she had thought of herself as being a strong, independent, and social woman who could stand her ground. She could not reconcile this former self-image with how she experienced herself now: small, scared, and insecure. Moreover, she noticed that she preferred to isolate herself these days. She also had the feeling that others did not understand her. The world also seemed to have changed. Her environment, in which she used to feel so safe, now seemed to be a dangerous place. In addition, she also started to have doubts about the meaning of her current job and her life in general. Life, which used to feel easy, had turned into a daily struggle.

Annabel showed the typical symptoms of a posttraumatic stress disorder. Her anxiety was very palpable during the first sessions. Her *basic trust* in life had been completely undermined (see Chapter 3). Annabel also clearly suffered from a loss of meaning: She no longer recognized herself, her bodily and emotional reactions, the others in her life, and the world. It felt like she had been teleported to a hostile planet where nothing—including her own life—made sense. She was suffering from a loss of meaning in the broadest sense of the word, and she felt reduced to nothingness. What she felt was existential anxiety as described by Heidegger (1999) and Tillich (2000): the fear of non-being, of nothingness, the fear of being annihilated or of not existing anymore.

As we can read in Annabel's story, unexpected life events can evoke an existential crisis (Arredondo & Caparrós, 2019). Our previous way of living has passed its expiration date. Besides the very concrete questions that often accompany traumatic experiences or losses, we start asking ourselves those ultimate questions: For example, Annabel not only asked herself why her body acted so strangely but also wondered what she was living for.

Traumatic experiences can evoke a heightened awareness of fragility and finitude. Annabel was disappointed that she was not stronger and wished she would have acted differently during the assault. She also felt disappointed in others. A sense of basic trust in others and herself made space for distrust (see Chapter 3). The whole experience was accompanied by fear and despair. But as Kierkegaard and Jaspers point out, by hitting rock bottom we can become more aware of what is essential to us, which, eventually, might help us to figure out who and how we want to be in the future.

Layers of Existing

Although the quality of our lives might resonate with the degree to which we are existentially aware, we do not stop living by being totally immersed in our day-to-day experiences. Everything we witness or experience, from the most trivial to the most extraordinary, is an expression of this existence. Yet we feel a qualitative difference between the mundane, the concrete, the routine course of events and those moments that stand out as being more significant.

In fact, as Holzhey-Kunz (2014) states, existential concerns such as death and the limitations of existence also play a role in our daily lives, regardless of whether we are aware of them or not. Our existential concerns might find their expression in such a mundane way that we might simply not notice them as existential. Inspired by Heidegger, Holzhey-Kunz (2014) calls these everyday situations *ontic experiences.* For example, many of us know the frustrating experience of being stuck in traffic, missing a connection with a train or airplane, or of having a flat tire. Each of these are recognizable ontic situations—and, in this case, very annoying. However, these situations are characteristic of a much broader and universal theme that we can identify as existential. In each of these instances, we experience the limitations of our existence and of not being fully in control, which ultimately show themselves in our mortality. Heidegger calls the latter the *ontological layer* of our experiences. This ontological layer transcends our concrete experience and our individual lives. What we experience *ontically* in these cases is the frustration of being stuck or running late while having to be somewhere else. Something in our situation is beyond our control, which might evoke a wide range of emotions or thoughts. However, whatever we feel or think does not have an effect on the traffic jam we are in. On an ontological level, we are facing the imperfect and the inescapable limitations of our existence.

We meet this ontological fact over and over, be it by failing a test, burning a cake, losing our keys, or hurting our back. However, as long as the situation is not exceptional, we seem to have little awareness of how our concrete situation refers to a larger ontological theme. There is indeed a big difference between a relational break-up and the breaking of a glass. While they are both ontic experiences, the first situation might lead more directly to an existential wake-up call. We might become more directly aware of the fragility and finitude of life by experiencing the finality of something that was meant to endure for eternity such as marriage. On a side note, it is not a coincidence that the breaking of a glass is incorporated as a ritual in Jewish weddings. Here, the ritual act of breaking a glass becomes an explicit reminder of this larger ontological theme of life and death (Frankel, 2005).

Existentialists such as Heidegger (1999), Sartre (2003), Tillich (2000), Arendt (2018), and Yalom (1980) tried to identify existential concerns or conditions that would characterize our ontological experiences. Tillich speaks of the *ultimate concern* of *being*: We are deeply concerned with being and fear that we, our loved ones, and life on earth will disappear one day. We can experience this ultimate concern vividly when we are confronted with our mortality, with any form of loss, with meaninglessness, or when we experience existential loneliness. In these moments we get a taste of this *non-being*, and it takes quite a bit of courage and a fair amount of basic trust to face and learn from this non-being experience (Missiaen & Vanhooren, 2021). Yalom (1980) calls these manifestations of our ultimate concern our *existential givens*. He distinguishes four recurrent challenges that summarize our ontological experiences: (1) death and the limitations of life; (2) freedom, choice, and responsibility; (3) existential isolation; and finally (4) meaninglessness (see Chapter 2).

Yalom (1980) assumes that these existential givens describe our human condition and that we all will meet these existential givens one day. A sudden confrontation or realization of these existential givens can completely overwhelm us. For example, through her traumatic experience, Annabel became painfully aware of these existential givens. On an ontic level, she was confronted with a jumble of emotions, an intense anxiety that ran rampant, insomnia and a constant vigilance that totally exhausted her. On an ontological level, she became aware of her fragility. She felt overwhelmed by agony, loneliness, and meaninglessness. Within an empathic therapeutic relationship and by exploring her bodily experiencing of her situation, she gradually could make sense of what happened to her (see Chapters 2 and 3).

Experiencing Existence Through Different Dimensions

Facilitating embodied existential awareness and experiential exploration within a safe relational environment is central in experiential–existential psychotherapy. By turning to our concrete embodied experiences in the here and now and by dwelling on our felt senses, we can notice how we are, who we are, and what really matters at this very moment (Gendlin, 1970). For Gendlin, the concrete ontic-embodied experience could serve as a portal to a larger—ontological—awareness (Lou, 2019). Holzhey-Kunz (2014) argues that our daily ontic experiences are indeed pre-ontological. By this she means that our lived experience of a concrete ontic situation always carries an implicit ontological meaning. Similarly, Rank (1932) points out that we often negotiate larger human issues through our daily experiences. He explains how this can be understood as micro-cosmic expressions of larger macro-cosmic dynamics. Painters often display larger concerns through their concrete artwork. Musicians might express in a single note the entire universe. Likewise, as we sense in our bodies what *something* might mean to us, we are also opening up to what is larger than ourselves (Frankel, 2005; Gendlin, 1962). Or in therapy, while sensing our concrete losses, we might also sense the larger issue of finiteness, which is not only linked to our concrete life but also to the same condition of all living beings.

Where Heidegger's and Holzhey-Kunz's understanding of ontic and ontological experiences seems to depart from the differences between them, Rank's (1932, 1936) *micro-cosmos* and *macro-cosmos* seem to emphasize how we as parts can sense the whole. Especially in the here and now, we can sense how the whole is expressed through us (Rank, 1936). Rogers (1961, 1980), Gendlin (1970), and Bugental (1999) build on Rank's work by pointing out the importance of working therapeutically in the here and now. Sensing into the here and now can lead to a deeper awareness of our issues and also—as we will see—transform them.

Somewhere between our micro-cosmic and macro-cosmic sensing, ideas about how we should think and lead our lives might prevent us from opening up to our micro- or macro-cosmic existence (Frankel, 2005; Rogers, 1961). As a result, they might stop us from growing and lead instead to a more rigid way of being. Dominating cultural and personal narratives might help us to make sense of the world, but we might mistake them for the direct experience of our existence itself. For example, religious stories can help us to sense the numinous, but they also can feel prescriptive and lead away from a direct experience of the sacred or cosmic (Schneider, 2013). Likewise, existential theories and concepts can help to illuminate existential awareness but can also distort or hinder a sensing into existence itself (Gendlin, 1973). Neither Hulzhey-Kunz's distinction between ontic and ontological experiences nor Rank's (1932) micro-cosmic and macro-cosmic experiencing highlights this in-between space of constructs, concepts, or narratives that are sometimes helpful or hindering. Therefore, we made a further differentiation between what we have called the micro-, meso-, and macro-dimensions of our experiencing (Vanhooren, 2018). Making human's ideas or stories more explicit as a meso-dimension has helped therapists and counselors identify problems and see opportunities to help clients make more sense of their existence (Vanhooren, 2019a). In reality, the micro-, meso-, and macro- dimensions are just different faces of the same whole, although problems in each of these dimensions might need attention and care in order to find new ways of living. Throughout this book, we will illustrate these three dimensions repeatedly as they can show us what—in Gendlin's (1997) terms—our *living process* might miss or need. To make it more concrete, we will examine what these three dimensions might look like in Annabel's story.

We can call Annabel's emotional confusion, her anxiety, her physical arousal, and her bodily sensations, the *micro-dimension* of her experience. The micro-dimension represents *how we are*, how we experience our lives in this very moment, in the here and now. It is in this concrete bodily palpability that we experience our existence (Gendlin, 1973). Although the micro-dimension might function as the most direct path to existential awareness (macro-dimension), this is not always the case. In any case, it is in the here-and-now that we can sense what is going on or what is at stake. As for Annabel, her body was showing her that she was in danger. It wanted to warn her and keep her safe. However, the chaos she micro-dimensionally perceived was also affected by what was happening to her in the meso-dimension of her lived experience.

We can regard the *meso-dimension* as an intermediate dimension that helps us understand our situation in more general terms based on our former life experiences. Our memories, our self-image, our identity, our story about the event, our life narrative, our family story, our worldview, our ideology, our values, and our norms all contribute to this domain. It is the space of our accumulated self-knowledge and knowledge about the world. The meso-dimension is about the question *who we are*, how we identify ourselves in the context of our life, our relationships, and our communities. To put it in more psychological terms, these are the mental structures or cognitive–affective schemas that have been developing throughout our lives (Greenberg et al., 1993). These structures help us to make sense of who we are in this world, to interpret our daily situation, and to make choices based on our former experiences. They also include mental and interpersonal structures that lie outside of us—such as cultural, religious, or ideological values and norms—that help us function and behave within our culture. While this meso-dimension is often helpful, it can also be stifling. As we shall see later, it can lead to self-alienation because our self-image might become *incongruent* with what we are bodily experiencing (Rogers, 1961). As a result, the stability the meso-dimension provides might also lead to a more rigid functioning. We might make choices based on convention or on survival mechanisms rather than on what we or the other needs in our current situation (Bugental, 1999).

In Annabel we see how the situation has a major impact on the meso-dimension. As is often the case with traumatic experiences, we see that guiding self-structures such as one's identity and world assumptions are at the edge of being shattered (Park, 2010). Tillich (2000) talks about *loss of meaning* in this context. The meaning system that used to give us shelter and direction—knowing who we are and what to expect from others—is now at a breaking point. The breakdown of the meso-dimension is frightening. When the framework that helped make sense of the ongoing stream of our bodily experiences is crumbling, it might feel like tumbling into an abyss. For Annabel, it felt as if she no longer recognized herself: She was no longer the person she used to be. Her autonomy and her firmness, which was an important part of her self-image (meso-dimension), completely disappeared. She was no longer that autonomous person. In a way, "she" vanished. Consequently, the traumatic experience and its immediate aftermath felt like a fault line in her life. There was a before and an after, and in the first therapy sessions she could not at all imagine what that "after" might be.

In the case of traumatic experiences, in which the meso-dimension crumbles, the ontological layer comes pounding in like a battering ram. In the footsteps of Rank (1932), we call this ontological layer the *macro-dimension* of our experience. It is the domain of our shared human condition, often expressed through major existential concerns and also the dimension of self-transcendent spiritual or cosmic experiences. The macro-dimension is about the mesmerizing awareness *that we are*, which often brings us to the impossible question of *why we are*. Depending on the situation—ranging from a beautiful hike in the mountains to a tragic accident—that leads to this existential awareness, we may feel either invited or challenged to re-engage with our existential reality. In Annabel's case, her traumatic experience was an abrupt existential wake-up call. Who was she? What was the meaning of her existence and of life as such? What was of essence to her? How did she want to spend her life from now on?

There are very good reasons to engage in this macro-dimension as a counselor or therapist. According to Schneider (2015), we only understand the full depth and breadth of our situation when we also ask ourselves what this situation means in the broader context of our existence. Only then we might fully understand what this moment means to us. Similar to Rank (1932), Schneider speaks of the *cosmic* layer of our experience, while van Deurzen (1997) and Leijssen (2013) speak of the spiritual dimension of our existence, and Rogers (1980) of the formative tendency in the universe that also runs through our organismic actualizing tendency. Whatever we call it, it refers to the layer or dimension that transcends us but also runs through us. It is about the larger existential reality that manifests itself through our current situation. The questions Annabel asks herself on this macro-dimension are not only about herself but also about humanity and existence in a broader sense. Asking ourselves these questions makes us dip into something larger or deeper. As we will explain further, exploring this layer of our experiencing opens new avenues and might help us to grow.

In the case of traumatic experiences and losses in general, it is precisely the struggle with this existential dimension that facilitates posttraumatic growth (Calhoun & Tedeschi, 2013). As Annabel engaged in a quest for meaning, she eventually could experience a new way of being herself. She also discovered a different way of being with others, which eventually led to a deeper appreciation of life itself.

Although working through one's existential concerns can lead to growth and more resilience, Hill (2018) notes that counselors and therapists can feel very uncomfortable when it comes to existential concerns. Psychotherapists note how they often feel afraid, unprepared, or unequipped to provide a space for the macro-dimension in therapy (Frediani et al., 2023, 2025). At the same time, one-third to two-thirds of clients who start therapy have implicit or explicit existential questions (Golovchanova et al., 2021). Counselors or therapists who feel unequipped to be present with these existential questions quite often seem to bypass these experiences (Frediani et al., 2025). As a result, their discomfort can hinder clients' exploration of this macro-dimension. How can we understand this discomfort in therapists and counselors?

The Cold Feet of Therapists and Counselors

May (1983) points out that clients not only enter the therapy room with their concrete problems but also with their entire existence. According to him, the heart of psychotherapy lies in the care for the client's *being*. The ultimate goal, May argues, is to help clients live their existence more consciously, setting them on a path toward more freedom and authenticity. Bugental (1978) sums it up: The goal is to nurture the client's presence in their own lives.

Presence is not only valued as an end but also as a quality of the therapist that helps the client become more aware of their own presence (Geller & Greenberg, 2012). However, being more present in and toward one's existence can be challenging. This is not only true for clients but also for counselors and therapists. If we as helpers open up to the client's macro-dimension, we also open up to how existence feels to us. *Existential empathy*, the capacity to be present and resonate with the client's macro-dimension and communicate this empathy, is often challenging (Vanhooren, 2019b, 2022a, 2022b). The clients' problems at the micro- and meso-dimension still seem somewhat "manageable" to the therapist. Usually, the therapist's life situation is different enough from their client's to allow the therapist to maintain a sufficient self–other distinction. The latter is necessary in order not to get confused or be overwhelmed by the experience of the client. However, when we meet the client in their existential space and sense the ontological meaning of what they are going through, it is harder to maintain this self–other distinction. The human condition of the client and the therapist are in essence not different. We share the same existential challenges, although our reactions or answers on the micro- and meso-dimension might look quite different.

Another element that might make it harder to empathize with the existential layer is that there are no solutions for our existential concerns. This might create a problem because in our Western culture therapists are somehow expected to solve any issue, including existential ones (Vanhooren, 2018).

Psychotherapy has not always been, and in some cultures still is not, a story of solving problems (Yang, 2017). May (Schneider et al., 2009), Rogers (1980), and Gendlin (1990) have been warning us about this increasing solution-focused orientation at the expense of the ability to be fully present with human suffering. Obviously, there is nothing wrong with wanting to alleviate the suffering of clients. On the contrary. However, the urge to solve what is inherently unsolvable seems to cause additional suffering. It is not a coincidence that the felt need to solve the client's existential concerns is often accompanied with a sense of powerlessness, helplessness, incompetence, or failure by the therapist (Frediani et al., 2025). Moreover, offering solutions or running away from the client's existential issues will leave the client feeling abandoned and even more isolated (Gendlin, 1990). As a result, our clients might sink deeper into a sense of existential loneliness and despair.

Sadly enough, this is more a reality than we might like to think. There are significant differences among therapists when it comes to existential empathy (Frediani et al., 2023, 2025; Vanhooren, Conrado

Veiga Bosquetti et al., 2022). Although different studies teach us that counselors experience difficulties with attending the existential concerns of their clients (see Frediani et al., 2023, for an overview), the study by Edberg and colleagues (2023) has probably been the most explicit. In their qualitative study with 139 health care professionals, Edberg and colleagues asked the participants how they would support their clients in talking about their existential loneliness. All participants agreed that being present was of absolute importance, but at the same time they confessed that attending their patients' existential loneliness was highly challenging. Some experienced fear and tried to steer their patients away from talking about their existential issue or instead tried to think of strategies to fix other aspects of their clients' situation. In one of our own studies, participants explained how they would conduct an assessment of the suicidality of their client in order to do something rather than just be present with their client who was wondering about the meaning of life (Frediani et al., 2025).

The latter not only points at our Western tendencies to intervene and solve. As Edberg and colleagues (2023) study suggests, counselors or therapists might also employ interventions because they cannot bear to be present with these existential concerns. Psychological interventions are then used as an instrument to avoid a sense of powerlessness or deep fear of the therapist. It is the therapist or health care professional rescuing themselves from being affected by what the client is experiencing. Indeed, for therapists who are not engaged in cultivating their existential awareness, the client's existential experiences might have the capacity to cause a sudden confrontation with one's own existential concerns (Vanhooren, 2022b).

Questions such as "Who am I? What is the meaning of my existence?" or the sudden realization of one's own mortality can not only waltz into the consultation room but also into the therapist's life. Not knowing how to stay present with the macro-dimension can lead to the therapist's sense of powerlessness and insignificance (Gordon et al., 2017). While the confrontation with deep human suffering and profound existential questions can lead to burn-out, compassion fatigue, or existential stress (Arrendo & Caparrós, 2019; Kjellenberg et al., 2013), it can also lead to an increased existential awareness, meaning, and secondary posttraumatic growth (Arnold et al., 2005; Tsirimokou et al., 2023). In a small U.S. study with 21 psychotherapists, 76% reported that throughout their work with traumatized clients they often were confronted with their own existential concerns (Arnold et al., 2005). Listening to existential questions initiated by their clients led to personal posttraumatic growth in these therapists. They described becoming more acceptant of both the beauty and the dark side of life. Likewise, they experienced a growing openness to spirituality. Because they dealt with their clients' suffering and didn't shy away from the existential questions that were evoked by this suffering, these therapists were able to connect with life differently—and in a deeper way. A systematic literature review by Tsirimokou and colleagues (2023) on secondary posttraumatic growth among therapists showed indeed that experiencing a deeper existential awareness and more appreciation for life is a common result of working with traumatized clients.

This is not only true for therapists who work with traumatized clients. Unrelated to the setting they are working in, therapists might notice a change in how they experience existence as a result of working with their clients. In one of our own studies, therapists and counselors expressed how they developed a different attitude toward existence during the course of their careers (Frediani et al., 2023). Not only had they experienced a shift from wanting to solve existential issues to being more present, they also sensed a growing appreciation toward working explicitly with existential issues. They felt gratitude for being a "witness" or a "midwife" of these intimate and intense existential experiences in therapy. At the same time, they also experienced that working with existential issues can be taxing. Finally, these therapists argued that while their capacity to be more present with their client's existential concerns grew over time, they also felt more existentially present in their own lives.

Rank (1936) was among the first to acknowledge that therapy is not a one-way street. In essence, client and therapist share the same situation at the moment of their meeting. It is a process of mutual influence, although the intention is that this should primarily help the client grow and not make the therapist suffer. Rogers (1961) would further describe the specific conditions needed in order to facilitate the client's growth process. However, Rogers (1942) also notes that we cannot get away from the fact that we—as therapists and counselors—are involved to some extent. While we can usually draw a line between us and the client when it comes to the ontic dimensions (our concrete experience, our identity, our life story), this line becomes thinner when existential concerns are expressed. There is no longer a clear difference between therapist and client at this point: We are all searching beings, struggling with the same concerns and more or less on the same path. An important question for us counselors and therapists is then: How can I remain present when death, suffering, existential guilt, loneliness, meaninglessness, and the desire to experience more freedom are expressed? Only when we feel we can be present and stay close to the client's existential concerns can the following question become legitimate: How can I help my client build a different relation with their ultimate concern? In order to be present, it is helpful to recognize these existential concerns not only in our client's life but also in our own (Vos, 2023).

Chapter 2

Existential Concerns, Processes, and Dynamics

It may sound strange, but knowledge does not necessarily lead to wisdom. Knowing about existentialism might look fancy in some social circles, and facts may bring structure to what otherwise seems chaotic. However, knowing about existential psychology does not guarantee a *lived* understanding. We could, for example, have a philosophical conversation about meaning in life with our client without actually touching or understanding their experience of meaninglessness. As a result, nothing might have changed at the end of the session, except for reinforcement of the feeling of not being understood at all. In order to understand what is going on in our clients' existential space, we need to be in contact with that space. In this case, it's also our space, and the client's subject is also ours as we share the existential space with them.

When we want to play it safe and limit ourselves to a rational analysis, the existential dimension itself seems to slip away. Gendlin (1973) emphasizes how theoretical concepts—even existential ones—can alienate our understanding of the lived experience itself. Rather than those existential concepts being signposts to a larger existential awareness and insight, they often lead us into a theoretical labyrinth where we can feel completely lost.

In addition to being too distanced from our clients' existential concerns by using a lobsided rational approach, the opposite can also occur. We can feel strongly affected by how the client experiences their existence. The way clients relate to life can infect us, so to speak. We can feel drawn into their agony, meaninglessness, and loneliness. When we fuse with their experience, we lack the necessary distance to stay close to them and relate to them. We might lose our ability to facilitate experiential exploration, reflection, and meaning-making. As a result, we might be too absorbed with ourselves and no longer be of assistance to the client.

Building a Grounded Relationship With Our Human Condition

In order to explore and understand the existential dimension of our lives we need a proper distance: a *relationship with*, not a coinciding with or a cut off from (Gendlin, 1996). Buber (1998) describes how we can approach existence in two very different ways. Our Western way is often characterized by what Buber calls the I–it relationship. In this mode of relating, we keep the person at a distance by objectifying the other person or our subject of study. When we walk in our neighborhood, we might act as if the other is not a living being with a personal history but rather an "it." Our knowledge often hints at this kind of object-ivity: We know from the outside. Although objectivity has its obvious value—we are lucky that brain surgeons know where the amygdala is—most of us do not want to live objective lives. We cannot fully grasp our lived experience in an objective way.

Imagine that your experience of chocolate is limited to its chemical formula, and the taste and sensation of chocolate is reduced to the biochemical-electrical reactions that the substance triggers in our bodies and brains. It becomes a poor and reductive description of what you experience when you have a delicious piece of Belgian chocolate (and be sure I know what I'm talking about). The chemical formula cannot match your lived chocolate experience. Sadly enough, the same strange objectifying and reductive tendency is often used when it comes to describing people.

For example, some clients talk about themselves as if they were talking about someone else, expressing their problems in almost technical terms and understanding therapy as a maintenance job where defective pieces need to be replaced. This kind of objective, technical approach is also prevalent in the counseling landscape (Schneider et al., 2009). We talk about psychological interventions and treatments at the risk of falling into this kind of I–it thinking. An intervention becomes something like a Lego piece that needs to be inserted. Therapy becomes a protocolized, step-by-step procedure that needs to be followed in order to solve the client's problem. In this way, we create a caricature of the highly complex process called therapy. Paradoxically, progress in neuropsychological research shows how deeply interwoven the therapist is as an embodied person in counseling and therapy (Lux, 2021). The deeper we understand therapeutic processes, the more it becomes clear that the result of psychological interventions is inseparable from the inter- and intrapersonal dynamics between client and therapist. It appears, for example, that therapists help regulate the client's emotions through their own nervous system and that a neurological synchronization develops between client and therapist during the course of therapy (Lux, 2021).

Rogers (1957) already hinted that therapeutic techniques only work insofar as they express a helpful way of relating. Indeed, also for Buber, change depends on how we relate. When we have an I–Thou encounter with the other, we are called to change. In this I–Thou encounter, we are meeting the other as a unique living being. The other becomes a person who is different, separate from our projections or preconceptions, and with whom we are connected, willing or not. These I–Thou encounters have something surprising and unpredictable. From this point of view, clients are not disorders to be treated but fellow human beings who are trying to make something of their lives. An I–Thou understanding is qualitatively different from an I–it knowing. We cannot come to an understanding without encountering. Furthermore, as Buber points out, we cannot encounter or meet without changing. In the therapeutic moment, meeting, understanding, and changing come together. Rogers (1980) emphasizes that a deeper empathic understanding goes hand in hand with the authentic encounter between therapist and client. According to Rogers, this authentic, empathic encounter forms the basis of a process that leads to a different way of being in the world. Referring to the quality of these moments of meeting, Mearns and Cooper (2005) speak about *relational depth*. The high quality of this therapeutic encounter is accompanied by a clear understanding of oneself and a feeling of being deeply understood and confirmed by the other (Rogers, 1980).

When we talk about existential concerns in this chapter, it is important to realize that recognizing existential concerns is only a steppingstone toward a deeper understanding that entails a deep encounter with oneself, the other, and life as such. Even more, we could speak of an existential space that we enter when we try to understand ourselves and our clients on the macro-dimension. We cannot understand or meet the client in this existential space without entering it gently ourselves. The brief discussion of existential issues and processes that follows is not meant to serve as a checklist. Rather, it is an invitation to explore this existential space for yourself and notice how you relate to these dynamics.

Four Major Existential Concerns and Processes

In his magnus opus, *Existential Psychotherapy,* Yalom (1980) describes four existential themes or givens that characterize human life. These givens are best understood as signposts; they are not the existential dimension itself. They help us to orient ourselves in this existential space, but the existential dimension itself is larger than these themes. As Sartre (1980) puts it, existence precedes essence. Trying to abstract themes or essences from experience is a very human thing to do, but life is larger than the words and concepts we use. The existential reality reaches beyond verbal, conceptual, and human thinking (Gendlin, 1962). It is no coincidence then that other scholars describe not four, but five or six existential givens (e.g., Hoffman, 2009; Vanhooren & Cooper, 2024). In this book, we have included other existential themes such as embodiment, not-knowing, time and space, and authenticity in the exploration of Yalom's givens. In Chapter 3, we will explore other existential themes that are usually not counted among these big four but describe important features of human living.

Existential issues are not solvable in themselves, Rank argues (Kramer, 2019). After all, they belong to who we are. They do not need to be solved because they also stand for what fuels us and makes us grow (Kaufman, 2020). Interestingly, Yalom mostly emphasizes the problematic and darker side of the existential givens over their life-affirming or generating power. In the footsteps of Tillich (2000), Yalom describes how these existential givens can drive us to despair and angst: His interpretation of the givens represent four different faces of how we are ultimately concerned about *being* and the threat of *not being* anymore. Tillich contrasts this ultimate anxiety about non-being with being itself. In his view, we can face threat and despair only when we are also rooted in being—life—itself. It is through this sense of connection or being grounded in life that we can find the courage to face our challenges, learn from them, and grow from there (Missiaen & Vanhooren, 2021).

According to Greening (1992), these four major givens challenge us at different points in our lives. The way we formulate our responses in the face of these challenges is not only indicative of how we relate to life. Indeed, a nihilistic or a one-sided negative relationship might sidestep the challenge of finding a path that does justice to both the brighter and darker shades of being. A one-sided positive response then might blind us and make us vulnerable (Greening, 1992). Therefore, in our exploration of these four major existential themes, we will not only address what can throw us off balance but also what can help us to deepen our roots and stretch our branches in order to feel more grounded in life. From there, we might find the courage to embrace life in all its shades and shapes; a challenging and exciting adventure for most of us.

But there is more. Gendlin (1997) emphasizes how existing is an ongoing process, and not just a matter of thinking or reflecting about existential questions when we feel challenged. For him, we *are* this ongoing process. We are a *living process.* This process does not happen in or to us but is a constant interaction through ourselves and our surroundings. However, this does not mean that there is no individual experience. We experience our living process in our own unique way. From this point of view, "existential" could be understood as the living process of being aware of its own living, its limitations and potentials. Yalom's or Greening's identified themes can be understood as moments in this process where this existential awareness increases through life's challenges and opportunities.

Indeed, our living process often gets blocked, deepens, or shifts when we experience losses, when we feel closer to our ending, when we try to make sense of our lives or seek connection where it fails, or when we are challenged to make important choices. However, moments of heightened awareness and peak experiences are also existential because they can lead to a deeper growth, integration, and fulfillment (Rogers, 1980). Living our lives openly and fully, experiencing meaning and having clarity, finding connection beyond oneself, and experiencing freedom as liberating are equally important moments as their "negative" counterparts. Furthermore, according to Gendlin, we are not just expressions of the human condition (Preston, 2007). We also carry existence forward as we make our way through life. We make life happen and life makes us happen. Through our living, we contribute to that living process. From this experiential–existential point of view, we are not just living the existential givens. We are also giving to existence through our living.

Finally, before we dive in, take note of the following. Although existential concerns seem to be universal, the way we respond to them also depends on our culture (Hoffman, 2009; Vos, 2022). As openly as we want to approach the existential layer in this book, our perspective remains undeniably Western. Our reflections are embedded in this particular culture and in this particular time. And this culture and this time are limited.

Death and Life

"You don't die because you are sick. You die because you are alive."
(Michel de Montaigne, 2006, p. 52)

Death and the Limitations of Life

Perhaps the most recognizable existential concern is about our mortality and our ongoing limitations in life. According to Yalom (1980), death is the existential given par excellence. He, therefore, wonders why mortality is so little addressed in psychotherapy. Although some people long for their life to be over, the vast majority are not looking forward to death (van Wijngaarden et al., 2020). Even among those of us who do have a death wish, there are many who have an ongoing wish to be alive as well (Verdegem et al., 2025). In some cases, experiencing that others respect your wish to die might paradoxically strengthen one's wish to keep on living (Verdegem et al., 2025). Most of us fear the process of dying rather than death itself. Nonetheless, in movies and stories, people try to outwit the allegorical death. The Grim Reaper or Pete the Death has to give way to the bright hero in many folk stories. In *Harry Potter and the Relics of Death* by J. K. Rowling (2007), a lot of magic is needed to keep Death at bay for a lifetime. Yet there is always a price to pay. I remember my grandfather saying: The curse of growing old is that everyone around you dies and that you, in the end, are all by yourself.

In our times, we do not use magic but rather medicine to buy us time. No matter how we exert ourselves, we have a "death line" and so do our loved ones. The end of things also shows itself in the wear and tear of our clothes and tools. No matter which detergent we use, the colors fade, though our favorite sweater may gain meaning as we wear it until it's in tatters. On a global level, finiteness and the limitations of our planet show themselves, for example, in climate change that threatens the existence of many species, not only humans. The agony we can feel when we are confronted with the accumulating floods and fires, shortages of water, the rising temperature, the changes in vegetation and the animal world has been called *climate distress* (Clayton & Crandon, 2024). It is the fear that accompanies the gnawing realization that a gigantic sword of Damocles is hanging over our heads. For the large majority of young people around the globe, this fear leads to demoralization, a loss of hope and faith in the future (Hickman et al., 2021). The fear of our finitude, in any form, can be so overwhelming that we would rather avoid this realization than acknowledge it.

However, it is precisely the denial of the limitations of our planet that has induced climate change. Paradoxically, the denial of limitations seems to lead to more limitations in the long run.

At least in our Western world, a tendency to avoid death and finitude has become dominant (Becker, 2011). A striking example of this avoidance is how we cope with aging processes. The ongoing fight with wrinkles, gray hair, and other signs of aging has led to an entire industry. However, the body does not lie, no matter how many layers of cosmetics we throw at it. Even plastic surgery will eventually have to give in to our aging cells. Our frantic attempts to master a natural process that shows the first signs of our mortality are hopeless. Change sets in even in directions we do not wish for. Our denial of death also shows itself in how we move through traffic. We take unnecessary risks while driving our cars and bikes, as if we are invulnerable. We also do not assume that when we leave our house in the morning, we might not see our family or roommates again in the evening. Bad luck is something for our neighbors, it seems. We often assume that sickness and death won't fall to us.

Poverty is a good example of how a limitation of financial, social, and cultural opportunities can deeply affect our lives and lead to psychological and physical distress. However, we rarely think that poverty may strike us one day. Limitations such as poverty and also others such as not achieving certain levels in school, sports, or at work are often portrayed as deficiencies or failures. Strangely enough, we assume that the sky is the limit while limitations are the rule rather than the exception. Everybody is limited, but still there is an expectation that things should be perfect.

Perfectionism is often accompanied by psychological suffering, showing itself as a recurrent ingredient of depression, obsessive–compulsive disorders, anxiety disorders, eating disorders, and the like (van Heycop ten Ham & van Megen, 2014). According to van Heycop ten Ham and van Megen, perfectionism is closely related to an intolerance of uncertainty. Indeed, how we relate to our limitations also shows itself in how we react to uncertainty. Sooner or later, something unexpected will happen. A date might not show up, we might not get the job we thought we would get, and death and its funerals never come at a suitable time. The unexpected teaches us that we are no longer in control. This suffering from a loss of control is hard for many of us. It punctures our illusion of being at the steering wheel of our existence. Sure, we are in charge, but we are not the only ones who make choices and direct our lives. Although we give direction through our choices, the outcome is always uncertain.

The unknown, the unpredictable, and the uncontrollable character of life has ultimately more impact than our illusion of being in control. We have already seen how Annabel's life was thrown out of its orbit by a disastrous encounter with a stranger. However, positive encounters also can turn our lives around. Partner choices are often based on such coincidental encounters. My parents met each other on the train. If one of them would have taken a train earlier in the 1960s, you would not be reading this book today.

As psychotherapy and counseling are in essence life processes, they are also characterized by a certain degree of unpredictability. Being able to tolerate the unpredictable is an important capacity to be developed by therapists, often referred to as *not-knowing* (Vanhooren, 2014). Although we can give direction to the psychotherapeutic process, the outcome of this encounter is unpredictable. Not-knowing implies that we can deal with the tension of not knowing the outcome. Interestingly, not-knowing is rather the antithesis of denial than of understanding. Denial stands for *not wanting to know*. In not-knowing, we manage to let be what we cannot know yet. Not-knowing provides a pre-conceptual and liminal space for what is still becoming. Change does not usually come from what we already know or have tried before (Vanhooren, 2014). The move toward change involves enduring moments of chaos and treading unbeaten paths (May, 1975). By not folding back on what should be, we are opening up to the new.

Unfortunately, Western societies often show little patience when it comes to processes of growth or becoming. Non-knowing is hard to tolerate, and the call for control is even louder in challenging times. The desire for and the success of authoritarian control-minded leaders who seem to have simple answers to complicated problems dwells on our intolerance of uncertainty. Rarely does this lead to constructive solutions to the benefit of all living beings. In other words, also in this case the denial of the complexity of life and living backfires in the end.

Ignoring death and the limitations of life comes at a great cost. On a societal scale, we deplete our physical and mental resources and thereby threaten our own existence (Afschrift, 2018). On a personal scale, the illusion of being invulnerable and infinite has a paradoxical effect on our quality of life (Yalom, 1980). The denial of death gives us license to postpone important steps until later—as if there will always be a later. The sense of temporality, however, may precisely enhance the intensity of feeling alive and increase our vitality. Realizing that our time is limited might reduce our unlived life or, in other words, our existential guilt, our muddling through or not daring to choose what is truly meaningful to us.

Existential guilt and death anxiety go hand in hand, argues Jessie Taft (1962). The fear of death is not separate from the feeling of not having really lived (Yalom, 1980). Contemporary research shows how death anxiety is related to different kinds of anxiety disorders (Arredondo & Caparrós, 2019; Iverach et al., 2014). People suffering from posttraumatic stress disorder, generalized anxiety disorder, panic disorders, phobias, and obsessive–compulsive disorders tend to experience more death anxiety than others. Our fear of spiders or getting on an airplane (ontic level), ultimately refers to our fear of dying or our extreme fragility through pain (ontological level). Annabel, for example, could not resist checking to see there was no one underneath her bed. She not only suffered from posttraumatic stress disorder but, clearly, also from death anxiety—the fear of being annihilated or destroyed. Her whole body was crying out for protection, to be delivered from death. Obviously, her level of fear was too high to function. In therapy, by regaining basic trust, accepting her newly felt fragility, and discovering new ways of living her fear disappeared (see Chapter 3).

Tillich already pointed toward accepting our non-being—in this case, our mortality—as an essential task. Studies confirm that the ability to accept our own mortality by embracing our humility while still giving meaning to our existence, decreases death anxiety (Iverach et al., 2014; Kesebir, 2014). Or to put it in Tillich's cryptic language: It is only by integrating our non-being in our being that we can fully live. It makes me think of Michel de Montaigne, one of the first humanists in Europe in the 16th century, who invented the literary genre called *essay*. In his essay "About the experience," he talks about death as an essential part of his life. He addresses the kidney stones that he suffers from as "my kidney stones," his lost tooth as an identifiable part of himself that already ceased to exist, and death as "my death" (de Montaigne, 2006). Interestingly, he writes with the same fervor about life, admiring his great example, Socrates, for taking dance lessons at old age and being lyrical about his own joys of life—despite or maybe thanks to "his" kidney stones.

Not all of us might be as keen as de Montaigne to embrace our finitude. Meeting our mortality might change the course of our living process deeply. This happened to Gunther, who was unexpectedly confronted with a deep fear of losing his wife.

Gunther and His Sudden Mortality Salience

Gunther, a 45-year-old Belgian father of three children, was a popular man in his circles. Gifted with an extraordinary sense of humor, he could make everybody laugh. His life was running smoothly until he received the news that his wife was stuck at an airport abroad. For an unclear reason at that time, he was suddenly engulfed by fear. It took her many days to be back home, but even then he felt terrorized by a sense of deep fear he could not get any grip on.

Looking for help was something new to him. He had never really asked for help and had no experience with therapy. During our first session, Gunther told me about his anxiety and how it prevented him from sleeping and working. He felt embarrassed because if felt silly to him. At some point during our first conversation, I asked him if he could notice this fear while he was talking about it; indeed, the fear was present. When I asked him where he sensed that fear, he pointed at his heart. Next, I asked him to describe to me exactly what he sensed around his heart. He was silent for a while as he was checking how his heart was feeling. He sensed a "very heavy pressure," the same feeling, of heavy pressure that he also felt during the night. It was this sense of fear, this precise pressure on his heart, that prevented him from sleeping.

Asking clients if they can feel what they are describing goes all the way back to Rank (1936) and Rogers (1942). It is the core of all experiential approaches not to talk *about* problems but to make the feelings around these issues present in the here and now. My questions to Gunther were informed by what Gendlin (1978) calls *focusing*, an experiential method to explore the edge of our awareness by zooming in on our pre-verbal bodily sensations about our current situation. Instead of thinking and repeating what we already know, focusing helps to sense the *texture* of our experiencing (Preston, 2007). It creates a liminal space where we can be with what we do not know yet but already sense. The meaning of what we sense is implicitly present. We enter the pre-conceptual or pre-verbal sense of our existence. We keep it company while not imposing what we think we already know about it. By sensing and becoming more aware of what this *felt sense* (Gendlin, 1978) means to us, the edge of our existence moves and shows itself eventually. We might become aware of what our living process needs in order to be carried forward, and by becoming aware of it, it has already been carried forward in a way.

Focusing is one of the main roads to explore the micro-dimension of our experiencing. By keeping the edge of our being company, we might experience how these sensations shift while we try to describe—not explain—them, and while doing so, we might discover new perspectives or a more holistic understanding of what is going on in our situation (see Chapter 4). We are experiencing a meaning-making process in action. Focusing on our micro-dimension circumnavigates patterns of thinking and living (meso-dimension) that often prevent us from discovering fresh insights. It gives us a chance to experience our existence or living process itself and might give us a sense of what it needs right now. Paradoxically, even focusing on our death anxiety can be life-affirming as it can help us sense what our living process needs in order to be carried forward.

I helped Gunther bring his attention to that pressure he sensed on his heart, that vague experience that overwhelmed him at night. As we do in focusing, I asked him if there were any words or images that would precisely describe how that pressure felt (Gendlin, 1978). Gunther talked about something that was "denting." By checking if these words really fit that felt sense on his heart, he found a better description. It felt more like a "heavy elephant's foot stepping on his chest." Yes, it was the feeling of not being able to move and of being completely stuck. There was something inescapable about it. It now became clear to him that his anxiety was about losing his wife. Or even more to the point, that his wife would die one day.

By exploring his fear at this micro-dimension, the meaning of his fear became clearer and more concrete. His anxiety was about the fear that his wife would die one day. The concrete situation of his wife being stuck at the airport evoked a sense of death anxiety. In Gunther's case this felt like being inescapably stuck under an elephant's foot pressing on his heart. Of course, we would not be able to keep his wife from dying; nor would it be possible to solve the existential concern of life and death. However, by listening and exploring his fear of death, we were able to keep it company and bridge Gunther's existential isolation. He had been really reluctant to talk about his fear and felt very alone in it. The large ontological theme of death had shown itself through a concrete, ontic situation and formed a challenge for his living process. It was like the situation was calling him to deal with loss and dying.

Just like Michel de Montaigne was able to explore his concerns about life and death and even developed a personal relationship with death in the shape of his lost teeth and kidney stones, we helped Gunther build a relationship with the elephant's foot on his chest. However, there is an important equilibrium to be aware of here. Clients can feel easily misunderstood when we only seek to personalize their existential concerns. By only talking about this elephant's foot, we would reduce Gunther's concerns about death and dying to its ontic dimensions. By only exploring or working around the micro- and meso-dimension, Gunther might still feel left alone with his larger existential questions or feel like there was no real space for it in therapy (Madison, 2010; Vanhooren, 2019a). After all, Gunther was not only experiencing the fear of losing his wife but also the human condition as such. There is a true art in balancing the attention for both our microcosm and our macrocosm. Together, they form a whole.

Still during that first session, I was also curious what precisely made him think that his wife would die. Somehow, I felt like the situation—his wife being stuck at an airport—was not directly linked to the theme of death and dying. What was it about him and his life that made this situation trigger death anxiety? So I asked him what made him think that his wife could be dying. I invited him to reflect on losses in his life: "How have you been dealing with death and dying in your family? Have any of your parents or grandparents died?" It brought us immediately to the meso-dimension of Gunther's experience.

Gunther explained that his mother had died a few years ago, but this was just the tip of the iceberg. Ten years earlier, his older brother died, probably by suicide. He told me that his brother was never able to cope with the death of their father. Their father died before Gunther turned six. He suspected that his mother was never able to help his brother mourn for his father, and she was no longer able to give warmth and love after the loss of her husband. Gunther did not remember his father that well. His memories were vague and mostly about his father being sick. The family story continued. Gunther never knew his grandfather because he also died at a younger age. It turned out that Gunther was the sole survivor of his family of origin. All men in his family died before turning 45. While he was talking about all these losses, I was wondering out loud if he himself received the necessary care from his mother or other people. Gunther looked surprised: He had never thought about that before. In his family, there was no sharing of feelings or thoughts. They all mourned by themselves and in silence, if they mourned at all.

By exploring the meso-dimension of death and dying, it became clear how death was overly present in his family story. No wonder he was scared about losing his wife. By wondering about his felt sense—the inescapable elephant's foot on his heart related to his fear of losing his wife—Gunther came to realize that it was time to mourn over his family members and face death. It was something he had been suppressing for years. Maybe it was not a coincidence that this was all happening right now. Gunther, at 45, was older than the male line of his family. They all had died before they reached his age.

As we were experiencing and exploring death, we encountered that other huge existential concern: the meaning of life. As if echoing the story of Gilgamesh, which was written 4,000 years earlier, Gunther wondered: "If life is finite, after all, what meaning does it have in the end?"

The Eroding Power of Finitude

The question whether life has meaning since it is finite may have something to do with the confusion between something being meaningful and something being useful. The usefulness of something ends when it stops functioning. Something that has meaning, such as an encounter that lingers after the moment is gone, retains its meaning or even increases in meaning over time. Nevertheless, the awareness of finitude challenges us. Even for those who believe that something of us lingers after death, this particular life comes to an end. Yet the idea that something of us remains can be comforting. Yalom (2008) explains how our lives might have a rippling effect long after we have gone. Just like a pebble that falls into a pond might have a rippling effect on the water surface, so can our actions have an effect on future generations—for better and for worse.

Maybe we become part of our family stories, or survive in family customs, certain values, the DNA we have shared. Or our names might be remembered through our family tree. Yet our particular lived story, with all its twists and turns, highs and lows, secrets and glories, will slowly fade. For many of us, this is a frightening thought. For others, it might be a relief. We feel, as it were, the eroding power of non-being. Inspired by his Jewish spirituality, Heschel (2011a) understands death as a portal that allows the individual to merge back into the whole. In Buber's terms, we could understand this merging back into the whole as the ultimate I–Thou encounter. According to Heschel, the desire for immortality is a distortion instilled by the ego desperately searching for individual prestige or meaning. Dying, according to Heschel, is life returning to its source. This idea also resonates with Rogers (1980). Somehow, we are part of that larger formative tendency, that larger process that has its own direction. Our personal process that reaches for fulfilment resonates with that larger process in its best moments and aches when it does not (Rogers, 1980). In whatever way, we have had the honor of being a personal and unique expression of life, and we have been able to give color to this entrusted life. Then we are reabsorbed into that *universe*. All this encourages humility, and humility—as paradoxical as it might sound—decreases our fear of death (Kesebir, 2014).

As we indicated previously, Tillich highlights the importance of integrating being with non-being. According to him, this is the way out of *despair*. The awareness of impermanence does not need to result in fatalism or nihilism. A popular story from Zen Buddhism is a good example of what Tillich means by this. In one of the many versions of this story, a disciple is having tea with his Zen master. The disciple notices how the master carefully handles an old teacup. Eager to challenge his master, the disciple asks him: "Why do you take such good care of that teacup, my master, if it will break one day anyway?" The master smiles and replies that because he knows the teacup will break one day, he is cherishing it right now.

The awareness of fragility and impermanence can indeed increase a sense of diligence and connection. However, we are often more familiar with the opposite. In our delusion of eternity and unlimitedness, we throw away this connection. This applies both to material goods—we rarely fix things in our Western culture—but also at times to human relationships. This is the perverse effect of a society where perfection is paramount and limitations are denied. Finiteness and vulnerability are linked to meaninglessness and uselessness. What is old and worn is ready to be thrown away.

The Zen story has made me think how to take care of and repair things. One of my favorite coffee cups has fallen about three times. Each time I have managed to glue the pieces together. As a result, I have developed a special bond with it, although I know that one day I will have to let it go. On the micro-dimension, I will then probably perceive some pain, but precisely this prospect gives a much broader meaning to my coffee cup currently. The coffee cup has become more than just the holder of my coffee. It has also come to symbolize the ontological theme of death and non-being (macro-dimension). Picking up the pieces and trying to put them back together also expresses my love of life, however fragile and finite it may be (macro-dimension). At the same time, I also experience warmth and gratitude when I think of all the stories that are associated with my coffee cup: I got it as a present from my sister on a holiday in France, I also associate it with having coffee in the kitchen of our former house, and with some particular life events (meso-dimension). The coffee cup has become a container of life, although it probably will not survive the next fall.

I feel the same way when I make up stories for our son, Jacob. One day he will not ask me to tell him another made-up story. So I am enjoying this blissful time right now, sharpened by the realization that this will come to an end one day.

My own life, too, will come to an end. I am not looking forward to my moment of dying—with or without suffering from "my" kidney stones—although I also notice something of an ambivalent curiosity (macro-dimension). Being aware that it will end helps me realize how much I love life and care for my loved ones. This awareness gives me a warm and tender feeling inside my heart, as if there is a gentle bonfire burning inside me, which we all can sit around and tell stories until late at night (micro-dimension). And this is how I want to live (macro-dimension).

Life as an Existential Given

There are many reasons why many of us fear death. Schneider (2023) explains how death anxiety might represent our deep fear of the Great Unknown. Maybe death itself is less anxiety provoking than the fact that we simply cannot imagine, symbolize, or understand what we are up to. The anxiety that comes with experiencing the completely unimaginable might be life enhancing, states Schneider (2023), as it might broaden and deepen our existential awareness and appreciation of life. Meeting—willingly or unwillingly—what we cannot understand might fuel our living process by challenging our way of existing: the "whole" in which we exist has expanded (Gendlin, 1986); or, inspired by Rank (1932), we might say that our deeper sense and embodied understanding of the macrocosm has affected and broadened our microcosm.

Death is not something most of us are looking forward to. On the contrary, the large majority wants to live as long and well as possible (van Wijngaarden et al., 2020): there is a deep yearning for life (Kramer, 2019). Even more, life is what we are. Although limited in time and space, life is our most profound existential given, says Arendt (2018), who calls it the human condition of *natality* (p. 9), which is inherent in all human activities. We are life, and we are passing it on. It is us and not-us at the same time. For just a moment, we are that unique and personal expression of something that is flowing through us. It is broader than us, and it will survive and encompass us. However, for that very moment, we can color it and shape it within the limitations of our existence. Within these limitations, however, there is a sea of possibilities, and finding our direction in this sea we might call growth.

Humanistic psychology shows that besides our need for a certain balance, we also have the need for growth (Kaufman, 2020). Growing as a human being stretches further than our physical growth and the development of our motor skills. It also entails deepening and broadening our cognitive–affective, social, and spiritual capacities. Rogers (1980) speaks about the organismic tendency to actualize our potential toward fulfillment. Growth arises when we try to understand the world around us and in us. It is fueled by our need to explore, love, and be of meaning (Kaufman, 2020). It also can be a result of having to survive in harsh conditions and having to make sense afterword of how we survived it (Tedeschi & Calhoun, 2004).

Rogers (1961) calls this whole phenomenon our *actualization tendency*. Gendlin (1996) terms it the *living-forward direction*. When we look around us, we see this phenomenon in everything that grows and develops, from the most rudimentary cell to the expanding universe itself. Although systems and organisms disintegrate at some point, there is also another observable law in our universe, in the living as well as in dead matter. Systems in our universe evolve into a certain direction as they go through time (Wong et al., 2023). They grow. And we human beings are good examples of such a process (Rogers, 1980). We see it in our children who learn to grasp, crawl, walk, and jump, and it all seems to evolve out of nowhere. It is this what makes us try, seek, and get up again. In later life, people sometimes show an amazing resilience during physical rehabilitation, as well as in picking themselves back up after a relationship breakup or some other type of loss. This does not mean that falling does not hurt or that our situation never looks hopeless. However, it is this power of growth that makes us get back up despite the potential risks and pain. While we cannot fully understand growth when we deny the circumstances and limitations we meet, very often it is precisely the challenges that make us grow. Rogers (1961) also speaks of growth toward maturity and wisdom as we learn to understand the complexity of life. In this way, acceptance of our limitations can also be understood as a distinct form of growth.

We can call this primal force that makes us grow an important existential given in and of itself (Leijssen, 2013). Georganda (2019) calls it *Oistros*: the desire to live, the capacity to keep going for life, and to participate in life fully. Where death and limitations might make things fall apart, life and love provide connection (Leijssen, 2013). The full experience of life can be overwhelming and leave us gasping for breath. Maslow (1964) describes in detail how peak experiences can turn our lives upside down. In the professional literature today, these types of experiences are called *awe*. They are boundary-pushing experiences in which we feel ourselves reduced and broadened to our true proportions: small and fearful. But at the same time such experiences are connected to something that transcends us (Schneider, 2009; Stellar et al., 2018). We might experience awe through unexpected encounters with people, art, nature, in therapy, or at any moment that transcends us. Awe experiences are in essence I–Thou encounters that put our situation in a different perspective. We can call them spiritual or expansive experiences. These moments can be very brief or for some of us ongoing (Heschel, 2011b). We might experience it in the Himalayas but also in our neighborhood park. Cottyn (2022) describes it this way:

> We were walking in an endless forest [...]. We had a map and a description of the trail. However the description was incorrect and we soon didn't see the yellow signs anymore. We soon got lost. In the beginning while searching for the trail, you still see the forest as consisting as separate parts, the wood, the trunks and the roots that look like chicken's feet, the branches that look tired, bark that only hangs to the trunk on a spider web[...]. All these separate parts, it is almost chilling. If you don't see the forest, you only see the rotting. We walked through thick packs of leaves, where we hoped our trail to be. Only then and there, on that imagined trail, when you lose yourself, you start to see the forest as it is: As a unit, as a sea. Each falling leaf adds to that thick layer of meaning. You begin to trust the forest. Nothing can happen to you. You float. The forest is in a constant process of recovery and decay, a tide of giving and taking. The tree is as merciless as it is generous. The tree is at the same time, running out of direction and time. This is how the forest lasts. Until another yellow sign shows itself again, pushing us out of paradise.

Gendlin (1996) reminds us that the situation we find ourselves in *carries* our lives *forward*. Being lost in the forest carried Cottyn's life experience forward toward a new experiencing of himself in this particular setting and a new understanding of life. It is as if the situation opened himself to a different kind of being and knowing. From this kind of experience, our lives are carried forward. People often know *somewhere* what could make their lives more meaningful. This is their felt sense of their next step, although it is not entirely clear to the mind yet. However, often it is only when the situation moves us into this knowing that we fully embrace the next step and our new understanding of ourselves in this world.

In the context of therapy, Rogers (1961) calls this also the *self-healing capacity* of the client. Rogers explains this capacity in terms of the client who knows somehow what is at stake, what to talk about, and what to explore. By attending to their concern empathically and unconditionally, it somehow starts to shift. It is a common observation in therapy, and no wonder that others, such as Bugental (1999), have described the same process. Bugental calls it the client's search when therapy is about their ultimate concern. As clients often try to make sense of what has happened in the past—but since they experience it now, it is very present in the current situation—we can also understand this process as form of *reactive growth.* It is a kind of growing through making sense of the past as it is experienced in the present (Gendlin, 1997) and, once we understand it, deciphering what it means for who we are about to be. It is the inscribing of our painful experience into our life story, which will alter the story itself. Integrating our painful—and joyful—experiences in our narratives will broaden our understanding of ourselves in this world. Here we are not growing in height but rather rooting more firmly in depth.

The self-healing capacity shows itself in how people spontaneously want to talk when they have experienced something extraordinary. They want to express it, share it, and make sense of it. How deeply we can process this experience often depends on the qualities and abilities of the listener but also of ourselves. The way we listen to ourselves and the way the other person listens to us determines whether we consider it safe enough to reveal the unknown or vulnerable pieces. Rogers emphasizes the importance of creating a safe climate that allows clients to engage in this kind of growth. The self-healing capacity, which Rogers initially formulated as being "in" the person, might be a part of the relationship the client has with themself and/or with the listener. For Rogers, the ideal environment is characterized as an empathic, accepting, and authentic therapeutic relationship (see Chapter 4). Gendlin (1997) further talks about a welcoming, gentle, and open attitude toward our felt sense about our situation. The empathic, genuine, and accepting relational qualities of the therapist become a model for how we can listen to ourselves or, more particular, to our felt sense (Gendlin, 1984). As a result, we might build a different relationship with ourselves and with existence as such.

We saw this self-healing capacity and growth clearly at work in our therapy with Gunther. The question of whether his mother had previously taken good care of him when his father and his brother died set in motion a long process of experiencing and reflection. Death anxiety made way for 40 years of delayed grieving. It was with a childlike shame that Gunther slowly opened up to mourn for his father. Once Gunther felt safe enough, there was room for tears, session after session, for the father he had hardly known. Gunther described our relationship as supportive and empathic, and when I asked him what was particularly helpful, he referred to "right questions at the right moment." Indeed, some of these questions, that only came to me by being attentive to what this moment needed, helped him to focus on to those vague felt senses or implicit meanings that hadn't yet received words. However, in my experience, Gunther also intuitively knew what to do. During therapy, he started visiting his father's grave weekly and twice went to clean it very thoroughly. This cleansing felt like a very deep experience, a ritual in itself. He hoped to be buried close to his father one day.

As Gunther was living through his grief in the micro-dimension, he also started to feel something missing in the meso-dimension. Now that everyone had passed away, the stories about his father were scarce. Gunther started contacting people who would have known his father. Later on, he started collecting stories about his brother and also about his grandfather. Interestingly, the new family stories shed a different light on his personal story. When he learned that his grandfather had been a gifted jazz musician, Gunther regretted that he never learned how to play music. However, it also made him think differently about his own son, who was playing music. It made him realize that it was important to encourage his son to develop this talent. Clearly, the meaning of music in his life had thoroughly shifted.

As Gunther was developing new ways of experiencing connections with his deceased family members as well as with his wife and children, other ontological concerns came to the surface. Topics such a meaning and responsibility came into focus. He became aware of the fact that he always played it somewhat safe during his life.

Fear of Life: Not Daring to Live to the Fullest

Rank (1936) points out that people not only may fear death but life as well. Life anxiety manifests by not daring to live life to the fullest, not taking steps in life, making choices out of fear, not daring to walk one's own path or show one's true colors. According to Rank, life anxiety, just like death anxiety, is part of our life process. Not engaging in life out of fear of getting hurt is a painful experience by itself. It could eventually lead to inauthenticity, as Kierkegaard explains, when we live only by the guidelines of the other in order to be approved (Gardinger, 2001). When life anxiety controls us, our unique voice might fade. Instead of living our unique life, we might live the life of the other. Yet authenticity does not necessarily mean that we always and only listen to ourselves. Rather, authentic living means that we are aware of our choices and responsibilities, and that we can listen to ourselves but also to the opinion of others. Authenticity does not necessarily mean doing your own thing or saying whatever you feel, regardless of what others might think. Authenticity has more to do with living consciously. In some instances, authentic living might entail choosing for the other and the greater good, while at other times it might mean choosing for oneself, although you might be scared to do so.

Fear of life is in stark contrast to that power of growth we just talked about. The grasping, crawling, and waddling baby does not wonder if it will be hurt. Nevertheless, fear is inherent to existence. Our first experience in the world, Rank (2014) argues, is one of fear. It is not the fear of dying, but the fear of being born—being torn away from a familiar unity and thrown into a completely unknown state of being. It is that fear that accompanies any separation, which is also part of becoming our unique selves (Rank,1996).

Life anxiety can be encountered in both its ontic and ontological forms. Rank especially emphasizes this ontological form of life anxiety. Even if we have the best and most loving parents, the best environment to grow up in, we still may experience that fear of living. As an example of this ontological fear of life, May (1983) explains how people experience fear when they are on the verge of self-realization and embark on the path of their dreams. Remarkably, when we get close to what we have wished for, we sense fear. Whether in love, work, or other areas of life, when important opportunities arise, many of us might flee. People then pass on expressing their love for that one person, taking that promotion, going on that special trip, and so on. Inherently, we sense that we are about to change. And there it is again, the Great Unknown (Schneider, 2023). Real growth, argue May (1996) and Taft (1962), involves a substantial change. We grow beyond ourselves. It is a *self-transcendent* experience (see Chapter 3). However, when we decide to play it safe and avoid our fear regularly, it might result in frustration and resentment, often projected onto the other or society. Clearly, the source is not the other but rather our own fear of life and our growing sense of leading an unfulfilling life. As a result, our world seems to shrink because we close down possibility after possibility to become our unique selves (May, 1996). It might start to feel as if we are missing the chances to be the unique expression of what we are or could become. It is the ontological dimension of our fear of missing out (FOMO) on our one chance to shape existence and be the tiny and timely co-creators of this world and this universe.

Disappearing from Your Own Story

Circumstances can have a huge influence and increase our fear of life exponentially. Our clients show how ontic life events can induce so much life anxiety that we almost disappear from our own story. Violence, abuse, and a continuous experience of insecurity make us seek shelter in order to survive. We fear for our lives and carefully scan the environment for signs of danger. In his book *The Discovery of Being*, May (1983) describes how people often sacrifice their own voice in order to survive. We might recognize growth in how we become very inventive in terms of survival. However, when the sensed danger becomes chronic, we might get stuck. We might not only crawl into our shells when we feel anxious but also start living in these shells. Slowly we might lose touch with who we are or can become out of fear of violent reactions from our environment. There is a real risk of losing track of our inner compass and sense of self. Rogers (1951) explains how the terror of rejection, negation, and the absence of love influences one's living process profoundly. After all, as human beings, we have this need for love, recognition, and appreciation from others (Kaufman, 2020). Many of us have a history of only feeling loved when we conform to the wishes of important others.

Rogers (1951) calls this the *conditions of worth*, or conditional love: "I will love you if…." Or even more painfully: "You only exist to me if…." For example, parents might react sharply to children's feelings when they themselves cannot allow or tolerate these feelings. People who have difficulties in experiencing anger might condemn the assertive anger from their children. The same, of course, also applies to sadness or enthusiasm, and so on. Not only parents but siblings, teachers, peers, and culture might reinforce these conditions of worth. When certain feelings or experiences we have are unacceptable to others, this might seep through in how we think about ourselves, how we value ourselves, and which feelings we allow ourselves to experience. Finally, these impressions leave their traces in our self-image and identity, our meso-dimension, so to speak. The consequences are often mild, but sometimes they are also destructive. When we shape ourselves and our lives only on the basis of what others approve or appreciate, self-alienation might eventually occur. Rogers calls the contradiction between a self-image formed primarily around the expectations of others and our own bodily sensing of ourselves and our situations *incongruence*. This incongruence is often noticeable in the difference between how we feel deep inside and how we show up to the outside world. It is the difference between the mask we are wearing and what we feel. In time, we might become so used to this masquerade that we end up ignoring our deepest needs and longings.

While we explored Gunther's fears in therapy, he not only discovered his fear of death but also of life. While focusing, he vaguely remembered once having to sing in front of his class when he was a little boy. He could not come up with the words, and he was laughed at by the entire class. He felt so embarrassed that he fainted, which made the situation even worse. This experience made Gunther keep anything at a distance that could be embarrassing. Among other things, this caused him not to share his family history with others, never to talk about his pain and loss, and hide these feelings so deeply that he was finally unaware of them himself. Gunther showed only his funny side to people. Not even his wife suspected that Gunther carried so much unprocessed grief.

This early experience of rejection and humiliation caused Gunther to play it safe on many occasions. This meant that he refused important promotions at work in order to avoid the possibility of failing. Therapy helped Gunther not only to grieve but also share and process painful and embarrassing feelings. As a result of this therapy, Gunther shared his evolving story not only with me but also with his wife, his friends, and eventually with his children.

The Right to Exist and Basic Trust

The conditions of worth can go so far that some of us do not have the feeling that they are allowed to exist (Rogers, 1980). Being confirmed as a human being that has the true *right to exist* is a fundamental existential need (see Chapter 3). Without experiencing the right to exist, many doors of life seem to close. Related to experiencing the right to exist is having a sense of *basic trust in life* (Frankl, 1967). This kind of basic trust goes beyond trusting others, which is often influenced by our earliest attachment relationships with people (see Chapter 3). Frankl (1967) describes this basic trust as the fundamental trust in what we can call the process of life. While our right to exist and our sense of basic trust can be severely affected by trauma and other adverse life experiences, it can also begin to falter when we cross our own boundaries.

This was the case of Ayla, an Eastern European, 34-year-old woman who was detained in prison because she killed her partner (Vanhooren, 2017). It all happened during a marital quarrel. For years, things had not been going well between Ayla and her husband. Previously, he had threatened her with a knife, and there had been several instances of physical violence. On the day of the killing, when Ayla was pregnant with their second child, they were arguing again. It completely got out of hand. The man grabbed Ayla's throat. She grabbed a knife, and a few moments later he was lying bleeding on the floor. Ayla was completely confused. She immediately called her mother, who notified the police and the emergency services. Ayla ended up in the prison where I was working as a psychotherapist at the time.

During our first conversations, Ayla told me in that she did not want to live anymore. She wanted her son to be adopted as soon as he was born. She had killed his father. How could she then take care of him, she wondered. On the day of the delivery, they brought her in handcuffs to the hospital, and a few hours later she found herself back in her prison cell with her newborn son. During the next few weeks, she slowly sank into a depression. She barely slept. She called it a state of a constant torture of her soul. Something in her did not want to live anymore, but something else told her she should not step out of life. Although she struggled with the feeling that she no longer had the right to exist, she did not want to end her life for her children.

Every day became a burden. Ayla had to learn to live with what had happened and she could not see how. Everyone is suffering, she told me. She felt she could not step out of life, as everyone had to live with what she evoked. She did not want to let everybody down again. She had to keep living for her children and thus learn to live with her guilt. The realization of how important her children were to her supported her. They were the remaining reason for her to carry on. Eventually, she started to find comfort and meaning in reading the Quran and in our sessions. As Ayla stated in one of our sessions:

> On the one hand, I am only a shadow of who I used to be. Or rather, I live somewhere in the dark shadow of my crime. Although it is a struggle to survive every day here, somewhere it has also deepened me. Through psychotherapy and my religious quest, I am trying to understand myself and the

> meaning of my life differently. As hard as it is to express this now, the value human life is priceless [...]. I feel that I understand others more deeply now. I also gained a deeper understanding of religion [...]. My therapy somehow helps me to accept the inacceptable. That doesn't solve my guilt, but somewhere I have to accept that it happened and that I will have to carry this burden for the rest of my life. It is a heavy backpack to carry, but there is no escape. I have to learn how to live with this guilt, and I will have to accept the challenge of explaining what happened to my children hundreds of times.

Searching for meaning was not a luxury for Ayla. For her, it was the only way to keep on living.

Meaninglessness and Meaning

Knowing why and what to live for not only can give people wings when times are good; experiencing meaning can also serve as a life vest during turbulent times. Viennese psychiatrist Viktor Frankl (2006) argues that meaning is not a luxury item that only comes in handy when our basic needs are met. Meaning is precisely what we need the most when everything else is lacking. Frankl experienced how meaning was vital during the World War II's Holocaust. Being Jewish in Europe, he was imprisoned in several concentration camps. His book, *A Man's Search for Meaning*, was a direct outcome of the horrible conditions he survived (Frankl, 2006). Frankl learned that those who still had some sense of meaning had a better chance of surviving. Some people managed to preserve their meaning by transcending the daily terror with simple acts of humanity such as helping the sick (Eliach, 1989; Frankl, 2006). Others who lost their meaning in life were more prone to suicidal thoughts; they also seemed to be more susceptible to physical infections, which usually resulted in a hastened death.

Frankl's book prompted an avalanche of research on the effects of meaning. Experiencing meaning in life might indeed help you to cope better with life challenges (Fortems et al., 2022; Steger, 2022; Vanhooren, Grosemans et al., 2022). Meaning in life has been robustly associated with different kinds of psychological well-being and with both mental and physical health (Delle Fave, 2020). On the other hand, the absence of meaning or lower levels of experiencing meaning has been associated with different many forms of psychological suffering such as suicidality, depression, anxiety disorders, eating disorders, self-harm, and addiction (Fortems et al., 2022; Vanhooren, 2019c). In two different studies, from one- to two-thirds of clients who seek psychotherapeutic help were implicitly or explicitly searching for meaning in life (Golovchanova et al., 2021, Hill, 2018). Furthermore, meaning-making can be understood as a core element of the therapeutic process (see Chapter 4).

Meaning as an Ultimate Concern

Just as the awareness of living and dying can be existentially challenging, so can our search for meaning and our quest for how to be with meaninglessness be taxing (Greening, 1992; Yalom, 1980). Discussing meaning and meaninglessness leads us straight into our existential space. Questions that belong in this domain include: What is my destiny? What do I want to live for? What drives me? What is of importance to me? What do I get up for in the morning? Who am I really? Do I matter? What am I doing here as a human being in this infinite universe? Does life have meaning in itself? Although we can identify some sources of meaning, we usually don't have answers right to hand (Delle Fave, 2020). There are indeed no definite answers to existential questions (Frankl, 2006). Within the context of therapy, the quest for meaning is not about finding a conclusive answer. Rather, it is about finding a way of living that feels meaningful to us (Rogers, 1961).

In general, it appears that a large group of people manage to experience their lives as meaningful. Based on our research among different populations in Europe and the United States, we can roughly distinguish four different ways that people experience meaning in life (for an overview, see Golovchanova et al., 2021). The first group of people seems to experience sufficient meaning and did not search for meaning at the moment of these studies. They are comfortable with themselves and with life as such. Possibly they will seek meaning when the need arises, but this is not the case for this group right now. Although the second group also experiences enough meaning, these people are constantly searching for meaning in their lives. As Hill (2018) suggests, they might also derive meaning from the fact that they are searching for meaning. Just like the first group, these people experience a sense of well-being. However, the way the second group moves through their lives is characterized by a more open and curious attitude toward existence.

A third group showed a lack of meaning. They experience more psychological suffering and less well-being compared to the previous two groups. This group is actively looking for meaning but does not seem to succeed in finding it. Finally, there is the fourth group. These people seem to suffer the most and show the least well-being compared to the other groups. What is striking about this group is that in addition to their lack of meaning, they do not seek new sources of meaning. In one study checking to confirm these findings in a population of prisoners, we discovered some additional characteristics of these four groups. The second group—which experienced meaning and was searching for meaning—showed significantly more posttraumatic growth than the other groups Vanhooren et al., 2016). Furthermore, the fourth group, which showed significantly lower levels of meaning and was not searching for meaning, included more prisoners who had been sexually abused as children. They might have given up on searching or might have been missing some building blocks to derive meaning from their experiences.

In sum, these recurrent patterns teach us that we suffer when we do not succeed in experiencing meaning in life. Moreover, when we give up searching, we suffer even more. So why do we need meaning in the first place, and why do we suffer from meaninglessness?

Human Beings are Meaning Makers

In order to answer these questions, it might be helpful to make the distinction again between the more ontic and the more ontological layers of experiencing our existence. At the ontic level, we see how we are constantly making sense and meaning. Usually, we do so without even realizing it. According to micro-phenomenological research, humans are essentially meaning makers (Gordon, 2013). Meaning-making is central to our human experience. Indeed, as Gendlin (1986) states, the process of being human implies meaning-making. Our hardware is designed to make sense of ourselves and the world (Gendlin, 1986).

At its most basic level, meaning-making happens almost unnoticed: We are constantly making sense. For example, when we see something that is flying around with wings and feathers, we make sense of what we see and give it the word "bird." Interestingly, when you recall the word "bird," a whole experience might open up to you, and you might also get a certain sensation—physically noticeable. Bird is then not just a word but stands for a whole embodied experience, which Gendlin (1962) calls the *felt meaning* of bird. As there are different birds, they might have different felt meanings. How does the bird owl or the bird swan *feel* to you? What are their felt meanings? Is there a difference? We not only try to make sense of what we see or hear but also of what we physically sense. What does your body sense right now? You might be sitting while you are reading. How does this sitting feel? You might not have noticed how you were sitting because the feeling of sitting was all right or good enough. Only when something happens or feels out of the ordinary will we *consciously* start to make sense or search for meaning.

We might start wondering what that stitch in our stomach is or what that look a stranger gave us means. When waking up in the morning, we might wonder what that unusual dream meant. When leaving to school or work, we might notice that the door was not locked and start producing different scenarios why the door was not locked. We are meaning-making in those very moments. We are creating small stories to fill in our meaning gaps.

For us human beings, language plays a special role in our meaning-making. It is hard to imagine a life without language. Images and words help us shape the experience of a meaningful world. It helps us understand what is going on. Words are good examples of ontic meaning. Anyone reading this sentence will understand what the word "table" means. However, the meaning of the word table shifts when we add another word to it. Just try to imagine a table (take a moment for the images you might get when you think of the word "table" and how that feels). Now do the same with kitchen table. After noticing what the meaning of a kitchen table does to you, replace the kitchen table with an operating table. Do kitchen table and operating table feel the same to you? Unless you are a surgeon and have your breakfast at the operating table, it probably will feel very different. You might have sensed how your body reacts differently to these words; a kitchen table and an operating table evoke very different bodily sensations and thus are very different felt meanings. Seeing a picture of your romantic partner or a picture of a car accident will evoke different sensations, although they are both compositions of pixels.

As you might have noticed, our meaning is embodied. As Gendlin (1962) explains, words, numbers, theories, and mathematics only make sense to us if they are somehow accompanied by an embodied process. The aha-moment, when we finally understand something that did not make sense before, comes with a bodily shift. The process of meaning-making involves our whole being. As Tillich (2000) puts it, we human beings do not have meaning; we *are* meaning.

The way we try to resist meaninglessness or losses of meaning makes this even more clear. A loss of meaning might be understood as a system failure. It threatens not only meaning but also us as human beings. Numerous experiments show that people interpret illogical or absurd situations in such a way that they make sense. For example, in a card game, people persistently interpreted a card with black hearts—which should be red—as a card of spades (Proulx, 2013). We interpret—make sense of—this situation in a way that meets our expectations. As a result, the situation does not threaten our sense of living in a meaningful and predictive world. Even when ambiguity arises in non-experimental situations, we assume the most plausible meaning. For example, when we see a car accident, we usually assume that the driver was speeding, distracted, under the influence of alcohol or drugs, or just had back luck, although we do not have the slightest idea (Proulx, 2013). We attribute a meaning to the situation that fits with how we perceive the world as a place that makes sense to us.

Funny situations, absurd jokes, and word games are often based on very mild forms of ontic losses of meaning. Interestingly, they make us laugh. However, even on this ontic level, a loss of meaning can make us suffer. In Annabel's story, we explained how a traumatic experience can cause a loss of meaning on an ontic level. Annabel was not able to interpret her feelings or her embodied sensations anymore. She felt alienated from her bodily reactions. Not recognizing her own emotional reactions was one of the sources of her anxiety. Another painful example of an ontic loss of meaning is what people experience during the different stages of dementia. People, places, and habits are no longer recognizable or make sense. The meaning of the known world disintegrates. However, as the long-term memory might still function, a sense of meaning can be found in the past (meso-dimension). Also, on the micro-dimension, people with dementia might still experience meaning through the here-and-now interaction with their surroundings (Dewitte et al., 2021).

Micro-Dimensional Building Blocks of Meaning

When people experience a lack of meaning, there could be several causes. Some of them can be traced back to the micro-dimension of our experiencing. In general, we can understand meaning as a surplus or the added value that arises from an interaction or a connection. For example, the letters *t e w a r* do not mean anything, but when we connect them in a certain order, the word "water" arises and its meaning cannot be reduced to its individual letters. On the micro-dimension, different basic aspects of interacting and connecting might be a source of a lack of meaning. In terms of experiencing ourselves in the world, essential building blocks on this level are: (1) our ability to be aware and/or be open to what we directly experience, (2) our ability to connect or attune to what we directly experience, and (3) our ability to symbolize our experiences in words, images, or gestures (Warner, 2013).

Let's have a deeper look at *awareness and openness*. Although at the most basic level meaning-making occurs almost unnoticeably, we can also become more aware of these processes. Neurophenomenology and neuropsychology shows how meaning-making occurs at the intersection of bodily, affective, and cognitive processes (Gordon, 2013). Not only do we feel clearly whether something is meaningful or meaningless to us, we can also find out what the exact meaning of the situation is if we zoom in on *how* we experience it. A pressure on our heart, a stone or butterflies in our stomach, a weight on our shoulders, a lump in our throat, these bodily sensations point at the meaning of the moment. Gendlin (1978) calls these vague bodily sensations our *felt senses*. We feel that what we are sensing means something, but this meaning is kind of implicit (Gendlin, 1962). The meaning is not yet clear. We might walk into a party and although we do not know what is going on, we sense that something does not feel right. We sense this through our body. Felt senses are different than emotions or feelings because when it comes to emotions and feelings, the meaning is mostly obvious. Felt senses refer to the intricate *interaction* we are involved in. The felt meaning and the felt sense are the surplus of our ongoing embodied interaction with our environment. This felt sense is a precise but murky implicit meaning of the situation we find ourselves in. It is not entirely in us (although many of us sense it at certain places in our bodies) but rather stems from the situation we are in. This situation stands for the interaction that takes place between myself and my surroundings, or between myself and just myself.

This felt meaning remains implicit as long as we do not pay further attention to it. Although mostly overlooked, this implicit meaning contains the most precise information about how we are, what is important to us right now, and what we need in this concrete situation. Bugental (1999) calls it *the living moment*. It is here that processes of change take place (see Chapter 4). For Gendlin (1970), the felt sense stands for the *core experience of our existence*.

In one of our own studies with 358 Belgian and Dutch participants, we discovered that people who are more aware of their felt sense on a daily basis (i.e., *focusing attitude*) not only experience more meaning in life, they also show more life satisfaction, less distress, and less existential anxiety (Vanhooren, Grosemans, et al., 2022). In a larger international sample with 1,217 participants, we replicated the negative relationship between this focusing attitude, existential anxiety, and depression, regardless of the participants' cultural background (Pellens et al., 2025). Neuropsychological experiments show that people who are explicitly attuned to their bodily sensations—called *interoception*—are also better attuned to the meaning of the situation and more empathic toward others (Ernst et al., 2012; Hlava et al., 2024). Tuning to our felt sense provides us with a particularly rich ground for authentic living because we can draw from the complex, multiple-layered meanings of our situation to guide our lives (Leijssen, 2007). Those who are attuned to their felt sense (micro-dimension) also avoid the risk of building their lives solely on the expectations that we have for ourselves, which are often based on the perceived expectations of others (meso-dimension).

Not everyone is aware and open to the bodily felt senses and miss this important source of deriving meaning. Also, some of us have trouble connecting *and* attuning to what our bodies want to tell us. We might be open to what we feel but find it difficult to be or stay attuned. There are multiple reasons why we might experience difficulties in this micro-process of attunement. Warner (2013) points out that not everyone manages to hold their attention to what they physically perceive. Maybe we did not learn how to slow down and to hold this kind of attention span, or lost this capacity along the road. In depression, for example, there is a kind of disconnection from one's bodily experiences (Fuchs, 2019), and as a result, the person loses their basic source of feeling alive and of making sense of their life. Life might start to feel like something that happens at a distance, in which they are no longer involved (Fuchs, 2019; see Chapter 4).

Indeed, attention and reflection presuppose a proper nearness or distance from our bodily sensations and feelings. Leijssen (1998) explains how some people stay too far from their bodily experiences and seem to feel nothing. This deprivation of feelings, or *alexithymia*, sometimes also experienced as emptiness, might have roots in childhood experiences such as neglect or violence; parents could not or did not help to mirror, hold, and name the young child's experiences. Usually, parents assist their children in making sense of everyday situations by taking a moment to reflect on what the child is expressing and give it meaning through language (Warner, 2013). The other side of the continuum represents lacking a certain distance from one's bodily experiences and emotions (Leijssen, 2025). As a result, we might feel overwhelmed or be scared of being overwhelmed by our emotions.

We fear in those instances being carried away, or we might become scared that our feelings will destroy us. In this case, meaning-making becomes difficult because there is no space to dwell on the implicit meaning of the moment. Some people might experience both and switch between being engulfed (too little distance) and being totally out of touch (too much distance). In such instances, cultivating an optimal distance toward our immediate felt experiences might help to make sense of what we are going through.

Sensing and meaning-making are unfolding processes through which the implicit meaning becomes explicit (Gendlin, 1978). When we bring our attention to our vague felt sense and accompany it by searching for words or images that fit what we sense and feel, we slow down our ontic meaning-making process. We are giving ourselves time and space to engage in an unfolding meaning-making process that reveals an insight in our precise personal-existential situation. Gendlin (1978) calls this slowed-down meaning-making process *focusing*. Focusing can be understood a specific form of self-exploration through which we make our implicit meanings accessible. Although many of us spontaneously engage in focusing without even knowing, Warner (2013) points out that others might recurrently experience faltering meaning-making cycles. She calls it *fragile process functioning*, a stumbling over one or more of the three micro meaning-making processes, which we explained as (1) perceiving and the capacity to be aware or open; (2) connecting and attuning; and (3) symbolizing what we are experiencing through different means of language.

Angus and Greenberg (2011) further speak of *un-storied emotions*. Here we are not talking about the more structural problems of fragile meaning processes. It is more about islands of feelings or emotions that we do not understand, usually feelings that we have not been able to process. After all, to process is to feel through our experiences and, by doing so, give space for their implicit meanings to unfold. The fear of being overwhelmed by what feels threatening inside prevents us from sensing its meaning. As a result, the need behind this is unknown and unattended.

The ability to connect with our felt experiences is not only a prerequisite for experiencing ontic meaning; it also provides the building blocks for engaging in a meaningful life. Abeyta and colleagues (2015) showed through a series of experiments that there is a link between the ability to experience both positive and negative feelings, on the one hand, and, on the other, having a more resilient meaning system that withstands existential threats. However, if we cannot or dare not to be open to our experiences, this might lead to problems on our meso-dimension and finally on the macro-dimension of meaning.

Our Perception of the World is Colored by Our Meaning System

The accumulation of meaning throughout various micro-situations will eventually shape our meso-dimension. As a result of positive and negative life experiences, we construct images of ourselves, our family, the world, and even of existence as such. Our self-image, identity, life story, family story, and cultural, ideological, and religious narratives are containers of meaning (Angus & Greenberg, 2011). Park (2010) calls this our personal *meaning system*. Our meaning system—this set of images and beliefs—forms the lens through which we view ourselves and understand the world. It helps us to determine how we want to connect with ourselves, the others, and the world.

Whereas meaning-making at the micro-dimension works bottom-up by deriving meaning directly from our current embodied experiencing of the situation, meaning-making at the meso-dimension works top-down through imposing meaning on the situation based on our former life experiences (Greenberg & Pascual-Leone, 2001). The meso-dimensional image we have of ourselves will help us to understand our own reaction in the here-and-now situation. Likewise, our culture will help us to understand the body language of others that are part of our culture. The structures of our self-image and world assumptions help us to quickly structure the meaning of what is going on. However, our meaning system might prevent us from being open to experiences that are different from what our meaning system expects. It might make us rigid and cause our experiences to be structure-bound as we interpret them based on our meso-structures (Gendlin, 1970; Rogers, 1961). It might prevent us from experiencing the newness of what we are experiencing right now. The polarization of visions and politics in society (Schneider, 2013) might be explained by the fact that we fear a loss of meaning on this meso-dimension. Consequently, people engage in fierce discussions and will even use false arguments and lies to convince the other of what is "right" to them, and, most of all, without having to risk rethinking their own positions. These discussions could be understood as "holy wars." There is a lot of energy that goes in preserving our own meaning system and our cherished beliefs (Park, 2010). A little burst in how we see the world might send us on a quest for meaning, which is often accompanied by anxiety and distress (Park, 2010).

Martela and Steger (2016) point out that people derive meaning from the extent to which their meaning-making system contains and maintains some degree of *coherence*. The coherence of our identity and corresponding values and choices as well as concrete goals can give us a sense of meaning. Contrarily, a lack of coherence can be experienced as a problem. The awareness of not remembering or knowing important pieces of one's life story can evoke a sense of meaninglessness. As Gunther showed, looking for stories about his brother, father, and grandfather helped him to fill in important meaning gaps and gave more meaning to his life. Some clients who grew up in orphanages or were adopted live with a sense of something missing concerning some elementals of their life stories. They might have been moved too often from place to place, and important basic information about themselves as children got lost. Other clients might not remember basic information concerning their pre-school or primary school years due to traumatic experiences and dissociation. To answer the question Who Am I? we need important building blocks on the meso-dimension.

Our *identity*, an important part of our meso-dimensional meaning system, arises like all meaning from interaction. We get to know ourselves by how we are understood or received by those significant others. If we cannot remember anything from our first years, we are dependent on others to hear about our very beginnings. Years ago, our son, Jacob, repeatedly asked me to tell him again and again "from when I was born." What I told him and how I told this story became a part of his life story. Significant experiences with our parents or others clearly color and shape our self-image, values, and norms. May (1983) and Rogers (1961, 1980) indicate how *conditions of worth* from others and society might strongly influence how we shape our self-image: Who am I supposed to be, am I allowed to be, am I allowed to exist? Adverse and difficult significant life experiences are therefore often a subject of psychotherapy. Experiential methods such as empty-chair work and two-chair dialogues from emotion-focused therapy or gestalt therapy can help to go through these stuck experiences from the past in the here and now in order to set them back in motion (Elliott et al., 2004: see Chapter 4).

Resonating with "Das Ganze"

Our sense of meaning of our life can be understood as the result of an intricate interaction between our bodies, our present experiential flow, our memories, our images of the future, our immediate and imaginary interactions with others, our world, and with what happens beyond our comprehension. The experience of meaning includes different building blocks that we can situate on the micro- and meso-dimension. However, our sense of meaning of the whole, the macro-cosm, or *Das Ganze* as Rank (1936) would say, transcends our micro-cosm as individuals. In the end, as we experience awe while gazing at the stars, our individual story does not seem to matter that much anymore. Here we are interacting with *the more…*, as Gendlin would phrase it. We can sense it inside, but it seems to be a trembling that resonates with the entirety of being far beyond our individual selves.

In those moments the micro-dimension and our macro-dimension of experiencing seems to overlap. Focusing, states Gendlin, can work as a portal to the experience of an ultimate (Lou, 2019). Indeed, focusing associated with meaning in life, life satisfaction, and less existential anxiety (e.g., Pellens et al., 2025; Vanhooren, Grosemans, et al., 2022). In a study with two diverse American demographic samples (n = 441 and n = 443), the openness to one's bodily-felt experiences was also associated with self-transcendent experiences such as awe and compassion (Hlava et al., 2024). Gendlin goes further, "within experiencing lie the mysteries of all that we are" (Gendlin, 1962 p. 15). These mysteries entail indeed the All (or the Nothing if this works better for you), which is more than what we can put into words. The meaning or meaninglessness we experience has a different character here compared to what we have been explaining so far. Knowing what our values or our goals are will not satisfy our need for a more ultimate meaning. Though we may have the experience that our life story is coherent and that we are able to formulate concrete goals, all of this seems to be peanuts when we place it in the broader context of the universe.

In the face of the macro-cosm, the pursuit of goals makes place for a search for our destination and fulfillment, our need for coherence might make place for our desire for existential significance (Martela & Steger, 2016), and the search for meaning *in* life might be enriched by the search for the meaning *of* life. Do I matter or have I mattered, and what is life all about? Wim, a 40-year-old prisoner whom I worked with as a therapist, came to the following realization: "If I would die right now, my life would have been meaningless. But if I could make a difference in another person's life, then my life would be a success" (Vanhooren et al., 2017a).

While reflecting on the ultimate question of meaning, some of us might sense the same fear of non-being that comes when we realize that we are finite. Given the fact that a sense of meaning arises from interaction, the feeling that comes with this question is already a result of how we experience this interaction between us and the entirety of life or, more correctly, the interaction we feel as timely human beings on a cosmic scale. This experience seems to be quite different for many of us.

For some, such as the French existentialists Sartre (2003) and Camus (1975), life might be quite meaningless. Although meaninglessness does not necessarily equal anxiety, for many this might be experienced as a threat-based awe (Gordon et al., 2017) in which fear, despair, existential loneliness, and loss of connection dominate. Indeed, for Sartre (1980) and Yalom (1980), there is no ultimate meaning of life. Sartre uses Heidegger's concept of *Verlassenheit* (i.e., being left to oneself) to describe that there is nothing else than oneself to lean on to make sense of one's existence. Yalom (1980) talks about groundlessness to explain the same condition. From their point of view, even though we might experience meaning on a micro- or meso-dimension, there is no ground under our feet. This groundlessness might be experienced as a powerful realization of this ultimate meaninglessness and ultimate freedom. It is the experience of non-being, as Tillich (2000) would put it. The universe might feel like a threatening void. Problems in making sense of the larger picture might lead to what Frankl (2006) describes as experiencing an *existential vacuum*. According to him, many people fail to experience their lives as meaningful. Despite their material well-being, their jobs, their family life and so on, something is gnawing at them. There is something missing that cannot be ignored: The missing of an ultimate sense of meaning.

On the other hand, there are existentialists such as Kierkegaard (2013), Buber (2010), Marcel (1969), and Jaspers (2003) who experience something very different when they sense their interaction with the entirety of life. In their connection with what transcends them, they notice how everything might make sense. Instead of experiencing groundlessness, they might feel carried by something larger than oneself. Instead of experiencing an emptiness or an absolute nothingness, they might sense something like an undefinable something. Rather than nothing, there is a *no-thing*, explains Gendlin (Preston, 2007). "It is not true that there is nothing at the bottom," he says. "The implicit life process is at the bottom" (Lou, 2020, 10:58)

It seems that the experience of this larger existential living space can feel very different to different people. It also might change over time. This makes sense precisely because the experience of this largest existential living space includes ourselves in our connection to this whole. It seems to be logical that our sense of ultimate meaning(-lessness) would change repeatedly. However, people seem to lean more toward one side of the continuum than the other. For many, it would be inconceivable to think that one might feel very differently about this grounded or groundless experience. This living experience might become solidified and guarded as a structure-bound experience on the meso-dimension. Losing or experiencing meaning on the macro-dimension might come with deep anxiety, as if the totality of one's existence is completely turned upside down.

One (negative) way of defending oneself against any cracks in one's meaning system is to think that the other is wrong and has to be converted into atheism or theism in order to see the true light or darkness. At this level, there is indeed a certain danger of *hubris*. We can notice a certain haughtiness when religion or a belief in an afterlife is framed as a form of denial of death or a kind of coping mechanism in order not to sense groundlessness. Likewise, there is hubris and disdain of the other when we want to convince others of an ultimate meaning of life. Clearly, the different position of the other toward the meaning of life can feel like a serious threat. A high dose of existential empathy, the cultivation of a not-knowing stance, and an unconditional positive regard for the experience of the other are the necessary ingredients for listening to the other in an open way (Vanhooren, 2022b).

Regardless of whether people may or may not assume existence has meaning, existential thinkers on both sides are convinced that we need meaning. If there is no ultimate meaning, Yalom (1980) argues, we still have to create it in order to keep on going. Sartre (1980) states that a person's meaning in life is built by their choices and actions. And although Frankl (2006) believes that there is an ultimate meaning, he turns the question of meaning upside down: What can I mean for life instead of what life might mean to me. It encourages us not only to enjoy life but also to lead a more engaged way of living.

The Content of Meaning

In addition to the distinction between ontic meaning and ontological meaning, an exploration of the content of one's meaning in life provides a different angle to understand problems in making sense of one's existence. The research literature generally distinguishes between eudaimonic and hedonistic meaning-making (Zegers, 2021). In the footsteps of the Greek philosopher Aristotle, *eudaimonia* can be understand as a kind of meaning-making that is not centered around oneself. It is inspired by values or virtues such as love, altruism, care, joy, and truth and is essentially directed toward the other, the community, the planet, etc. (Leijssen, 2013). *Hedonistic* meaning is characterized by its immediate gratification. It is focused on pleasure, experiential thrills, material well-being, and so on. Whereas hedonistic meaning is more characterized by *getting*, eudaimonic meaning is more by *being*.

While enjoying good food, a hot tub, and summitting a mountain can be an expression of one's joy in life, it appears that people who primarily derive their meaning from hedonistic sources are more vulnerable in the face of adversity. As Frankl already observed, people who are more engaged in eudaimonic meaning-making not only appear to be more resilient. they also show higher physical resistance to infections and inflammations on a physical level (Delle Fave, 2020; Ryff, 2012). Socioeconomic or gender differences do not seem to explain this link: Overly depending on hedonistic meaning is a risk factor for dying earlier (Becchetti et al., 2019). In the absence of eudaimonic meaning, hedonistic meaning-making is also associated with depression (Telzera et al., 2014). Adolescents who are primarily focused on pleasure are more likely to experience depression than their counterparts who are committed to nature, social, or other self-transcending goals. Hedonistic pleasure does not seem to be durable. Once its effect vanishes, hedonistic pleasure leaves us with emptiness, which makes us look for more pleasure in order to fill the gap it left in the first place. As a result, we end up in a cycle that leads to a sense of meaninglessness and hopelessness (Telzera et al., 2014).

This is what happened to Aisha, a 21-year-old college student who was stuck in this kind of hedonistic downward spiral. However, this was not obvious at the start of our therapy. All I knew at the beginning was that she suffered from symptoms of depression, bulimic binge eating, and self-injury.

Aisha, Searching for a Way out of the Void

During our initial sessions, Aisha reported that she experienced great fatigue that caused her to spend her days in bed. She realized that by constantly being tired and staying in bed, she would not be able to live a meaningful life. Indeed, she wanted just the opposite. She wanted to be a significant person, to leave a mark, to do something she would be proud of. Yet she could not rouse herself to action. Although she did not want to lead an average life, she knew she got little done. For Aisha, life in itself had no meaning, but at the same time she wanted to be the most attractive, the best, the most interesting person within her group of friends. Life had to be fun. However, she—and life as such—could not live up to this expectation.

Very early in therapy, we discovered that anything showing the opposite of what she hoped for was accompanied by a deep dip in energy. Sometimes Aisha would crawl into bed, and at other times when she felt too upset she tried to cope with this void by binge eating or by self-harming behavior. There was a need to be at the center of attention. If her partner was not around, she would fall in love with someone else or seek immediate sexual attention. Aisha realized this was not leading to a life she was hoping for: "How can I ever have a steady relationship and a family if I forget about my partner when she is not around?"

Aisha was stuck in a downward destructive spiral in which, paradoxically, everything was supposed to be fun. Her hedonistic way of living did not fill her hunger for meaning. Aisha lived from thrill to thrill, but her existence remained empty. In order to help her experience more meaning in life, our challenges were multiple.

On the *micro-dimension*, it became rapidly clear that it was difficult for her to sense her body. It was also hard for her to describe her feelings or symbolize her felt senses. She could not respond to my questions about what she was feeling or sensing in the here-and-now. When I asked her to describe what she was feeling just before she would binge eat or injure herself, she would only describe a kind of numbness that she tried to get rid of by self-destructive or impulsive sexual behavior. By not being able to attend her bodily feelings and not knowing how to use words to describe her inner world, basic meaning-making on this micro-dimension was faltering. One of our first tasks in therapy was to learn how to attend her felt sense, her feelings, and her inner world. When we lose touch with ourselves, we miss the basics to experience a meaningful life. During the first stage of this therapy, there was a lot of focus on expanding her bodily and emotional awareness and learning how to use language to describe and explore her inner world. As a therapist, I used my empathic capacity to the fullest to help her articulate what was noticeable inside her or in interaction with others.

Aisha would often honestly respond with "I don't know" when I asked her to describe what she was feeling at the moment. I had to rely on what we call *re-experiencing* and *crossing* (Ikemi, 2017). During this re-experiencing, the therapist tries not only to be aware of what the client is experiencing but also of their own felt sense and will tentatively communicate this experiencing with words. The therapist engages in this micro-dimensional meaning-making process in an active and cautious way. With Aisha, I tried to be aware of what she could not put into words. I was tuning into her pre-verbal felt sense by attending my own felt sense of her situation. I encouraged her to check if the words I used to describe what she might be sensing matched with what she was experiencing. By continuously using this re-experiencing throughout the first sessions, Aisha's openness to her inner world significantly increased. We call this *crossing*: Her capacity to experience and symbolize her felt sense and derive meaning from her experiences was growing in richness and depth. Eventually, by focusing on what she was sensing, the initial emptiness and numbness transformed into a deep sadness. This sadness, which initially seemed to come out of nowhere, was accompanied by a lot of tears, which surprised her. The meaning of this sadness would only unfold during the following sessions. But for now, it was remarkable to see that by allowing herself to experience her sadness, her fatigue and depressive symptoms decreased.

On the *meso-dimension,* we met a different challenge. As Aisha learned to attend the reality of her inner world, she became aware that she had to face the outer reality as well. Her meaning system with its overly high expectations needed revision. There was a clear dissonance between her high expectations, on the one hand, and what life had to offer, on the other hand. It led to a constant disappointment. In therapy, we explored where those expectations came from. As is often the case, it turned out that her expectations had some strong roots in her family story. In her experience, her family placed a strong emphasis on performing and exceling. "Just being" was not good enough; only shining achievements were met with cheers and love. These conditions of worth nestled deeply in her experience of her existence: She only had the right to exist if she was better than the rest. As a result, she expected herself to excel constantly. It also made her look down on people who lived "mediocre" lives, including herself. By reflecting on these expectations, she eventually came to realize that there was injustice in how she looked down on herself, others, and on life as such. Life could not meet these expectations. At this point, the meaning of her sadness and sorrow on the micro-dimension unfolded through these meso-dimensional explorations: It was the sorrow of her deep loneliness and her desire to be accepted and loved for who she was—not for the person who excelled.

As a result of these discoveries and realizations, Aisha started to wonder what could really give her life meaning. On the *macro-dimension,* she expressed early in therapy that life was ultimately meaningless. Yet she wanted to mean something as a person and make sense of her life. As we progressed through the micro- and meso-dimensions, Aisha experienced a shift concerning meaning at the macro-dimension as well. Initially, she thought her life could only be meaningful by doing something deserving of a special place in history. However, she came to understand meaning in terms of contributing to the bigger picture and to the well-being of others. She made an explicit shift toward a more eudaimonic sense of meaning. Instead of asking herself whether a situation was nice, she now asked herself what would be important in this situation. This made me think of Frankl's (2006) *de-reflection*: the reversal of the question "what is the meaning of life" to "how can I be of meaning to life itself." Aisha was very concerned about climate change and wanted to actively work to turn the tide. In addition, she committed herself to a long-term relationship, although she was deeply afraid of failure and conflict. It only now became clear that it was her fear of failure in intimate relationships that made her feel so dreadfully lonely. However, she no longer allowed herself to be dictated by her fear of life. Instead of trying to live up to impossible expectations, her acceptance of possible failures was precisely what opened the door to a more meaningful existence.

As we go deeper into Aisha's story, we will see how she not only found meaning in her relationships but also by how she made some risky decisions concerning her future. As studies repeatedly indicate, people usually experience meaning through their connection with others and through personal growth (Delle Fave, 2020). Aisha would derive meaning through both of these sources.

Personal Growth and the Other as Sources of Meaning

Personal growth that leads to more meaning is characterized by, among other things, an openness to and an encounter with what is happening in and around us (Kaufman, 2020). We can only grow when we open ourselves up to what we do not know yet. From a humanistic point of view, therapy is always a form of growth. Psychotherapy and counseling is not just a matter of removing or alleviating suffering. Therapy is also a process of broadening and deepening our existence. In fact, from this humanistic point of view, suffering and symptom relief is understood as an outcome of meeting the challenges that bring us to therapy in the first place. Likewise, we could see how Aisha's suffering shifted while she was growing as a person through therapy. The subsequent shifts on the micro-, meso-, and macro-dimensions can be understood as personal growth or development, resulting in a more authentic relationship with herself and others.

In addition to experiencing meaning from personal development, people generally derive meaning from their relationships with others (Delle Fave, 2020). Not surprisingly, clients also experience more meaning through the therapeutic relationship (Fortems et al., 2022, Rim et al., 2022). The therapeutic relationship can lead to a corrective experience when the client feels seen, accepted, acknowledged, and appreciated by the therapist. As a result, clients not only start to experience the relationship to themselves differently but also to experience more meaning in their relationships with others (see Chapter 4). People derive much of their meaning from their interactions with their parents, children, friends, family, or their community (Delle Fave, 2020). Others experience meaning in contact with nature, the universe, or the mystery of life. This resonates with what Heschel (2011a) means when he argues that no one's ego is worthy to be their ultimate goal.

It also resonates with belonging as a source of meaning (Delle Fave, 2020). Belonging involves a deep sense of being part of something that is larger than ourselves. Belonging goes beyond our attachment to people or places, as we can also feel deeply at home in ourselves, in our bodies, or in the whole. Those who can feel at home and belong to the Great Unknown might experience a stronger sense of basic trust (see Chapter 3). For some of us, being part of a larger whole might feel threatening, while for others the realization that they are unique might be frightening. As Rank (1936) describes, for many of us relating to others while staying true to our colors might be a real existential challenge.

Isolation and Connectedness

In between the lines, you might have found in the stories of Gunther, Ayla, Aisha, and Annabel that connecting to others is an important source of meaning. In our own lives, we derive meaning and value from being a romantic partner, friend, colleague, family member, or parent. When something does not work relationally anymore, we often suffer or experience a multitude of feelings. For people in general, relationship break-ups and social exclusion are draining when it comes to their meaning in life (Stillman et al., 2009). Just like meaninglessness, loneliness has been robustly associated with mental and physical health difficulties (Constantino et al., 2019). Yet this does not mean that those of us who constantly spend time with others automatically feel good. As human beings, we equally need time and space to spend with ourselves and to find our particular path in life—at least within Western cultures. This dual need, wanting to be unique but also wanting to feel connected, often leads to struggles that color our life stories. Novels, songs, and movies are often built around this existential challenge: the need to be wanted and loved, grotesquely portrayed in the search for the ultimate love and often impossible relationship, on the one hand, and the need to be unique, on the other, shown in the architype of the suffering superhero who saves the world.

The desire for affection, sexuality, love, and friendship can consume us like fire. Some of us would give up anything in order to establish that romantic relationship or to become a member of this special group. However, being absorbed into another person or a group can make us lose touch with ourselves. For example, you may suddenly realize that you are putting aside your own needs or aspirations just to gain approval, appreciation, recognition, or love. Self-alienation for the sake of the other is therefore not an exceptional phenomenon.

But there is also that other side. Along with the need for security and love, we also have the need to make a difference, to be significant, original, and our own person. We look up to people who have made exceptional achievements or speak their minds without being afraid to be expelled from the group. Although both desires—the desire to be unique and the desire to be included—do not necessarily need to clash, people often swing between these two poles (Rank, 1936). Rank, the forerunner of humanistic and experiential therapies, discovered that many of his clients seemed to be suffering from their inability to find a balance or a solution between these two needs—to find their own voice while also feeling connected and accepted by others (Kramer, 2019).

The Longing to be Whole Again

According to Rank (2014), the trauma of birth or the splitting of the original mother–child unity is the starting point of the desire to feel whole or complete again. Once born, we have become identifiable individual beings. From that point on, there is a yearning to retrieve an ultimate wholeness, states Rank. During some instances, we might again feel immersed in something larger. However, we might feel pushed out of these wholesome moments after a while, accompanied by a mourning that we have lost it once again. Moments of experiencing an intimate connection with a romantic partner, friends, nature, and the universe are good examples of this kind of connection. The pain of having to leave these people or experiences behind feels like leaving something of ourselves behind. Regardless of Rank's theory of the trauma of birth, people tend to seek a deeper connection, be it inside or outside themselves. Different theologies and psychological theories describe the soul as that part of the self that can bridge our microcosm and macrocosm (Leijssen, 2009).

According to Rank, the desire for wholeness can also be an expression of a longing that transcends our individual ontic experience. On a more ontological and spiritual level, this desire is a reminder that we were once whole before we were born and that after we die, we will merge with that larger whole again. The ontic concrete experiences of our search for oneness are an expression of this larger existential theme. Since fusion means the end of our individuality, it can release a deep fear of death (Rank, 1936). It is not a coincidence that the orgasm—into which we disappear for a moment as a person—is also called in French *la petite mort* (the small death). But even before and beyond bedtime, we can dissolve in our relationships like a fizzy tablet. This fear of losing ourselves can be so strong that we no longer dare to engage in an intimate relationship.

Besides the ontological desire or fear for oneness, we can also experience the fear of being thrown back into our individuality. On an ontic level, this becomes noticeable in how people respond to relational disillusionment. Some of us only engage in relationships while keeping an eye on the emergency exit, while others might endure anything out of fear of being alone. Whether prompted by fear of death (to be absorbed in wholeness) or by an anticipated terror of being thrown back on ourselves, avoiding the ontological desire for oneness comes with a price. The pain of not feeling deeply connected and not belonging might come with feelings of being forlorn. However, this is the price that some people would rather pay. This, too, can be an authentic, meaningful choice.

The desire for uniqueness and the expression of our individual voice stands for the other pole of this existential challenge.

The Equally Strong Need for Separation

Besides the desire to surrender to a whole, there is also the need to exist as a separate entity. How we respond to this might be influenced by our culture, but in Western societies many of us have a need to make our unique contribution and to make a difference in the world. Curiosity might help us explore different paths in life that set us apart from the other birds in our original nest. Developing our own passions and interests might help us develop our own sense of self. In addition to curiosity, the will is one of the engines of our growth toward uniqueness (Rank, 1936). The will is a pulsating force that might help us to go against the grain if necessary. We flex our will when we discover the word "no" as a toddler. Standing up for our own opinions belongs to this domain. Where curiosity can set us on our path, our will helps us to make choices, cut knots, and overcome our fears. It can help us liberate ourselves when we get stuck in unhealthy habits or dangerous situations. It helps us face our challenges, achieve our goals, and cope with the unexpected (Maddi, 2013). However, the will also has a shadow side. When we are hyper-focused on what we want, we might become blind regarding our need for connection and fail to consider the needs and desires of others as well.

Our growth toward uniqueness is not always met with applause. Tension, conflict, and disapproval—or our fear of these possible reactions in others—are often the toll we pay. Depending on our relationships with our parents, caretakers, or peers, the road to become our "truest selves" can be quite rocky. Not only can disapproval be painful, we might also feel really guilty of being disloyal when we make different choices. In relationships, the rising need for uniqueness can evoke a deep fear of being abandoned. Separation—tearing ourselves away from our relationship with others or taking a different position within these relationships—can be tragic. These breaks might be accompanied with loneliness, guilt, and grief. Withholding oneself from becoming oneself out of fear of experiencing these feelings could be considered as another dimension of one's fear of life (Rank, 1936). Life anxiety can keep us from taking our next steps. By avoiding these next steps, we might become overly dependent on others and develop a deep sense of frustration toward them, ourselves, and life. We might start avoiding being alone in order not to be reminded of our unfulfilled needs or wishes.

Interestingly, Moustakas (1972) argues that we need periods of solitude and silence in order to experience personal clarity. While it is true that we discover ourselves in relation to others, it is equally true that we can only experience ourselves when we notice what is happening inside. It is through personal reflection that we discover and develop a relationship with ourselves. Kierkegaard notes in his renowned *Sickness unto Death* (2013, p. 269) that the *self* is actually a relationship that relates to itself. It sounds a bit complicated, but it becomes clearer when we realize that we often have inner dialogues. Indeed, we regularly engage with different aspects or parts of ourselves (Mearns, 2002). In some therapies, these parts are given names (e.g., the inner child, the supporter, oppressor), although they might be different for everyone, change over time, merge, or disappear. We can understand these parts as colored glasses through which we experience ourselves in certain ways. We might start talking to ourselves from these different self-perspectives. We can understand Kierkegaard's idea of the self "being a relationship that has a relationship to itself" as the ongoing inner dialogue between our part-selves or voices—some very loud, others silenced. We might notice how these intra-relationships play out when we are in conflict with ourselves and others. When we lack a certain degree of personal integration, we might feel very confused and miss a sense of direction in our lives. Längle (2018) emphasizes the importance of living with inner consent, an endorsement of one's way of being in order to pursue our path to fulfilment.

True autonomy can be recognized by feeling at ease with oneself and being grounded in one's being. It might sound like a paradox, but autonomy might open the door for a deeper and less complicated connection with others (Rogers, 1961). When we are more firmly connected to ourselves, we are more able to recognize the other as a person with different needs and feelings. The deeper our self-empathy develops, the more we can be empathic to others. At those moments, both needs—being connected to ourselves and being connected to others—are met.

Existential Isolation and Connectedness

In addition to our desire to connect and to be ourselves, existential psychology teaches us that we can never feel completely connected constantly or ever exist completely apart from others. The concept of *existential isolation* refers to the experience that no one will live like you have lived and therefore rarely, if ever, will you have the feeling of being completely understood (Yalom, 1980). We may experience this isolation as loneliness, but this is not necessarily so. Those who can be with themselves can also enjoy being alone (Moustakas, 1972). Also, the reality is that we do not exist by ourselves.

In addition to Kierkegaard's notion that the self is an ongoing relationship, Heidegger (1999) describes how we are in constant interaction with what surrounds us or, more correctly, that we are interaction. On a biological level, we are completely part of our ecosystem. We are mammals on this planet. As human beings, we also live entirely within the subjective reality of culture, language, and meanings. We cannot escape that either. Even when we dream, scenarios unfold that are about ourselves interacting with others, animals, or our environment. In therapy, we notice how people keep struggling with important others, even when they have not seen them in years or when they died. Although we may be existentially isolated, we are equally interdependent and connected. Both our existential loneliness and our ultimate connectedness are, in a nutshell, expressions of our selves, the relationship that we are, or the many ways in which we experience our *dasein*, ourselves-being-in-our-world. From this point of view, we can understand our loneliness as a type of relationship we are having with ourselves in our world. We cannot escape the relationship we are having with ourselves and with others, although we might not be able to share how this feels or what it means because we experience it in our own unique ways. This might feel very lonely. However, our unique feelings of loneliness might help us to reach beyond the field of interhuman relationships and feel as one with nature and the universe.

How we experience the existential challenge of isolation and connectedness might depend on the situational quality of the relationship we are having with ourselves and others.

Quality of Contact

Just as we can distinguish substantive differences between hedonistic and eudaimonic meaning, there are essential differences in how we encounter ourselves, others, and the whole. We already mentioned Buber's (1998) distinction between I–it and I–Thou encounters. In the first kind of encounter, we have already defined the other, ourselves, or the environment based on theories or previous experiences and do not enter this meeting with curiosity or interest. For example, we may buy bread at a bakery without being fully aware that we are interacting with another person. Similarly, we might have dinner with our family without really engaging with one another. These are lower quality meetings because we are not really open to the potential that each encounter holds. We are available neither to the other nor to ourselves. We are unaware that this encounter is unique and finite.

Sometimes we actively employ this I–it mode when we want things to remain unchanged. For example, we may avoid experiencing and encountering our family members' or the client's suffering by minimizing the family member to what we think they are or the client to a "disorder." When we see people on the street, we might reduce them to their looks or how they behave. We reduce the other to that one aspect that is different (or similar) from who we are or how we think that people in our culture should behave. Especially when we see people who seem to look poor or odd, we tend to reduce them to what we interpret as their difference. This not only prevents us from really meeting them, but we are also alienating the other. We might easily project our fears on that person. The other becomes a symbol for what is essentially our death anxiety: our fear of poverty, of the unknown, of the potential harm that we might experience when we would engage with that person.

Interestingly, we also seem to vary in how we meet ourselves. Cooper (2015) talks about an I–me relationship, where we turn a deaf ear to all kinds of inner signals. Not listening to our body, our intuition, our felt sense, or hiding difficult emotions or thoughts are signs of this kind of I–me relationship. Traumatic experiences and the anxiety of being overwhelmed by our own emotions might eventually lead to a poorer relationship with ourselves. A good but sad example is how little we pay attention to our dreams. While in native and ancient cultures dreams were regarded as important information regarding one's health and the well-being of the group, within the Western culture we mainly have lost the art of tending our dreams (Moss, 1996). Instead of dreams being a source of meaning, wisdom, insight, and creativity; for many of us they have become trivial and "non-sense."

The imposed silencing of the inner world is draining in the long run (Larson et al., 2015). Just as we distort the other into a caricature, our self-image might become a parody of who we are when we close ourselves off from our experiential flow. Whereas I–it relationships might lead to prejudices and racism, our I–me relationship might lead to *inner xenophobia*: the fear of the inner great unknown or the stranger within ourselves. Unvisited places become a wasteland, and the parts that we silence might become our demons (Missiaen & Vanhooren, 2021). Silencing or avoiding our inner voices might lead to loneliness because of the poor connection with ourselves (I–me; micro-dimension). The roots of this loneliness might have something to do with tragic life events and how these influenced our life story (meso-dimension), feeding our fear of what is percolating inside. In addition, we might also realize that there is always something of ourselves that we do not seem to understand. Here, in the midst of our self-experience, we bump into the existential unknown. In more archaic terms, that which we fail to understand might be our soul (Leijssen, 2009), that something that is in us but not us, that process of living that transcends ourselves but runs through ourselves.

Neglect, violence, and abuse—in short, all unsafe situations and relationships as well as the unexpected tasting of the existential, ontological, and spiritual layer in our self-experience—can make us frightened and run away from ourselves. However, we might sense that in order to live more meaningfully, we actually need to turn to ourselves again and listen more carefully to our inner whispers.

The other form of meeting Buber describes is the I–Thou relationship. It represents the here-and-now encounter in which we do not narrow the experience down to our expectations or projections. This kind of fresh encounter creates the opportunity for change. I–Thou encounters bring movement. We might have I–Thou encounters with people we never met. We also may have unexpected conversations with people we have known for years; free from the ascribed roles of the past, we might engage in this encounter as if we are meeting this person for the first time. Encounters between children and parents can have this special quality once they are able meet each other from the standpoint of person to person. These meetings have the potential to change this relationship deeply and leave precious memories afterward.

Buber does not limit these I–Thou encounters to meetings between people. We also can experience I–Thou encounters with animals, nature, the galaxy or with the spiritual realm. We can be thrilled by meeting a wild animal in the forest or simply by seeing a dog on the street. The self is at that moment nourished or touched by the meeting that is something of the whole. This experience of awe broadens and deepens one's existential awareness (Schneider, 2009, 2023). A good example of a deepening I–Thou encounter is to be found in one of Rank's early diaries (Taft, 1958). Rank describes how he felt really moved by a coincidental meeting with a dog:

> Today I saw a dog, trembling and with tail between legs, sitting on the street. From his sad eyes shone all the suffering that was ever endured in the world. The sight brought a lump to my throat and tears to my eyes. I had to turn away and go quickly. But I could not forget it, so unspeakably sad was the picture… (Rank, February 18, 1905; in Taft, 1958, p. 44)

Rogers (cited in Anderson & Cissna, 1997) reminds us that this kind of meeting is not limited to people or beings in the outside world. We can also be surprised by what is happening inside us. In his dialogue with Buber, Rogers reveals how we can be surprised when we open up to ourselves and dare to meet our unknown inner layers. Openness to what presents itself not only increases the quality of contact but also takes us beyond our narrow self-concept or limiting identity. Needless to say, our dreams constantly invite us to meet ourselves and others differently. Dreamwork can help us to develop a qualitative I–I relationship, an open-minded and open-hearted encounter with ourselves that is different from the narrow I–me encounters with ourselves. Meeting ourselves with curiosity and openness and meeting others through I–Thou encounters can lead to a continued openness to our inner experience. The awareness that the process we are can grow beyond our stranded identity (Rogers, 1961).

It is important to realize that I–Thou/I–I and I–it/I–me relationships are on a continuum. Except for the mystic, few people continuously reside in an I–Thou encounter and, conversely, people rarely meet others only through absolute I–it relationships. Also, people rarely reside only in an I–me or I–I relationship. Perhaps there is a tipping point somewhere on this continuum where we either experience a more authentic quality in our interpersonal and inner relationships or are more caught up in constrictive encounters with ourselves and others. However, depending on circumstances and our choices, this also might change.

Therapy can help us to move toward more authentic relationships (see Chapter 4). Sometimes the road toward authenticity is long and steep. Early traumatic experiences can lead to a deep distrust of others and one's own inner world (Gunst & Vanhooren, 2018). Short-term therapies will usually fail to change these inter- and intra-relational patterns of distrust (Coppens, 2024). It is the long-term *corrective* experience of the therapeutic relationship that can help clients eventually. In addition, experiential methods such as focusing as well as chair dialogues from emotion-focused therapy can help clients meet themselves differently (Elliott et al., 2004). However, in severely traumatized people, trust in self and others rarely develops without a struggle.

The Therapeutic Relationship as a Corrective Relational Experience

Rank (1936) was the first to identify the quality and experience of the therapeutic relationship as the crux of profound psychotherapeutic change. In his footsteps, Rogers (1942, 1961) argued how psychotherapeutic change could be understood as a consequence of restoring the client's capacity for growth by offering an empathetic, accepting, and authentic encounter. These moments of authentic encounter allow the client to feel so accepted and understood (need for interpersonal connection and acceptance) that they can discover and develop themselves as a unique person (need for separation and uniqueness) without compromising this sense of connectedness (Rank, 1936). As we described previously, this dynamic of experiencing the need to develop as a person, on the one hand, and experiencing the need to feel connected, on the other often, leads to difficulties, fractures, resentment, and tons of guilt. In the accepting, authentic, empathic encounter, however, there is the opportunity for a corrective experience. At this point, Rank and Rogers argue that clients can grow beyond their former painful inter- and intra-personal experiences (Kramer, 2019). In these empathic I–Thou moments, a new possibility to *be* differently with oneself and the world unfolds.

Feigned empathy or superficial presence will not do the job. Decades of therapeutic research has shown the robust association between the therapeutic relationship or empathy and therapy outcome (Elliott et al., 2018; Flückinger et al., 2018). This also means that when the therapist's endeavors are not perceived as empathic by the client, it will have a negative impact on the therapy outcome. As a result, while therapists might have acquired a lot of techniques and experience, they cannot hide behind the role of expert. There is a real art to being fully present while also using one's expertise to help the client.

However, as existence is limited, so is therapy and the extent to which we can maintain this high quality of presence. Although there are differences between therapists when it comes to their quality of presence and attunement (Castonguay & Hill, 2017), it is precisely the formal limitation of this encounter in terms of space (the therapy office or an agreed-upon setting), time (the session length and/or number of sessions), and intention (a therapeutic relationship and not a friendship or love relationship) that makes this condensed therapeutic encounter with life possible. The therapist or counselor is only fully available and present within the limits of this framework and within their personal limitations. Although there is a threshold when it comes to therapists' interpersonal and reflective capacities—without which therapy would not be possible (Castonguay & Hill, 2017)—the finiteness of therapy and the fact that the therapist does not appear to be perfect also offer the client an opportunity to detach from therapy, to practice with autonomy and to eventually spread their own wings (Rank, 1936).

Within these boundaries, however, therapy can provide a space to meet the other and oneself in a corrective new way.

Interpersonal therapeutic presence (I–Thou), however, will not bear fruit if it does not enrich one's inner experiencing (I–I). Or, as Kierkegaard would say, we can only be fully in relationship to the other—who is in relationship to themself—by also relating to the relationship we are with ourselves.

Relational Depth as Quality Presence

Mearns and Cooper (2005) call those moments of high relational quality where the therapist and client are both fully internally and interpersonally present *relational depth.* In these instances, the therapist has the experience to fully understand the client, and the client is aware of being fully understood. In addition to this understanding, there is also the awareness of each other's otherness. Feelings of being deeply connected but also being different and unique are simultaneously held by this momentary encounter. This is a good example of how a specific microcosmic or ontic here-and-now moment of therapy also expresses a macrocosmic or ontological living process. Rank already described how the therapist and the client can meet in such a way that they not only meet each other but also feel included in what he calls "das Ganze" (Kramer, 2019). Gendlin (Preston, 2007) would say that they not only experience or express this whole in their unique way but also carry something of this larger macrocosmic whole forward, since this whole is not a static but rather a living process that keeps evolving. However, we understand that these moments, these meetings with a high quality of relational depth, have an impact on the client as well as on the therapist. They both feel moved by this encounter. And this is exactly what Buber meant when he was talking about I–Thou relationships.

Besides being touched in a positive sense as a therapist or counselor, an authentic I–Thou relationship makes us susceptible to painful experiences in the therapeutic relationship. By being present, we can notice the cracks in the therapeutic relationship, which is never a pleasant experience. Safran and Muran (2003) draw our attention to how the therapeutic relationship, like any other human relationship, has its highs and its lows. It is subject to the same existential dynamics, sometimes resulting in moments of relational depth but also in ruptures.

When we do not feel met or understood in therapy, we might feel painfully thrown back on our existential isolation. Instead of having a corrective experience, our sense of disconnection might feel reinforced on the macro-dimension. On the therapist's side, the inability to connect with a certain client might feel as a deep failure. In this case, regardless of what the micro- or meso-dimensional causes might be, we might suffer from not having met the other or not having found a way to be separate from this client. Also in this situation, we are expressions of this existential dynamic but this time on the suffering side instead of on the growth side.

For Rank, the need for connection and uniqueness are not only one of the most important sources of our suffering, but they also form the backbone of the therapeutic process. Growth in autonomy means increasing one's capacity to be together with oneself while being with the other, or not losing connection with oneself while losing connection with the other. Rank sees his clients growing through becoming close with themselves but also by experimenting with allowing themselves to be different or by becoming closer to the therapist. Clients who previously felt the need for connection out of anxiety to be separate may thus experiment at a later stage of therapy the desire to differ from the therapist. Therapists and counselors who have difficulties with being separate might struggle when their clients start to detach, experiment with being different, or provoke conflict. Helpers who are more likely to experience difficulties with closeness might bite their nails when their clients seek approval, the safety of the relationship, and attachment.

Furthermore, the therapist's I–Thou and I–I relationships are usually not immediately reciprocated with the same quality of contact on the client side. Very often, clients arrive with relational distress, difficulties with interpersonal contact, and/or a poor connection to their inner world. Because of this keeping the quality of the therapeutic relationship high is often a matter of hard work. Caring for the I–Thou relationship can be challenging when the client wants to hold the boat evoked by fear of failure or distrust. Based on former suffering, clients might be insulting or passive-aggressive out of self-protection (Gunst & Vanhooren, 2018). How clients relate to the therapist (I–it) and to themselves (I–me) can be confusing and alienating for the helper. As a result, as therapists, we might be confused because our inner experiencing is influenced by our interaction with our client (which is influenced by how they interact with themselves). Cultivating inner presence as a therapist is not a luxury. Being aware of our inner flow of experiences as therapists is what Rogers (1957) calls *congruence*. It is through this congruence that we remain sensitive and attuned to what is going on in the therapeutic relationship, and in the client's and our own inner relationship. This congruence was a highly necessary instrument for me when I was working with Aisha. She did not have words for what was going on inside her.

Aisha's Search for Herself in the Whole

When Aisha first came to see me, I had no idea how this therapy would unfold. In those first sessions, Aisha talked about how she struggled with depression, with binge eating, and a little later—when she felt more safe—about her self-injuries and what she called her sexually impulsive behavior. She worried deeply about having a long-term relationship as she had experienced that she could fall in love instantly with anyone else. Aside from her search for meaning, the existential dynamics of isolation and connection were equally important during this therapy. Although Aisha managed to maintain connections to others, they were mostly characterized by I–it and the I–me encounters.

On the ontic micro-dimension, Aisha experienced very little contact with herself (I–me). In a way, her relation to her inner world was rather silent, dormant, or blocked. She also had a hard time finding words that matched her inner experiencing (which caused problems at a meaning level). On this micro-dimension, the existential dynamic of isolation and connection showed itself through this disconnection with herself (I–me). However, the way she talked about herself revealed a harsh and inner critic voice, which was ready to take her down at any moment.

This active negative and critical attitude toward oneself has been called the *inner critic* (Stinckens, 2008). Although we situate the inner critic further on the meso-dimension, here it manifested itself by not taking any feelings seriously. As Aisha put it, "Having feelings and self-compassion is for the weak." And she did not want to be weak. However, there was something about our therapeutic relationship that made her give these explorations of feelings a chance. She felt that there was somewhere a click between us. I remember putting a lot of effort in establishing an accepting, authentic, and empathetic I–Thou relationship to facilitate a I–I relationship with herself. However, as there was nothing resonating inside, she did not know how to explore this nothingness.

There were moments—especially with friends—when she could sink completely into this nothingness. When we dwelled on what was happening during those moments, it was noticeable that Aisha felt cut off from herself and felt alone in her group of friends. She then sank into something she could not name yet. It was a grim experience that made her feel extremely tired. It took a lot of empathic guessing and re-experiencing on my part to get in touch with what she could not explicitly sense. "I don't know," she said, referring to that nothingness inside. But even nothingness and emptiness can change over time, as long as we keep it company (Vanhooren, 2010). We took our time—many sessions—to dwell on this nothingness, during which I tentatively gave words to what this nothingness evoked in me, and let her check what these words did to her. Step by step, I was trying to help shift her alienating I–me into a more personal I–I relationship.

Our experiential explorations of this nothingness often made Aisha feel nervous. She was afraid that this would make her stay in bed for days. However, when she eventually managed to engage in self-exploration and stay close to her experiences on this micro-dimension, this nothingness shifted into a deep sadness. "Something is holding me down in there," Aisha told me, although it was unclear what was holding her there. Admitting sadness in the shape of tears while being in the presence of another person was new to her. On the one hand, there was shame in feeling seen in her sadness, but, on the other hand, it was also a sign of her trust and our growing I–Thou relationship. Simultaneously, there was also an inner relational shift. As Aisha was able to admit her sadness and became less afraid of it, her fatigue and depression disappeared. The generalized and impersonal tiredness and depression turned into a sense of sadness and later a sense of grief.

Eventually, by staying close and giving space to this grief, it became clear what this was about. Even though she wanted to excel as a person and do something unique and special in order to give her life meaning, she felt immensely lonely. Aisha's grief was about her existential loneliness, and she felt completely trapped in it. It was that great loneliness that overpowered her whenever she had a sense of losing attention from her friends. It was that same loneliness that made her seek sexual pleasure at random. She fled into fusion rather than have to experience that unbearable loneliness.

While focusing on her existential loneliness, we tried to build a different inner relationship with her feelings of being deeply lonely. I asked Aisha how she imagined this lonely feeling would look. My intention here was to make this macro-dimensional ontological experience concrete on her ontic micro-dimension. Maybe, something of this larger ontological process that was experienced by Aisha could be carried forward by interacting with it. By searching for an image that would fit her felt sense of this existential loneliness, we might be able to relate to it more directly and understand more deeply what it needed in the context of her living process. To our surprise, the image Aisha had was that of a small boy. There was something pure about it. When I asked what this little boy needed from her, there came the need for comfort and care. I suggested that if she would sense that deep loneliness, she would picture that little boy. I asked if she would notice and comfort this little boy. It was an active step to help shift her former harsh inner I–me relationship into a more compassionate and caring I–I relationship. We had come a long way. Her initial tiredness and depression had transformed into a nothingness and emptiness, to an undifferentiated sadness and a more defined grief, and now to a sense of existential loneliness that took the shape of an innocent little boy. These different experiences show the many steps or shifts from her I–me to her current I–I relationship. Once she discovered how to care more for herself and to ask for help when needed, she achieved more autonomy. The quality and color of her inner relationship was changing. Kierkegaard would have been very pleased, I think.

While exploring her life story (meso-dimension), we discovered that her loneliness was also linked to significant adverse life events. For example, she remembered how during kindergarten she had experienced difficulties connecting with other children. She had a clear picture of how she stood alone while the other children were playing during recess. There was also that time when her parents had explosive arguments. She would flee to her room to feel more safe. Their ongoing conflicts made a deep impression on her and made her afraid to invest in a long-term relationship. Whatever was not "funny" could indicate an upcoming conflict, so Aisha just wanted things to be and to stay fun. As a result, she found herself mostly being engaged in more superficial I–it relationships and felt troubled when she realized that she judged others on a spectrum of whether or not they were fun. What or who was not funny was essentially dangerous and had to be avoided.

It was the shift in her inner relationship through our work on the micro-dimension that gradually also facilitated a shift in how she related to others. Her more compassionate and caring stance toward herself—initially to that innocent boy inside—made her listen more mindfully to others. However, this created a new problem. She became so concerned with others that she started to neglect her inner relationship again. Aisha now needed to find a balance between taking care of and being taken care of. It eventually led to conflicts. Friends were not used to the fact that Aisha was also taking care of herself and was not available all the time. It was quite a confrontation to realize that she was not perfect, that the others were not perfect, and that finding a perfect balance seemed to be impossible.

The therapeutic relationship also changed throughout this process. During the first stage, the therapeutic relationship mainly functioned as a vessel to build a different relationship with herself. However, during this second stage, the therapeutic relationship itself became a subject in therapy. Something about our togetherness had changed, and it took us a while to notice what had happened. Just like in the outside world, something of conflict and difference appeared during the sessions. Thanks to our previous work, Aisha was able to articulate what she needed. Searching for words and inner exploration was less necessary now, she claimed. Rather she needed to figure out how to deal with her conflicts with others. Being able to express what she needed was, as Rank (1936) would have put it, a courageous act of will and growing autonomy. Aisha had outgrown the therapeutic relationship as it had shaped itself during the first stage. The therapeutic relationship that was briefly on the verge of a rupture was fortunately able to grow along with her. As a concrete move, we invited a friend whom she had a hard time being with. Aisha wanted to be open with this friend but did not know how to talk with her friend without completely jeopardizing this relationship. In therapy, she was able to explore what she needed from her friend, and in the session itself, she was able to communicate this message. All of this helped her to engage in a long-term relationship in which Aisha took steps in tolerating closeness but also in continuing to take care of herself.

On the macro-dimension, Aisha realized that having a life full of fun was an illusion. Allowing herself to realize this illusion was a painful process. Accepting that conflict was part of being in a relationship but that it did not have to be the end was a difficult lesson. Aisha realized that life came with being hurt but also—even non-intentionally—sometimes with hurting others. At the heart of her search for connection and uniqueness, she came to describe this ontological issue as follows: "Am I allowed to be just as I am? May I exist with my imperfections without constantly having to criticize myself? May my relationships be imperfect, and may I not always have to have it my way." There was no definite formal answer; however, she answered with her young life, taking steps in relationships in a very different way than before therapy.

Finally, and with a similar sense of risk, Aisha wondered if she would change majors as a student. For a long time, she dreamed of becoming a doctor, but she had never dared to start out on that path out of fear of failure. If she did, she would have to work much harder and might have to realize that she would be aiming too high (a possibility she had been avoiding so far). But now she realized that if she never tried, she would blame herself for the rest of her life. Not trying would lead to *existential guilt*. Trying would mean giving it her best shot. She would be responsible for her failure but also for her eventual success, and trying already seemed to be more dignified than not trying at all. This choice, and even the consideration of making this choice, required a great deal of courage.

Freedom, Choice, and Responsibility

With Aisha's reflections on her new choice, we arrive at Yalom's final theme of freedom, choice, and responsibility. Yalom (1980) refers regularly to the widely known philosopher and existentialist Jean-Paul Sartre. Sartre, an active resistance fighter during World War II in Nazi-occupied France, is quite radical when it comes to freedom and responsibility. According to him, we cannot outsource our choices and responsibility onto anything or anyone. We are fully responsible for who we are because there is nothing else to fall back on (Sartre, 1980, 2003). Our societal rules are made up, and nothing that can guide us how to live. For him, we are doomed to be free because our existence is groundless. Our freedom is a given. Our responsibility is inescapable unless we fool ourselves. According to Sartre, we flee from freedom when we list reasons why we don't change our miserable situation. When we complain about injustice but act as if we do not have any influence, we only betray ourselves. There is no mercy for not taking responsibility over our lives, according to Sartre.

Indeed, Sartre's vision on freedom and responsibility is challenging. In his way of thinking, we become who we are by the choices we make (Sartre, 2003). Although we can never fully assess the consequences of our decisions, we remain responsible for the paths we take and for the opportunities we ignore. From this perspective, we are always accountable for our existence. However, we are also fully responsible for the suffering of the unknown other, according to Sartre. Closing our eyes to the suffering of the other does not mean that we are no longer responsible. We evade the appeal that lies in the gaze of the other, as Levinas puts it (Keij, 2014). Perhaps we can try to defend ourselves by arguing that we did not choose to help that unknown other. Sartre would not be satisfied with this answer. Not choosing is also a choice, at least for the status quo (Sartre, 1980). It is a choice not to fully engage, a choice not to fully bear our responsibility, or a choice to let the world be like it is. Indeed, we are not only fully responsible for ourselves and the other but also for the world at large (Keij, 2014). After all, how we shape our lives also affects the lives of others. Our freedom is relational, argues Arendt (2019). A freedom that oppresses the other ultimately oppresses ourselves. From this point of view, guilt seems to be inevitable.

Unlike New York's proud and self-confident Statue of Liberty, Sartre's picture of freedom seems to be burdened with the heavy loads of responsibility and guilt. However, there are also other voices when it comes to this existential challenge. Not only do other existential philosophers oppose that life would be groundless (e.g. Preston, 2007), but still others would argue that there is no unlimited freedom. As Greening (1992) reminds us, while it is true that we have more freedom and choice than we might realize, we are also limited and determined. Arendt (2018) explains that human existence is always a conditioned existence because we create. Through our actions and creations, we shape new human conditions that are different from the natural physical conditions that also determine us. Artificial intelligence, for example, is a new human condition that creates new possibilities as well as new limitations and threats. The real question seems not to be the extent to which we are free or determined but *how* to be free and take responsibility for our existence while being aware of our limitations.

Freedom as a Spatial Experience

Just like meaning can fluctuate and change over time, so does freedom. According to van Deurzen (2018), freedom is not a given but rather an awareness that increases by realizing what determines us and how we want to relate to these influencers. We are indeed influenced by numerous factors that might limit or enlarge our degree of freedom; these include our genetics, our culture, our sociodemographic conditions, our family history, our current relationships, and our physical environment. But we are never fully determined by our surroundings, states Frankl (1967). Even in the most restrictive circumstances, we still have a choice in how we want to relate to our situation. It is a powerful thought, particularly when we feel helpless and small.

By juxtaposing harsh external circumstances and the freedom to choose how to be with these circumstances, freedom could be understood as a spatial experience. Existential therapy and counseling are often about regaining this space and discovering new possibilities to move one's life in a different direction (Schneider & Krug, 2026). Rogers (1942) noted early on how learning to experience inner freedom also creates the possibility to make new life choices or reaffirm choices once made. However, it often takes a lot of dredging before our ship can sail out into the open sea again.

The open sea can feel too big at certain times. Some of us need a safe harbor instead of having a new wild adventure. According to Schneider (2015), when it comes to freedom, we seem to move on a continuum between expansion and constriction, depending on what we need but also depending on where we get stuck. Limitless freedom—too much expansion—can feel very threatening. There is no harbor to return to. But not every expansive experience has to be destructive. Many of us long to travel and to discover the world. It seems a healthy thing to do as long as we have a place to come back to. Out of fear of the unknown, some of us might flee into a state of constriction. Here we are dealing with our life anxiety again, which can lead to existential guilt. We might feel trapped in our life situation, and sense that we must get out of this place. In depression, constriction is so strong that there does not seem to be a way out. Our living environment has shrunk, and time has come to a standstill (Fuchs, 2019). Help will have to come from outside because our inner resources have dried up. In less paralyzing situations, we might notice that we have been hanging around in the same harbor for too long. We might sense that it is high time to hoist the sails and go on an adventure. However, sometimes we blow off our travel plans at the last minute when the fear of expansion sets in. This *fear of life* is understandable because once out of port we will not be the same—for better or for worse (May, 1996).

Positive moments of constriction, in turn, are situations where we begin to take better care of ourselves and isolate ourselves for a while in order to slow down and take time for reflection. Therapy is therefore not only or always the search for expansive freedom but perhaps rather about finding a new balance between constriction and expansion. For many clients, counseling and therapy are primarily about expansion. They want to get rid of a kind of restriction and be in a different place in life—preferably as quickly as possible. In certain situations, however, good care is more a matter of finding a new constrictive safety, especially when our haven seems to have been washed away.

Although constriction and expansion seem to be opposites, when combined they provide an optimal non-paralyzing experience of freedom. Possibly we experience the most freedom when we can maintain a direction once we sail on the open sea. The high seas are no longer completely overwhelming when we have a notion of our direction and know how to consult our inner compass or the stars. Indeed, the therapeutic process described by Rogers (1961) and Gendlin (1996) is about being more in touch with our own felt sense of direction. Direction is limiting on the one hand but is also liberating on the other: We have a sense of where to go, which means we can reject countless other directions. This positive constriction allows us to make our way through the abundance of impressions and to feel open and free. This sense of direction is not random, according to Gendlin (1997). Once we resonate with our embodied knowing, we might sense our next step. In therapy, people often get a clear sense what move to take. Some call it intuition. The question is if we really want to listen to what our inner wise felt sense wants to tell us.

It is not uncommon to shy away from our embodied wisdom. Again, we might prefer not to know about our next life steps because our existence itself as we know it will change. In not wanting to know, we restrict ourselves, although the sea is calling. Quite often we impose restrictions on ourselves without being aware of it. Bugental (1999) speaks of *self-imposed limitations* that often arise from unprocessed life experiences or survival strategies. Survival strategies are ways of living that help us get through difficult situations. They are often aimed at easing or numbing the pain, at hiding or getting around risky situations. However, survival strategies do not help us in the long run. May (1983) explains how survival strategies can eventually lead to non-being at the cost of being, a sense of not living while being alive. Self-imposed limitations can eventually lead to helplessness, powerlessness, and despair. We have restricted ourselves from the world of possibilities, from our future, and closed down our sense of spatial freedom. Helplessness, powerlessness, missing a sense of agency, and despair can be understood as the negation of having freedom, choice, and responsibility. They appear when we no longer have a sense of having an impact on our own existence.

Marie's story shows how self-imposed limitations and guilt can completely block our living forward process and how experiential–existential therapy might be helpful in regaining one's freedom to exist.

Marie's Story, or How Everything Was Under Control

Marie, a 30-year-old woman, was referred to me by her general practitioner. Marie had been taking anti-depressants for about ten years. Her existence felt hollow, gray, cold, empty, and joyless. She sometimes felt like she was already 90. She was looking for something that would change her current situation, but nothing had helped her so far. It seemed like her life was frozen and would stay immobile for the rest of her days. She had seen a psychologist before, but it had no effect. In addition to her depression, she also suffered from an obsessive-compulsive disorder. She had to get up early every morning to clean her house. She had two cats who were not allowed to go outside, which made cleaning—in her opinion—even more necessary. The grass in her garden had to be carefully raked, and when at work, she kept a clean desk. Marie also looked impeccable. With everything under control, her days looked quite similar, too. Holidays would disturb the routine, so Marie never took a vacation. I noticed during our first conversations that there was something self-punishing about her way of living. I kept this impression to myself during these first sessions because I could not relate this impression to anything she was talking about.

Phenomenologically, obsessive–compulsive disorders could be an expression of a need to keep life under control and the anxiety of losing control over life. In Marie's case, anything that could throw a spanner in the works such as a trace of dirt, dust, or any other unexpected turn of events had to be avoided. Marie not only kept control of her house, her garden, and her cats, she also kept control over her husband. He was not allowed to touch her. More than that, to make sure he would not seek intimacy, Marie would scold him at night. As a result, he stayed at a safe distance, physically and emotionally. Actually, Marie also found him unattractive and did not feel any love for him. Yet she did not want to leave him. Just as the cats were deprived of their freedom, Marie also kept her own life chained. It was a far-reaching self-imposed limitation, keeping her life fully restricted. There was no freedom to be sensed, only a kind of frailty and a heaviness beyond that immobilized way of living.

It did not take a long time before I also got the feeling of being stuck in our conversations. As often happens, her current existential concern became a living dynamic of our therapeutic process (see Chapter 4). Since we are fundamentally interactive as human beings, her way of being also influenced how I experienced myself throughout our sessions. On the one hand, this allowed me to get a taste of what it means to be Marie. On the other hand, it allowed me also to notice how it would feel to be part of her environment or lifeworld. I not only noticed that there was something self-punishing in the way she treated herself and life, but I also sensed something of how her cats and her husband might have felt restricted or limited, just like I sensed being stuck during our interactions. I also felt my freedom shrinking while being in conversation with Marie, and, ironically, noticed how our tomcat Pol was running freely in our front yard while chasing an insect. Free as a bird, he came peeping curiously at the window. He reminded me of how my client's cats were "safely" inside while our cat was enjoying the early spring weather outside, enjoying his free, exciting life. I felt like taking a quick run in our garden, too, but naturally stayed inside. However, the feeling of wanting to escape for a moment made me realize how my interaction with Marie felt restricted. I missed a sense of freedom, spontaneity, and creativity. However, I also noticed a certain sympathy for my client. Beyond the thousand chains that kept herself and her surroundings under control, I could also hear a distant echo of something like warmth and a zest for life. During unguarded moments, especially when Marie greeted me at the beginning or at the end of the session, I could sense her authentic human warmth. I experienced something of hope and a knowing that we would be able to work things out.

After a couple of sessions, I realized that I had to feel sufficiently free while being with her to bring movement to our interaction and, hopefully as a result, also into her stalled life situation. I used an interactional method we call *immediacy* or *disembedding* (Safran & Muran, 2003). It is a meta-conversation about how we—client and therapist—are interacting in order to liberate ourselves from a recurrent and stuck interpersonal pattern. It takes a lot of self-reflection on the therapist's side because we need some clarity before we engage in this conversation. We also do not engage in immediacy before we are sure that we are not just playing out our own interpersonal patterns in therapy with this client. First, I tried to observe what was concretely happening during our interaction that made me feel stuck. I also focused on my felt sense about this situation. Regarding my felt sense, I could feel how something in our contact narrowed my inner space and made me feel trapped. It was a shrinking sensation that threatened to minimize my inner relationship to an I–me encounter. While our interpersonal encounter had potential, it felt like a deserted place. I felt alone and there was something of sadness in our therapeutic relationship, although Marie was actually very present in one way but absent in another. Our therapeutic relationship had an I–it quality. I felt stuck, and it was understandable that something in me wanted to run free as our cat did. All of this alerted me that I needed to do something. Observing our interaction closely, I discovered that when I tried to contribute something in the shape of a reflection, a question or anything else, Marie would not hear me or would not let me finish my sentence. She would just talk over me. It seemed to me that I didn't have a place in our relationship. I didn't have an impact, or at least this was not clear to me. I decided to interrupt her to discuss this recurrent pattern.

Of course, I conveyed my message with sensitivity and concern because I was aware that what was happening here probably had a lot to do with her stuck life situation, and this why she came to look for help in the first place. I made clear that I wanted to discuss something difficult with her, indicating my impression that what I was trying to ask or tell her during our sessions did not seem to get through. It felt like she was not noticing or hearing me, and that there seemed to be no room to dwell on what she was feeling or noticing in the here-and-now. To my surprise, Marie recognized what I was describing. Marie explained how she prepared each session carefully and knew beforehand precisely what she would be talking about. My attempts to bring something in was a possible threat to her plan. This beautifully shows how the therapeutic process can mirror how clients shape their existence. The way she engaged in therapy was an extension of how she dealt with life: Nothing was allowed to escape her control. Of course, she did not respond to my invitations to check her feelings in the here-and-now. Marie indicated that she was afraid to dwell on what she felt. That was too unpredictable. Just like her cats, her husband, and me, anything she could sense inside had to be controlled. She could not stand silence, here or at home. The radio played constantly. When I asked her what she would expect if she were in a silent space, she didn't have to think very long: "Something very unpleasant, something terrible." She was frightened of what she might encounter there.

Putting Something in Motion: Small Steps on the Road to Freedom

As Schneider and Krug (2026) put it, therapy is essentially a path to freedom. People seek help because they are stuck in one or more aspects of their lives. Help would not be necessary if their living process would just carry itself forward. The experience of being stuck is usually the starting point of many counseling sessions. The process that we are is blocked. Our river no longer flows; instead, it has turned into a pool of stagnant murky water. Person-centered, experiential, and existential approaches often focus on helping the client's situation move or flow again. No matter how we think about therapy, without movement we seem to get nowhere. As therapists, we rely on the living process itself, argues Gendlin (Preston, 2007). We assume that by attending and interacting with our core pains or woundedness differently, the living process will resume its carrying forward tendency.

In their search for how to bring movement to their clients' blocked living processes, Rogers (1961) and Gendlin (1973) discovered that a shift in how people relate to their experiences ultimately brings movement. Here we are at the micro-dimension of our experience. The I–me inner relationship, characterized by either being overwhelmed by what we feel or by being completely out of touch, curtails our inner experiential freedom significantly. In the case of feeling overwhelmed or acting impulsively, we speak of an under-regulation of our feelings. For some of us, this flooding also creates anxiety because we then feel we are no longer in control of ourselves or the situation. In those moments, we might feel scared that we will drown in our stormy inner ocean. In the therapies with Annabel, Gunther, and Aisha, there were moments when they felt afraid of not being able to overcome their emotions of anxiety or sadness. Indeed, just being delivered to our inner or interpersonal storms does not make us feel free. Although everything seems to move, nothing is moving at all. Marie, however, was mostly out of touch with her inner world. She hardly sensed anything. Here we meet that other form of an I–me relationship: an over-regulation of our inner world. Instead of being in a storm, over-regulation reminds us more of a stranded ship on a sandbank.

Sometimes people go from under-regulation to over-regulation and vice versa. People who over-regulate often have the sense that there is something beneath the surface, and that's exactly why they invest in controlling. Marie started to sense that something was peeking through. It felt like "something terrible" was waiting there for her, and so she wanted to keep it at a distance. By closing all the cracks that would let her inner sounds get through, Marie closed herself down. As a result, she was out of energy, so far removed from her inner well and life around her. It was a high price to pay.

It was Rank (1936) who first understood that it is not the talking that makes therapy helpful. Rather, it is the here-and-now experiencing of our concern within the safety of the therapeutic relationship that brings movement (Rank, 1936). Interestingly, in Marie's case, it was our here-and-now meta-conversation about our interaction that brought a first movement. It made her more aware that she was holding off—without knowing what she was afraid of. In the following sessions, Marie would consciously allow me to ask her exploratory questions and make reflections. Now that our interaction was moving into an I–Thou direction, I tried to help her relate differently to herself in the here-and-now. Because she felt apprehensive for what would come up if she gave it her attention, we took it slow and easy. We were looking for what Gendlin (1996) calls a *workable distance* (or a workable closeness): not to be overwhelmed but also not to lose contact with inner experiential world. In this way we created, in Rogers' (1961) words, more *openness to experience.* This openness to our felt experience is the equivalent of freedom on this micro-dimension. Being free to notice what we are sensing without being overwhelmed or having to run away from it is related to progress in therapy and counseling (Gendlin, 1996). The attitude of being able to dwell freely with ourselves in the here-and-now, also called the *focusing attitude,* is not coincidentally associated with less psychological suffering, less existential anxiety, less depression, and more life satisfaction (Pellens et al., 2025; Vanhooren et al., 2022).

One concrete way to cultivate this focusing attitude, and, thus, this inner freedom, is to engage in what Ann Weiser Cornell (2013) calls *self-in-presence.* It is a form of friendly self-observation, like sitting next to an old friend (our inner experiences) on a bench, listening to their fears, pains, or joys, without giving any advice or leaving it alone. Self-in-presence helps us to be with our inner ripples as well as with our storms without getting caught up in them. The latter is also called *disidentification.* However, it is not a detached but an engaged, interested, and curious being-with. Our felt sense has always something of the unknown and the unpredictable. Here our felt sense stands for what we cannot entirely grasp or understand. It easily slips away and changes even before we fully get it. We might fear it somehow. We do not really know what it—or what life—wants from us, because it always *becomes.* We enter something of the macrocosm that runs through our microscopic embodied sensing. It is the wild unknown all wrapped up in that particular murky feeling. Here we encounter Levinas's gaze of the other appealing to our responsibility, but this time the gaze and the call come from within; it is *the other within us* that wants to be seen and heard. In therapy, this otherness is sometimes about important neglected needs or unprocessed experiences but also about very recent experiences that ask for attention. Specific ways of using language in our therapeutic reflections and explorations can actively help clients to meet their inner experiences at a more workable distance. A great example of this use of language is to be found in Lize Spit's 2016 novel *It Melts*. Spit describes how her main character Eva becomes aware of something particular while at the grocery store:

> *Something* is missing then, *everything*, as if I had once been more complete and *something* in me remembers how that felt. *It* also strikes me every time I'm standing upright in the bath tub. Then *something* comes to lie on my skin. *It* closes in on me, tightens, makes it clear to me that I am in the wrong place. (Italics added; pp. 20–21)

The main character notices a certain felt sense, a vague physical sensation, which she is in touch with without getting overwhelmed by it. Specific words such as "something" and "it" in this excerpt, help the main character maintain a workable distance. As a result, she remains present with herself and this vague *it*, with its very specific implicit meaning. Another example may make it even more clear. For instance, when I say that "something is afraid in me," it allows more space and reflection than when I say "I am afraid." Saying "I notice that something is afraid in me" might even create more space. "I am afraid" means that I fully identify with my fear, whereas "something in me" creates a certain distance. It also creates a certain curiosity, an invitation, a concern, but without being overwhelmed. It somewhat enlarges our experiential freedom. There is more space.

Although disidentification really helps to regulate our inner distance or closeness and creates a space to explore our inner senses, using "something in me" is not always fruitful, particularly when we explore our meso- and macro-dimension (see Chapter 4). For example, when we are about to make a choice saying "something in me chooses" impoverishes the life force that is noticeable in "I choose." When our full being is engaged in our situation, using the sentence "a part of me or something in me" minimizes what we truly experience. And that is not what we are aiming for.

Interestingly, our experiential freedom at the micro-dimension is often related to our degree of freedom at the meso-dimension and vice versa. The way we define ourselves and understand our life story and the world around us often limits or expands what and how we are experiencing. Significant life events, unprocessed episodes in our story, and the way significant others have responded to us in the past or present help shape our meso-dimension. The incongruence between the restrictive image we have of ourselves and how we experience our situation is often noticeable as a form of bodily tension, a restlessness, or some other vague sensation (Rogers, 1951). All too often, this tension does not feel very inviting. However, it is precisely by paying attention to the felt sense of this tension or restlessness in the here-

and-now (micro-dimension) that we will expand our experiential space and freedom, which will also lead to changes on our meso-dimension.

Marie and Her Fortress

This was also noticeable with Marie. Our meta-conversation about what happened between us helped her to be more aware of how controlling she was toward herself and others. During the next sessions, Marie tried to be more open and aware of her inner experiencing as well as of the presence of others. It was not easy for her. She was so used to taking control over life constantly. There were times that she slipped into her old habits again; however, she was more aware now of the effect this had on herself and others. She also started noticing how her old pattern was not always "on" anymore. For example, she would catch herself enjoying being with others. She was also surprised that she spontaneously bought olives for herself. This felt really new to her. At other times, she would sense how difficult it was for her to receive any care from others. She became painfully aware how difficult it was to talk to her husband about how lonely she felt.

Another positive sign was that Marie did not prepare for the sessions any longer. It was a conscious decision after she realized that preparing the session was not only a way of being in control but also a form of withholding care. She took a big leap into the unknown, and our therapy started to feel like a true adventure. It felt like we were entering a jungle where there are no set paths. There was the fear of monsters that were lurking under the trees, but there was also a growing awareness that there might be treasures to discover. She realized that control would not only prevent her from experiencing pain but also from enjoying life. Soon she started to have moments when she felt like herself again. But as she experienced more hope and life, she also started to get a clearer picture of the obstacles that prevented her from living freely. For example, she noticed a deeper distrust of others (see Chapter 3). There were times that something sounded an alarm, and she could feel how she was crawling back into her shell. In the eleventh session, Marie explained how this back-and-forth movement felt to her:

> **Marie**: I really got into it, trying to let go of control this week. All of a sudden, I was enjoying the sun. That was so nice! Man, I really haven't been able to enjoy the sun for years. But there are those other moments... It can feel so chaotic. I really can feel a lot of tension then.

Siebrecht: I hear you naming both sides. So by being able to let go of control, you can enjoy yourself again, and that amazes you.... And then, on the other hand, there is that chaos when you let go of control, accompanied by tension in your body....
Marie: Yes, I am beginning to realize more and more how I have been avoiding sadness and emotional pain all these years. If I see something in the newspaper that might affect me, I quickly turn the page. But there was a little bird on our driveway recently, hurt by another animal. I can't let nature take its course... I would like to stop nature's course.
Siebrecht: That seems like an impossible task, controlling nature...
Marie: Impossible, I know... It exhausts me... I'd rather crawl away then....
Siebrecht: It seems like you prefer to crawl into your self-constructed fortress then, where everything seems to be under control; but life outside that fortress cannot be controlled... I don't know if it's true, but it seems as if the life inside your fortress, which is then under control, also doesn't flourish when it's being cut off from the free nature and life outside...
Marie: Yes, inside it is safe. I have everything under control there... But there is almost no life left inside... I am so tired living such an isolated life in there, keeping everything to myself. But there outside… is a hard world.
Siebrecht: A hard world... What exactly do you mean by a hard world?
Marie: All of those things that can go wrong. Your children can fall out of their beds like my sister's youngest recently... Also, with what's going on in childcare these days. I would be afraid to have children today and leave them in childcare.
Siebrecht: Being afraid of having children... What exactly would you be afraid of?
Marie: To lose them...
Siebrecht: That's what you're afraid of...
Marie: Yes...
Siebrecht: Have you experienced that before?

This piece of exploration nicely illustrates how Marie gained insight by reflecting on her inner experiences. Where she used to shut down from her experiential flow, she now seems to have acquired more experiential freedom (Schneider, 2015), which helps her notice how she hides in her fortress and what the consequences are of doing so. Along with this increasing awareness, she also notices how nice it can be to surrender to the direct experience of life itself. The taste of olives and the experience of sunshine feel like a real discovery. While she notices how she enjoys the sunshine (and sunshine can be a real treat after a dark and grey Belgian winter), she also becomes painfully aware of how she feels isolated in her former I–it relationship with living.

While Marie develops a kind of basic trust that exploring and experiencing difficult issues in this safe environment might lead to something new, she also is getting closer to her deeper woundedness. With woundedness (Barret-Lennard, 1990) or core pain (Elliott et al., 2004) we refer to the deeper wound or a profound missing (Gendlin, 1997). Something important that our living process needed in order to live forward remained unfulfilled. As a result, our living process had to take a turn and to go on living with this missing piece, although it became really affected by it, maybe came to a standstill, or was in survival mode (Gendlin, 1997). Something we deeply missed from ourselves or others during a significant situation can influence all further choices we make. As this often refers to unfinished significant life events, we can situate this on the meso-dimension, but it also influences our experiential flow (micro) and our way of experiencing existence in general (macro).

It was this woundedness or this missing that Marie was afraid to get in touch with. It was against experiencing this terrifying something that Marie built dams and fortresses. It was something painful, some hurting part of life that she tried to keep under control, but by doing so she started to feel she was lifeless. To put it in other terms, she swapped being for non-being. By trying to do so, her whole living process kept circling around this missing so that her whole life was turning on an eternal roundabout. Her existence came to a standstill in the shape of depression and an obsessive–compulsive disorder. However, during this eleventh session, this "being afraid of losing children" led to a buried memory. Marie remembered now how she underwent an abortion about ten years earlier. She remembered how she had felt so terribly alone and isolated, as if no one else was there. She remembered how she was yelling. Her abortion was the last time she was intimately touched, which she never allowed again. She left the hospital with tons of guilt, a realization too heavy to bear. Marie closed herself off from this experience, and any path that might have made her remember this unstoried event was severely guarded. The care and attention she needed that day had been waiting for more than ten years. This missing had been ruling her life until this very session.

Guilt and Responsibility

For us human beings, there seems to be no escape from feeling guilty unless we close ourselves off from the suffering of others and our planet. However, by cutting ourselves off from our environment—which never really works—we also become estranged from life, as Marie's story shows. Guilt feelings are very human and normal. They show us that we take life seriously and that we care. However, guilt feelings do not make life easy. When we have feelings of guilt, we don't feel complete or whole. They might function as a sign that we have some unfinished business with life. We might have the general sense that we didn't do enough or, more concretely, that we have wronged a person. At other times we also might feel guilty toward ourselves. We might have let ourselves down at some point. All of these instances might form a stoppage in our living process (Gendlin, 1997)—something that keeps hindering ourselves in relation to world as long as we do not pay attention to it.

Existential guilt might be understood as a special case of guilt where we are guilty against existence. Existential guilt also can be explained as our regret about our portion of unlived existence. We might regret the choices we made and not having lived our own lives to the fullest. There are those missed opportunities: "If I would have known, I would have...." However, as human beings, we are limited and so is our time on Earth. Acknowledging our limitations can help us to be gentler toward ourselves, others, and humankind as such.

Frankl (1967) notes that in case of real guilt, when damage beyond repair has been done to ourselves and/or others, acceptance of our limitations will not be sufficient. In those cases, we face a different task. Real guilt deprives us of our freedom, Frankl argues, but by no means absolves us from our responsibility. On the contrary, asking for forgiveness and attempting to put things right is essential in order to heal the breach made to the other and our own sense of being (Vanhooren et al., 2017a). Precisely when the damage is beyond repair—for example in case of physical, emotional, and sexual violence— the situation calls for personal transformation. In my work with victims and offenders, I have learned that both parties need to go through some form of personal change in order to move on with life. As in Annabel's case, even when symptoms of PTSD diminished, she still needed to find a different way of being herself in her changed world.

She had to reinvent herself, which required a deep search for new meaning. She had to get to know herself and the world around her anew. This process of personal transformation might eventually result in posttraumatic growth (Tedeschi & Calhoun, 2004), which could be understood as the living process's new way of being in the world. It has been carried forward by the existential challenge the person went through. Posttraumatic growth is often marked by a deeper appreciation of oneself, the other, and life as such. I have often witnessed a similar kind of process on the offender's side (Vanhooren et al., 2017a, 2018). Ayla, whom we also already met, was convicted of manslaughter. She had to find a way to be and live with her guilt, which could not be altered. Not only was she challenged to understand how this could have happened, she also had to ask herself how she could go on living knowing that she had killed her husband. The guilt called into question her own right to exist. Although the pain of the damage probably never disappears on both sides, the only way to go on with living seems to be one that can carry the guilt and the pain. For Ayla, this meant living her life with more awareness. She was conscious of her future challenges and took full responsibility for them.

Responsibility does not mean leading a flawless life. The great mystics, saints, prophets, and righteous across religions and cultures have been very aware of their daily errors (Buber, 1991). The ability to respond lies in our reaction to our daily and more existential challenges. How do we respond to the ontic and ontological challenges of our time? In consciously searching for an answer; taking our possibilities and limitations into account based on what is important and meaningful to ourselves, the others, and the planet; and transforming our answers into concrete choices and actions, we take steps toward an authentic existence. By our actions, we design who we are to become (Sartre, 1980). We shape our values and norms, our life story, and our identity (meso-dimension). However, different than Sartre, we acknowledge that it is our experiential freedom (micro-dimension) that creates the possibility to realign ourselves to our living process. As long as there is no experiential freedom, actions often are halted because there is hardly a sense of direction (see Chapter 4). Also, our recourses seem to be out of reach, energy is lacking, or there seems to be no future to aim for.

In Marie's case, attending to her woundedness and guilt (micro- and meso-dimension) helped her to take responsibility over her life and to make choices that would redirect her way of being in the world (macro-dimension).

Carrying the Past into the Future

Marie started to understand why she had been denying herself pleasure and joy for years. More than a decade ago, she really had been a person who enjoyed life fully. She had a nice romantic relationship. However, the unplanned pregnancy created an unpredictable turn of events. At that time, Marie did not have a space where she could express the full scope of her ambivalent feelings around her pregnancy. Her family and her boyfriend pulled the abortion card. Marie was not fully convinced, but thought they were probably right. In the hospital, during the operation itself, she started to have doubts. But it was too late. During our next sessions, Marie expressed how guilty she felt now. She also became aware of her anger toward her parents and her ex-boyfriend as she realized that she did not have a real voice in the conversation at that time. She also did not feel cared for in the aftermath of the abortion. While she was able to sense all of this (micro-dimension), her life narrative changed due to this new insight into her past (meso-dimension). Inspired by Gendlin, Ikemi and colleagues (2023) call this the *carried- forward was.* Marie's past was carried forward or changed because we were able to attend and listen to her missing or unmet felt senses of that time. As a result, her life story had been altered, which would carry forward her future. Indeed, by realizing what really had happened then-and-there during the here-and-now and how it influenced her entire being for a decade, she wondered how to continue her life from now on (macro-dimension). She could no longer continue to live as she had been living for so long. By realizing that she did not speak up for herself at that crucial moment in the past, she could not go on without expressing what was important to her in her current life. This only would bring more depression, misery, and suffering. It felt so crystal-clear right now. It would do injustice to her unborn child and to all the pain she had gone through since then.

In a next session, we used an empty-chair dialogue (Elliott et al., 2004) to help Marie relate to her guilt by facilitating a conversation with her unborn child. Experiential methods such as focusing and chair dialogues (Elliott et al., 2004) can help clients meet their missings and their unfinished business from the past and carry forward their living process again (see Chapter 4). During this empty-chair dialogue, Marie contacted her felt sense of her unborn child and spoke to it from a different chair. During this dialogue, Marie spoke directly and honestly to her child about how confused she was at that time. She also empathized with her baby. The conversation was challenging and difficult but also beautiful because of its authenticity and depth. This session made her strongly aware of how important the question was of how to live her life more authentically. An observer would have noticed that we were explicitly immersed in the macro-dimension during these sessions. Marie wondered what she really wanted. Focusing helped her realize that she no longer wanted to be that "unhappy old lady who was tired, empty, and had lost her purpose in life." She became aware that she wanted to open up to life itself. It was remarkable to notice how we had been moving since the beginning of our therapy from a strong constricted way of living toward a longing and expanding way of existing. For Marie, it was now time to set sail.

Her growing openness toward life showed itself in multiple ways. First, Marie tried to explain to her partner what happened to her before they met and how this impacted her life and their relationship. They decided to go on holidays, and they enjoyed it. Marie heard herself singing at home and was surprised by it. Her changed attitude had also important consequences for the other creatures in the house: The cats were allowed to go outside. In sum, Marie felt redeemed and liberated. Therapy was no longer necessary. However, life decided differently.

One year later, Marie was pregnant, but her baby was stillborn. Marie contacted me again, and we had some sessions where we grieved for her stillborn daughter. Marie also came to question her relationship with her partner, whom she never really felt in love with. She wondered if she wanted to continue her relationship. Eventually she cut some difficult knots and choose to leave. Coincidentally, I happened to run into Marie years later. She was married to a new person and was the proud mother of two children. She was really smiling. Her warmth and zest for life were radiating.

The Question of How to Live

On the macro-dimension, the existential theme of freedom, choice, and responsibility might be about the question of how to live one's life. Values associated with religious, ideological, and cultural frameworks that we situate on the meso-dimension might point in a certain direction or to a possible path. Commandments and prohibitions are deeply rooted into our cultures, our family stories, and our identities. We are often unaware of how these values serve as implicit guidelines. They help us determine our choices. Ancient commandments such as "Thou shalt not kill," as well as the prohibition of incest and other transgressive acts, are based on millennia of accumulated human wisdom that such behavior causes deep harm to the victim and the perpetrator as well as to the community. In addition to our empathy for the suffering and well-being of others, it is this kind of wisdom that keeps us from profoundly damaging others and ourselves. The greatest common denominator of world religions and certain other ideologies has been described as the golden rule: the instruction to treat your neighbor as you want to be treated, to love the other as yourself. It is a call for empathy, righteousness, and unconditional love. Eudaimonic values and meanings are often derived from this golden rule. Anyone reading between the lines of these widely held values will quickly discover that connectedness with the other and with life is the underlying factor. However, as we already mentioned when we explored meaning and meaninglessness, not everyone shares the experience of feeling fundamentally connected.

The question how to live might be more challenging when the experience of the absurdity, meaninglessness, and the groundlessness of existence prevails. The question of how to live, as Sartre (1980) notes, might have a shattering quality. Without anything to hold on to, there does not seem to be any compass or a constellation that might help to navigate. There does not seem anything other than oneself, and this also might be quite groundless and even dangerous. In this context, Levinas does not trust the individual as the measure of what is right or wrong (Keij, 2014). For example, Hitler was probably convinced that his Nazi ideology was righteous and meaningful. According to Levinas, the ethical measure of how to live one's life is the welfare of the other. And not just the other who belongs to our group: all others. This might conflict with extreme ideologies and also with Western individualism. Did not Kierkegaard revolt against following the habits of the other and called it inauthentic living? How about that?

For Gendlin (1973) and Merleau-Ponty (2002), the answer lies in the fact that our existence, and the experience of our existence, is an interactional embodied happening. Authentic choices might be those choices that emerge from our most open experience of the situation. We can taste the full scope and complexity of our situation by opening to our felt sense, which is, according to Gendlin (1962) and Petitmengin (2017), a preconceptual knowing. This means that we experience the situation before it is assigned by our cognitive operations to how we usually divide our world: body or mind, emotion or thought, object or subject, me or the other. The felt sense contains the richest immediate implicit knowing that has not been narrowed down yet by our usual patterns. When we tune into this felt sense and ask what this situation needs, it can help us to sense the desired direction. However, in addition to consulting our felt sense, it seems wise to base our choices also on good external information. The broader our openness to experience, the richer our felt sense and the more responsible our choices will be—for ourselves and the whole.

The fact that we can never fully assess the consequences of our choices but still have to choose makes choosing a real challenge for many of us. There often is no right choice. Sometimes there are several right choices, and at other times there are none. In the latter situation, it might take a lot of courage to choose because we sense we might hurt others or ourselves by taking a certain "right" direction. Bitter choices are hard to be made. Marie's choice to leave her husband was such a choice. Breaking off relationships rarely makes one happy, but these, too, can be authentic choices. At other moments, we might make choices that hurt ourselves to the benefit of others. Basic trust and the attunement to our integrity might help us to make those difficult choices.

Responsibility, Integrity, and Anavah

Integrity, which literally means making whole (Vanhooren & Schneider, 2026), can be understood here as making consciously considered choices with the full awareness of all sides of the story in which we personally bear full responsibility for the choices made. It also reminds me of the Hebrew word *anavah*, which is a central notion in the Jewish spiritual–ethical practice called Mussar (Morinis, 2007). Anavah is sometimes translated as humility or modesty, but the actual meaning is somewhat lost in translation (Morinis, 2007). Anavah represents taking our own rightful place in the world without being too modest or immodest or between self-debasement and arrogance. Morinis's phrase "no more than my space, no less than my place" helps us to understand what this Jewish spiritual idea is about. Responsibility in terms of anavah means that we try to take our proper place in every situation. Taking our place also essentially means being our answer or our *response-ibility*. As our place is situational (Morinis, 2007), our responsibility in every situation is different.

When we do not take our place, we might be fleeing our responsibility. Conversely, we can also feel over-responsible, acting as if our space is larger than it actually is. As a result, we risk taking the other person's place and depriving that person of their opportunity to grow by taking responsibility over their life. Also, by assuming that our place is larger than it is, we might take on more responsibility than we can carry and cause a lot suffering. The search for the right place—no more, but also no less than our space—is a true quest by itself. We might overestimate what we are called to do (Morinis, 2007). Conversely, turning our backs on the suffering of others because we think we did not cause the problem denies our place in the situation. Even if we do not have anything to do with the cause of the harm, we still might have a role to play in the healing of the problem.

Anavah calls us to attune to our situation and to situate ourselves within it. It calls us to discover our destiny and purpose in the concrete circumstances we are living in. We are not called to sit on all the chairs or to act as if we are not present. It calls us to take our rightful place in our history and to act as if only you or I can act as unique beings. Buber (2010) refers to a Chassidic story that matches with anavah. Shortly before he died, the wise Rabbi Susja made the reflection that at the final judgment he would not be asked why he had not been like the great prophet Moses. "No", Rabbi Susja said, "I will be asked why I had not always been Susja."

Gendlin (1973) notes how people somehow know what the next step in their lives should be. He talks about the carrying forward of the situation we are a part of. However, quite often, we seem to resist this next step, or we still miss something in order to live forward. A great example might be found in the backstory of Stefan Hertmans' (2018) novel *War and Turpentine*. The novel is based on Hertmans' grandfather's diaries about his life as a soldier during the First World War in Belgium. Hertmans received the diaries of his grandfather but resisted reading them for many years. He felt somehow that he had to do something with these diaries, but it just did not happen. Hertmans kept struggling with them until he found the courage at some point to surrender to this living-forward direction. As long as he resisted, that part of his life felt incomplete. Eventually, he opened the diaries and knew he had to write a novel about them. It was not a coincidence that writing this novel also carried his living process forward as a new whole. Writing the novel not only helped him to better understand his grandfather but also his own history. His book was eventually translated from Dutch into twenty languages and was rated as one of the ten Best Books of 2016 by The New York Times Book Review.

Aisha's story showed us that her life would not be whole if she would not have accepted the challenge to pursue her study of medicine. It was a step that had to be taken. Quite often we know what we should be doing, ontically and ontologically. In the case of Marie, we witnessed how there was no other way forward than listening to what wanted to be heard. Her life had come to a complete standstill out of fear to face her next step: listening to her guilt and ambivalent feelings about what happened ten years previously. By doing so, she carried her life forward, which unfolded in unexpected ways.

Our discussion of freedom and responsibility might remind us of our daily call to develop our own idiosyncratic path in a direction that feels right within the bigger picture of our life, connected to others and with what transcends us. That paving our path does not always run smoothly was evident in the lives of Annabel, Gunther, Ayla, Aisha, and Marie, and maybe in yours too. Perhaps you have been recognizing the four major existential challenges we discussed so far. Maybe you also noticed that you might have been responding in a similar way to all of these existential challenges, or how the four mayor existential themes are deeply intertwined. In the next chapter, we will reflect on existential suffering and profound growth, especially when we feel insecure, have learned to distrust life, and don't have the feeling that we have the right to exist.

Chapter 3

On Existential Suffering and Growing

You cannot heal from life, says Emmy van Deurzen. Suffering, from physical to mental pain and distress, is indeed a significant part of life. Taft (1962) argues that suffering and growth can go hand in hand. At a minimum, suffering can be an invitation to grow in terms of making sense of our existence. Any suffering has the potential to lead to a deeper understanding of life, spiritual learning, and experiencing life more fully. If we understand growth as a deepening of our existential awareness and understanding, we can view the obstacles on our path as important teachers. These teachers nor the lessons to be learned might have been the ones we were looking for. Nonetheless, when obstacles arise, there is no real turning back. If we do so, we seem to meet the same obstacle or challenge at the other end of the road. Challenging obstacles such as trauma, emotional and physical pain, or loss might lead to wisdom and posttraumatic growth if we engage with the existential concerns that arise (Tedeschi & Calhoun, 2004; Vanhooren, 2022b).

Growth itself, even when it is not evoked by adversity, is also often accompanied by pain, fear, or loss (Taft, 1962). We call them growing pains. We might experience fear and apprehension at different growth steps: When we are about to start college, change jobs, move to a new place, or starting to date a person we really like, we might sense fear and tension. Growing also often means leaving something behind as we take our next steps in life. Just like the snake in the story Gilgamesh, in order to transform or change we have to let go of our former skin. We need to let go of something that has been familiar to us. This "skin" might be a habit, a way of being, a person, a social role, or many other things. Symbolically, as Taft (1962) points out, growth can be understood in terms of being born as well as of dying. It can be scary to change precisely because something of us might cease to exist while our next self is not fully born yet. This liminal place, between the former and the next, is a fragile moment, explains Van de Veire (2024). Therefore therapy, as a place of becoming, is often a space of mourning for what we are letting go of, and a space of being *no-thing-yet*-ness: What we are to become has not developed its new shape. We cannot identify with it because it hasn't yet acquired its new shell, wings, words, or other structure. It is still an implicit something. It is in the making, evolving out of our implicit sensing of who we might become. With this becoming, our situation and our environment will change, and often a part of us does not want it to happen. The human beings around us—and something in us—might resist or welcome it, which might feel odd or stressful, especially because we might feel shy and uncertain, having not fully identified ourselves with this new "me."

Beyond our human interactions and social roles, growth in terms of existential awareness might entail a deeper understanding of being, such as fully recognizing one's limitations and vulnerability or understanding oneself in terms of being a tiny and temporary part of an ongoing eternal unfolding galaxy. Moore (2024, p. 158) argues that "...the continuous development of self-awareness [...] will most reliably lead to an opening-up to a larger reality." Rogers (1980) suggests that our ongoing becoming is part of a larger becoming that he calls the *formative tendency*. Gendlin (1986) explains that as our living process further unfolds, our experience of the whole expands as well. It seems like our micro-dimension and macro-dimension carry each other forward. Eventually our direct experiencing might open up to what can be sensed as that larger process that runs through us, but it is at the same time also not us. Concepts such as awe (Schneider, 2009), opening up to the Bigger System (Leijssen, 2021), and being in touch with *das Ganze* (Rank, 1936) refer to that kind of experiencing that enlarges our sense of being and at the same time deflates our egos.

However, letting go of our former shapes, habits, and ways of being, is not an easy thing to do. It is very human to seek the familiarity and safety of our habits, even when they are destructive to ourselves or others. We might not feel ready to trade the familiar for the new, which initially comes with a sense of insecurity and not knowing. Indeed, here is that life anxiety of Rank (1936) again. However, sticking with the old often comes at a price. Not only do we close ourselves off from our possibilities (May, 1983), we might also get stuck in ways of being, situations, and identities that become obstacles in themselves. When we try not to change or grow, we might still sense that something is wrong, although we might do our best to silence it. This is what Rogers (1961) refers to when he speaks of incongruence. It could be understood as a kind of self-concealment, which ultimately leads to more suffering (Larson et al., 2015).

Gendlin speaks of a *structure-bound experiencing*, an imposing of our former experiencing on our current situation (Rogers, 1961). It is a narrowing down of what we allow ourselves to sense, feel, or be. We limit our range of experiencing to a certain structure or a belief of how things should be. These beliefs could be positive (e.g., "Everything is great between us") or negative (e.g., "We will never be able to work things out"). By clinging to these beliefs, positive or negative, we both delude ourselves and limit the ability of our life-world and life as such to grow or change. We are not allowing ourselves to be carried forward into that enlarging whole that would deepen our experience of living. As a result, our living process, or at least a part of it, has been temporarily parked or stopped (Gendlin, 1997). Eventually, our incongruence may lead to choices that are not attuned to what we are missing and need. It might lead to defining ourselves based on a structured-bound experiencing of ourselves, rooted in former unfinished ways of being. This kind of stoppage (Gendlin, 1997) might express itself in what we call symptoms.

Symptoms can be understood as signals or signs of a structure-bound experiencing of oneself and the world. They are the sensation of the pain, anxiety, or suffering of being stuck, the signposts of what cries for our attention, the woundedness or missing that has been waiting to be heard and healed, the part of ourselves that wants to grow. The symptom refers to that unfinished life situation that continues to define our lives as long as it did not receive the care it needed. In this sense, a symptom is similar to the German word *Denkmal*, a memorial, something that remind us of a place where a task still awaits us. As Fuchs (2013) points out, symptoms refer to smaller or larger existential challenges that are waiting for our response.

Symptoms should not be confused with negative feelings that are just part of life. Fear, sadness, grief, anger, and other potentially distressing emotions are healthy reactions in the face of danger, loss, or boundary crossings. In essence, all emotions are part of healthy functioning; they want to make us aware of where we are in life. Some of us might talk about good or bad emotions. This betrays a value judgment, as if negative emotions were morally reprehensible or as if a good life consists of only positive emotions. Without our so-called negative emotions, we would not be able to live. We would not flinch at the sight of a bear but act carelessly. Without grieving, we would not be able to say goodbye to previous situations and experiences and take them along with us on our developing path of life.

When I think about my own life, I cannot help but realize how my path was shaped by negative as well as positive experiences. For example, a relationship break-up not only brought me to my knees; it also opened the door to my current life. I am pretty sure I would never have met my partner if I had not gone through the pain of that earlier relationship break-up. It was the pain that evoked a widening toward people and the world. Because of this openness, I took the opportunity to hike for five weeks to Santiago de Compostela in Spain. I learned how to travel by myself and be open to whatever came along my path. Interestingly, I started having a recurrent dream that I would traverse a wide river and meet a person that I recognized as being my new partner. A year later, I traveled from Belgium to the United States (over the ocean) and met my current wife at the borders of the Hudson in Garrison, New York. Only later would a colleague point out that this recurrent dream had come true. The adventurous story with my wife and our international marriage would carry me further. I had to reconsider my beliefs and understandings about many aspects of life. I was confronted with the realization of how culture deeply colors our perceptions. Our new situation also led to the beginning of an unplanned academic career. The birth of our son opened up a totally new dimension. I came to cherish parenthood as one of the most important aspects of my life.

Although this part of my life story might sound romantic, growth is clearly not a synonym for happiness or only the bright side of life. While translating this book into English, I was experiencing severe facial pains caused by a neurovascular problem. It not only produced neural pains but also high levels of anxiety. I experienced a new kind of vulnerability. It invited me to grow by appreciating my embodied sensitivity and to evaluate how I was living my life once again. Growth is not a synonym for reaching goals and realizing one's dreams. From an experiential–existential point of view, growth is understood in terms of becoming more attuned to the intricacy of living (Gendlin, 1997; Rogers, 1961).

Relating to Existence

Appreciating the intricacy of life, experiencing a deepening of one's existential awareness, and enlarging one's openness to experience are often the result of working through old pains or new obstacles in life (Moore, 2024; Vanhooren, 2022b). For some, or even most of us, it is not easy to maintain this openness toward life and its continuous challenges. There might be when we are barely surviving, or as Marcel (1969) calls it, *under-living* as an undergoing of life. Our process seems to be parked or stuck for a certain time. Difficult circumstances can teach us to live in a certain way in order to survive. These survival modes can lead to constrictive ways of being, such as being overly pessimistic and distrusting in order to avoid disappointment or overly optimistic in order to avoid negative thoughts and feelings. Although life challenges can sharpen our existential awareness, we are not always provided with the means to overcome and learn from these challenges.

One-Sided Positive and Negative Ways of Relating to Existential Challenges

Existential challenges can be understood as typical life situations that have the capacity to make us more aware of our human condition and invite us to deepen or reconsider our way of existing. They might also invite us to broaden our embodied understanding beyond our microcosm into a more macrocosmic plain. However, when we are existentially challenged, it might feel more like we are crawling on our bellies through the mud or into a stinky swamp. We might feel hopeless and powerless, waiting for something or someone to save us from our misery. That's exactly why we look for help and go to a therapist. The prize of gaining a deeper understanding and wisdom often only comes after we have been wrestling with this existential challenge (Tedeschi & Calhoun, 2004). Until then, an empathic listening person at our side might help us to digest our experiences until they reveal a different understanding of who we are in our current situation and which roads might lie ahead of us. In fact, these new paths represent our potential new selves.

However, we might get stuck while being existentially challenged. It is a very human reaction to get stuck in those moments because existential challenges basically invite us to change, which can be a scary and lonely experience. Greening (1992) describes two major ways of how people get stuck when they are facing existential challenges. The first one is maintaining a one-sided positive attitude toward existence, which ignores the negative or painful aspects of life we are facing. One-sided positivity might lead to a certain vulnerability, states Greening (1992). We cannot keep a one-sided positive view of the world or of ourselves unless we continually distort reality. It might make us vulnerable when we are confronted with life's tragedies and dangerous situations. Paradoxically, it might also unleash our own destructive powers.

In my work as a psychotherapist with prisoners, I witnessed how an overly positive or optimistic attitude toward oneself could lead to disasters (Vanhooren et al., 2018). Some of the prisoners I worked with realized that they had been hiding pain and other negative experiences from themselves in order to maintain an overly positive self-image. It was particularly difficult for these people to acknowledge that they had been the source of harm and destruction. Although the offences they committed were hard to deny, there was still a strong disbelief: "This wasn't me. I would never do this." Facing our personal shadow sides and those of the world we live in can challenge our constructed life stories, identities, and worldviews (meso-dimension). Reviewing our life story might confront us with old pains and traumas. For offenders, the only way to take responsibility for the damage done and learn to empathize with their victims' pain is to work through their own traumatic experiences (Vanhooren et al., 2017b). Only then can they empathize with the victim's pain and reconstruct a less positive but more realistic understanding of who they are.

Greening (1992) further explains how people might relate in a one-sided, rigid way to one or all four major existential concerns. Some of us might have a more nuanced relationship concerning loneliness and connectedness but a less nuanced view when it comes to finitude. Others might lean toward a one-sided positive view toward all existential concerns. We might imagine that we are invulnerable and pretend that this life will not end. We might imagine being constantly connected and flee every possible situation in we find ourselves alone. Some might maintain that their freedom is unlimited and that they are not responsible for the consequences of their actions. On top of this, some of us might assume that life is meaningful at all times and that our vision of what makes life meaningful is always right.

Greening also argues that we can get stuck by holding a rather negative or pessimistic vision when we are existentially challenged. For example, when being confronted with issues concerning death and life, we might get stuck by understanding ourselves only in terms of our vulnerabilities and limitations. In terms of meaning, we can get bogged down in nihilism and cling to the vision that life is utterly meaningless and absurd. Frankl (2006) explains how we can get stuck in an *existential vacuum* by failing to give our lives meaning. Furthermore, we can also retreat into our solitude or assume that we have no choice or impact on our lives. We can even use some parts of our life narratives as an alibi to convince ourselves that we are doomed and that our life situation will never change (Swildens, 1997).

The challenge, as Tillich (2000) already suggested, is to learn to be open and even integrate non-being and being—and everything that lies in between—in order to find the courage to be. Interestingly, people who manage to integrate the vulnerability but also the beauty of life show a more robust meaning system when they face adversity (Abeyta et al., 2015; Tedeschi & Calhoun, 2012), experience less death anxiety (Kesebir, 2014) and exhibit more wisdom (Weststrate & Glück, 2017). Indeed, as Greening (1992) concludes, the true challenge seems to lie in finding a balance or an integration: to love and engage in an I–Thou relationship while knowing it will not be perfect and that one might be disappointed, to search for meaning although life seems to be totally absurd at moments, to make choices while not knowing the consequences, to engage oneself in making the world a better place while others make war and don't care about others and the planet, and to celebrate and care for life while knowing it is finite.

Existential Transdiagnostic Suffering

Experimental research shows that an openness to experience positive and negative feelings fosters a more robust meaning system when experiencing existential challenges (Abeyta et al., 2015). People who seem to react in a rigidly negative way when they encounter existential challenges also report different kinds of psychological suffering. It makes sense because all suffering is existential at the end of the day. Death anxiety, a phenomenon we can understand as a stuck relationship with the major existential concern of death and life, has been identified as a *transdiagnostic factor* across different kinds of psychological suffering (Iverach et al., 2014). Transdiagnostic factors are recurrent ways of thinking, feeling and acting that play a role in causing and or maintaining psychological suffering over different forms of psychopathology. For example, Iverach and colleagues (2014) found that death anxiety is associated with various forms of anxiety disorders, posttraumatic stress disorder, obsessive-compulsive disorder, depression, and others. Meaninglessness and losses of meaning have been linked to various forms of psychological suffering (e.g., Delle Fave, 2020; Glaw et al., 2017; Li et al., 2020). A lack of meaning has been associated with depression, posttraumatic stress disorder, suicidality, addiction, among other conditions, (Fortems et al., 2022).

Existential isolation and loneliness have also been identified as transdiagnostic factors. They have been associated with poorer psychological and physical health (Constantino et al., 2019; Coyne et al., 2025; Maitland, 2020) but also with a poorer outcome in counseling with general psychologists and social workers (not trained in humanistic or existential therapies). Finally, when it comes to the existential concern of freedom, choice, and responsibility, experiences such as hopelessness, helplessness, despair and the feeling of having no impact on one's own existence also have been associated with various forms of psychological suffering (Cheng et al., 2013; Ejdemier et al., 2021).

Obviously, how people relate to their existential challenges is influenced by their cultural context. For example, people might differ in the extent to which they feel the need to have an impact on their existence. In cultures where having a choice or an impact as an individual is less important, the relation between having less impact and psychological suffering is still existent but the effect size is noticeably smaller (Cheng et al., 2013). Also, people from more collectivistic cultures derive more meaning from connectedness than from their personal achievements (Yu et al., 2016). However, one of our own studies shows that the focusing attitude (i.e., one's openness toward the felt sense in a daily context) was associated with less existential anxiety and depression regardless of one's culture (Pellens et al., 2025). This shows that on an implicit bodily level we share basic ways of being or interacting with our existence.

Suffering and Existential Sensitivity

Within our different cultures there are still differences between individuals. One of those differences is our sensitivity and affinity regarding the macro-dimension. Depending on one's culture, some people might become psychotherapists, counselors, priests, rabbis, imams, elders, chaplains, healers, shamans, witches, or choose similar life paths. When it comes to psychotherapists, not all of them are wounded healers, but there is a certain affinity with suffering (Cruciani et al., 2024). As a kid, I was tormented by a recurrent nightmare night after night for almost a decade. I was afraid of going to sleep knowing that the same dream would come and haunt me. I was crushed between the floor and the ceiling in this dream and had to follow my path through a dreadful forest. Schneider (2023) reveals how he needed therapy as a young child following the death of his brother. Jung (1994) and Rank (Taft, 1958) both had their portion of significant psychological suffering. Likewise, as Moss (1996) explains, the initiation of a shaman is associated with pain, suffering, and dreams about danger and death. However, the key to become a sensitive psychotherapist or counselor with an affinity for the spiritual and the existential lies not only in the suffering. Cruciani and colleagues (2024) highlight that people who become therapists are more rightfully called healing healers than wounded healers. Healing healers are people who also have experienced positive and helpful relationships, are invested in self-healing and gaining insight, and experience an altruistic and eudaimonic motivation to help others. There might be a parallel with the shamans, who experience not only death but also rebirth in their dreams and experience a vocation to become a healer within their own communities (Moss, 1996).

Interestingly, Fuchs (2013) and Holzhey-Kunz (2014) observe how their clients seem to be more receptive to the existential layer of life than the average person (who does not exist, by the way). According to Holzhey-Kunz, people who suffer psychologically might look and search beyond the average. However, their existential awareness might not always be accompanied by knowing how to creatively cope or be with their sensibilities. Existential awareness happens to them, writes Holzhey-Kunz, like an unchosen path that seems nothing more like a dead end. The helplessness, hopelessness, and despair we described in the previous chapter are part of their experience. Fuchs (2013) describes how this sensitivity does not guarantee a way of relating to this existential realm, which would help them navigate through life's storms and challenges. They might be painfully aware of the macro-dimension, which he calls *Existenz* in Jasper's terminology (Fuchs, 2013). In this context, Jaspers uses the beautiful metaphor of the ontic house that we need in order to live in this ontological landscape. Without this house and having no place to shelter, wandering in this landscape might become a continuous frightening experience, a mission impossible. This shows itself not only in terms of classical psychological symptoms but also through many other aspects of life.

Phenomenology—a specific philosophical movement and scientific methodological approach that seeks to understand phenomena through personal experience (Reynaert, 2006)—describes how this kind of structure-bound experience shows itself in the experience of one's own body, self, consciousness, emotions, moods, and the experience of time, space, the other, and society (Stanghellini et al., 2019). For example, Fuchs (2019) outlines how mood disorders such as depression, burnout, and mania, are characterized by a general sense of not participating in the shared experience of time as most of us do.

Whereas in depression the experience of time is slower or even stationary, in mania time is experienced as accelerated. In depression, the body and physical movements also seem at a standstill. When it comes to spatial experiences, in depression everything seems to take place at an almost unreachable distance (Fuchs, 2019). When we get stuck in our relationship with our existence, we usually get stuck in different registers of our lives. How could it not be, as our pain and our joys are about being.

In his search for what "being" means, Heidegger (1999) started his enterprise by studying the human being. The characteristic of the human being is that this kind of being is always in a relationship with something else: the *there*. It is always up to something (Gendlin, 1962). A human being is a *dasein*, according to Heidegger; literally translated this means *being there*. This "there" can be anything—something of ourselves, something from the past, the now or the future, the other or that which we cannot grasp. The process of living seems to stagnate without a there, or when the way we relate with the there no longer flows, freezes, or petrifies. Gendlin speaks of a *frozen whole*, by which he means an experience that is structure bound and flows no longer. When our ontic homes are endangered or disappear, we find it difficult to relate. Then things just happen to us. When we reflect on what happened and how it happened or is still happening, we start building a relationship with the there again. On a mildly critical note, I find the word "there" a poor translation of the German word "da" because da can also be translated in Dutch as "er," which means a place that is not somewhere yonder but much closer. It could refer to presence. Dasein could then be translated as "being present" instead of "being there." It supposes a more conscious way of being, a sense of a higher awareness of being, and resonates more with an experiential–existential approach.

The etymological meaning of existence (van Veen & van der Sijs, 1997) points in the same direction. The original Latin word *ex-sistere* means to emerge, arise, come out, or become. It is a compound of *ex* (from) and *sistere* (to make stand, to bring into a state). Existing means to relate but not to coincide with its present state. Once stuck, we lose our margin of freedom in the face of our situation. The moving or emerging is frozen, and we lack the space to look at it. We coincide with our situation, and as a result, we no longer "exist," philosophically speaking. We should take the latter, as far as I'm concerned, with a serious grain of salt. However stuck we are, there is usually something in us that longs for our situation to be different. That itself already means that we don't fully coincide with what happens, and that there is some carrying-forward energy in every situation (Leijssen, 2021). This does not take away from the fact that we might feel desperate at times, thinking that nothing seems to change at all, making us feel completely hopeless. scared, and stuck forever.

Getting Stuck at the Bottom of Living

For many there are moments—and for some of us entire episodes—where we feel completely stuck in our lives. In those instances, breaking down our existential suffering into different existential concerns according to Yalom's theoretical framework does not bring a lot of perspective (see Chapter 2). This kind of stuckness or stoppage (Gendlin, 1997) resonates more with a structure-bound experience or frozen whole around one's dasein itself. It might feel like being stuck at the bottom of life and being continuously blocked, where nothing really moves in one's relationship with life (macro-dimension). We encounter it as a way of experiencing—or not-experiencing—the here-and-now (micro-dimension). This stuckness is often linked with adverse life experiences in the past and present, coloring our outlook on our self, the other, and life (meso-dimension). We will mainly focus here on what this kind of frozenness, this falling apart or stoppage, might mean on the macro-dimension.

In existential and other literature, concepts like ontological insecurity, basic trust, epistemic distrust, experiencing the right to exist, the inner critic, and others are used to refer to this kind of being stuck at the bottom of existence. They partially overlap but also highlight different aspects of ways of existing that breathe fragility, hopelessness, and despair.

Ontological Insecurity

Ontological insecurity was first described by Laing (1965) as a disruptive experience that undermines one's sense of existence. We could say that ontological insecurity describes a way of hitting rock bottom at the macro-dimension. Laing argues that people who are sufficiently ontologically secure can distinguish themselves from the world quite easily. They experience their bodies as their own, they have a sense of being an entity, and their lives feel real. There is a continuous experience of time. There is some form of internal felt consistency or coherence. For people who do not have this sense of ontological security, life is experienced quite differently. We see ontological insecurity emerge in people who are suffering from psychosis or dementia, but milder forms might also be experienced by anyone else.

When ontological insecurity is paramount, any daily experience can pose a potential threat to one's basic experience of living. Just having an everyday conversation might disrupt an already fragile sense of self. Spinelli (2005, p. 159) describes how ontological insecurity affects our most basic experiences: "There is no longer a certainty that we are, what we are and who we are." The experience of reality in times of acute ontological insecurity feels like it cannot be shared with or understood by others. All this can be accompanied by a profound experience of existential loneliness and high levels of anxiety (Laing, 1965). Existing might feel like a precarious balancing, easily disrupted by anything from the outside or the inside world.

Eneman and Vanhee (2011) emphasize how these experiences in the context of psychosis can imbalance one's meaning system. Sips (2019) explains how losing meaning was a central part of his own acute psychotic experiences. His meaning system, his meso-dimension, crumbled from intrusive experiences that he could no longer tie together with how he had known himself and the world. It reminds us of how Annabel suffered a loss of meaning after her traumatic experience (see Chapter 2). However, what triggers this loss of meaning during a heightened sense of ontological insecurity does not need to come from what we usually would identify as something that crosses our personal borders. During times of ontological insecurity, borders that keep ourselves together seem particularly fragile. Imagine an extremely fragile water dam that could collapse due to the weight of a leaf falling from a tree or by a cat walking over the dam. Anything random could trigger such a breach, even positive experiences. Sips (2019) describes how he first became overwhelmed by a series of existential insights or breakthroughs. In his diary, he writes:

> I don't know if I will be able to explain, but I believe to have understood the essence of my existence... The word to which it all seems to boil down to, and which makes me different from most other people, is goal. Many people do not explicitly ask themselves what their existence is about, and why they want to reach certain goals apart from the happiness it brings, or furthermore, that this happiness is more than a feeling, something that can't be touched, from something that is actually in their brains. (p. 953)

However, the initial sense of clarity and "aha" experience was countered by what he called "anti-aha" experiences (Sips, 2019). While aha experiences connect and reorient, anti-aha experiences undermine one's existential position and beliefs about the world (Sips, 2019). In the acute stages of psychosis, the meso-dimension, which includes one's position toward oneself and the world, seems to be weakened. Anything that might disconfirm the meso-dimension might make it crumble. The self disintegrates and a shared mode of being in the world is endangered.

According to Eneman and Vanhee (2011), ontological insecurity involves not only a loss of meaning in the meso-dimension but also a meaning deficiency in the micro-dimension: It is no longer possible to attach meaning to one's here-and-now experiences. The top-down framework that the meso-dimension provides to give meaning to daily experiences no longer functions. The here-and-now experiences can no longer be understood through this framework. Hypothetically, the micro- and meso-dimensions might function separately now. The meso-dimension is no longer corrected by here-and-now experiences. As a result, one's top-down meaning system might start to drift away, and the way the person interprets themself and the world might be confusing and frightening for themself and alienating to others. The micro-dimension and macro-dimension can no longer be understood through a (socialized and culturally adaptive) meso-dimension, which might leave one to flounder in an endless sea of angst.

If this ontological insecurity takes on a chronic character, which does not always happen, experiencing meaning and building a new meaning system can be quite a task. Not only is there the quest to give meaning to one's psychotic experiences; existence might continue to feel like a shaky house that can collapse at any moment. The concern and care for one's fragile existence might further alienate oneself from society. It can be accompanied by a deep sense of meaninglessness and worthlessness. A 50-year-old man, a master of philology, expressed how his search to live with his existential fragility took a toll on him (Eneman & Vanhee, 2011):

> I feel really worthless. When I look back on my life, I see that I am just at the same point as thirty years ago. My life is a synonym of immobility or spinning in circles. I have made nothing of my life. I feel I have contributed nothing to society. I am a useless part of society. What do I have left to expect from my life? Wait until I turn eighty and die of an infarction? (p. 20)

Searching for meaning in life and a new understanding of oneself and existence are important pillars of recovery. Sips (2019) explains how connecting to others and how they understood reality was a necessary intermediate step during his recovery. Connecting to a shared intersubjective reality can be a grounding experience, providing a more solid symbolic surface or membrane from which the world can be experienced and make sense again (see Chapter 2). During fragile moments of ontological insecurity making contact with the other and with one's body and the environment can help to support one's sense of meaning. Prouty (1994) developed pre-therapy, a person-centered experiential approach that aims to restore this basic contact in people who are experiencing ontological insecurity. In his pre-therapy, priority is given to strengthening contact between oneself and one's environment. The therapist helps by literally repeating what the client says or by describing what the client does in order to bridge the feeble connection between them and their body, the other, and their immediate environment. Language helps here to gently reconnect, generate basic meaning, and retrieve a sense of connection with the world.

Basic Trust and Deep Mistrust

In addition to experiences of ontological insecurity, there are others that strongly affect our basic sense of being. Overall, most people have some form of trust that underlies their relationship with existence (Janoff-Bulman, 1992). This trust is almost unnoticeable. It is expressed in how we deal with ourselves, people we meet on the street, animals, objects, and whatever we interact with. This general sense of trust seems to permeate our way of interacting, as if there is something of a larger safety net to fall back on if something would go wrong. People might feel carried by something or have the sense that in the end things will be all right. A meta-analysis of nearly 1,000 studies involving over 2.5 million participants (ages ranging from 6 to 84 years) from China, the United States, and the United Kingdom shows that higher levels of general trust are robustly associated with well-being, health, and longevity (Bi et al., 2025). Over time, trust and well-being seem to reinforce each other. In this study, trust was not only measured toward others, but also toward instances, and life in general.

Frankl (1967) describes a *basic trust in the universe*, beyond our ratio or intellectual understanding. It reminds us of Kierkegaard's (2013) *leap of trust*, something that we can rely on beyond our knowing. Frankl locates it somewhere "at the depth and center" of the person

(Frankl, p. 61). Frankl does not refer to a literal place—although it can remind us of our felt senses that are often experienced around our chest—but to the core of our being. The theme of basic trust also returns in Gendlin's (1996) trust in the living process and carrying-forward experiencing. It resonates with the phrase that has been attributed to Israel ben Eliezer, a Jewish mystic also known as the Baal Shem Tov: "Let me fall if I must fall. The one I will become will catch me."

As described earlier, our sense of basic trust is at least partly nurtured by our experiences with people (see Chapter 2). Research on attachment shows how our early experiences with significant others such as our parents have a profound impact on how we interact with others and ourselves. Shaver and Mikulincer (2012) further explain how people who know how to attach securely also cope better with existential challenges. They are more likely to seek support from others when confronted with death or loss of meaning. Also, these people may succeed better in establishing more meaningful relationships, experience more meaning in life, and also face the world in a more open way (Dewitte et al., 2018).

Research suggests that our basic experiences with people might also color how we interact with other aspects of our lives. Studies have shown that there is an association between attachment patterns with people and ways of relating with animals, places, and symbolic others (Cassiba et al., 2013; Christian, 2020). These studies suggest that people who feel more securely attached to others are also more likely to attach more securely to non-humans. This basic trust in non-human relationships might become more important in old age when our peers die (Van Assche et al., 2013). However, these studies do not suggest that being securely attached to people equals basic trust or being securely attached to life. For example, Zilcha-Man and colleagues (2011) argue that a secure attachment relationship with pets does not simply mirror one's attachment relationship with people. When our basic trust in people is dented, contact with pets, places, nature, and the bigger picture might serve as an important shelter. For people who feel severely and deeply hurt by others and society, the felt connection with pets, nature, and the universe might be the last stronghold where they can sense something of safety and warmth. Taft (1962) rightly notes that the relationship with ourselves also might provide a foundation from which we can rebuild our basic trust in life. Actually, when we get closer to ourselves and grow beyond the masks that no longer fit us, we might discover a more direct relationship with the universe. When things go really wrong, finding something that still feels true and authentic in oneself or in relation to a place or an idea might be a lifesaver.

Annabel, whom we met earlier, had a difficult relationship with her mother during her childhood (see Chapter 1). She rarely shared anything with her mother. It just did not feel safe. She also had a difficult relationship with her older sister, who could be quite aggressive. As a consequence, Annabel had learned to keep things to herself. She would not show her vulnerable sides or share her deeper experiences with others. The trauma she suffered intensified the feeling that others were not to be trusted. Incidents following her excessive alcohol consumption also made her not fully trust herself anymore. At the beginning of therapy, I noticed that Annabel had little she could trust. Nevertheless, we could identify some old, isolated places that still preserved some seeds of trust. In the first sessions we would practice how to experience a safe space through guided imagination. While we sought a safe space for her, she suddenly remembered her old tree house.

As a girl, Annabel had often fled to this treehouse when her parents argued or when she just wanted to be by herself. I assisted her to visualize this treehouse and helped her to experience finding peace and safety in this imaginary place. It would help her to rebuild something of basic trust. We also discovered another old place that instilled basic trust in the past: her faith. Prayer helped her connect with the God in whom she trusted; it was a kind of contact in which she felt safe and heard. I encouraged her to pray for what she really needed. Eventually, the therapeutic relationship would also become a safe haven, making it possible to reconnect to herself differently and connect to others in more authentic ways.

While some of us might experience a loss or a lack of basic trust, others might rather experience a kind of basic *distrust*. When experiencing basic distrust, the other is characterized as being untrustworthy and attributed with negative or evil intentions. Basic distrust might be the consequence of having been through an accumulation of harmful experiences while having missed a positive counterbalance of love and care. In the end, it is precisely the lack of positive experiences that might make one swing from experiencing a lack of basic trust to distrust. With a lack of positive experiences and human loving kindness, there is little to draw from. It might also feel safer not to expect anything from oneself and the other or expect that things will change for the better. This kind of self-defense strategy might make the other suspicious, whether they want to help or not. Society might turn to an unsafe place filled with people having only evil intentions. However, this does not take away one's need to be understood and cared for. While the other is basically not to be trusted, sometimes the opposite is projected on a charismatic leader, who will come and save one's world. Blind faith rarely leads to salvation, which again reinforces that basic distrust.

Precisely because our need to love and to be loved never ceases, and because there has been an ongoing experience of relational damage, people can plunge blindly and rapidly into new relationships (Swildens, 1997). The new person can be experienced as the savior, but this can rapidly change when something of their woundedness is touched. Love might turn quickly into anger and hate. As the other might switch from angel to demon and the other way around, life can feel like an ongoing guerilla war (Swildens, 1997). Orme and colleagues (2019) speak of a lack of *epistemic trust* and *epistemic distrust*: What the other says or does is suspicious and cannot be trusted.

Living with basic distrust makes life hard and painful. There are no places to rest. One is a fugitive in one's own existence. There is hardly room for *ex-sistere*. There is no house or home, as in Jaspers metaphor, to take shelter and reflect from. Shifting from one storm to the next, there is not a lot of experiential freedom or *self-in-presence*. The therapeutic relationship plays a crucial role in therapy (Swildens, 1997). This relationship will be the center of the therapy, which can help the client stay connected to themself and the therapist while experiencing—relational and transferal—turmoil. Slowly and steadily something like basic trust might unfold as the other might not give up holding the client. Learning to slow down and dwell on one's meso-dimensional meaning-making processes (how meanings are attributed to oneself and the other, often called mentalizing) and learning how to symbolize one's felt senses on the micro-dimension might eventually help hold on to and trust one's own living process more deeply (macro-dimension; Warner, 2013). However, none of this would be possible without the client experiencing the basic trust embodied by the therapist. This is not an easy job for the therapist, who also senses the basic distrust of the client. However, the therapeutic relationship might counterbalance that basic distrust through an authentic interest in and care for the client's history of relational harm and pain. It might shift the cycle of extreme negative and extreme positive expectations. It might invite the client to come and live in the world of mixed experiences—a world that is neither hell nor paradise, where there might be a rightful place for oneself among the other mortals who are trying to make sense of their existence.

One's Right to Exist

Whereas ontological insecurity might be understood as the insecurity and profound doubt "that we are, what we are and who we are" (Spinelli, 2005, p. 159), one's *right to exist* reflects the question and, hopefully, the confirmation that we are allowed to be. For many people, there is no doubt about having the right to exist. It seems so obvious that it is never questioned. However, for others this right to exist does not seem to be a given fact at all. Having doubts about our right to exist can impair our basic sense of being. Pommerenk (2018) writes in her blog:

> Last night I asked myself: "What is at the root of ways I am getting stuck in life right now?"
>
> I have revisited this process, over and over and over again, almost daily for the past 10 years, for myself and also for those around me. I used to be a therapist. I am now a coach. I have been on a ride of transformation for the past 15 years. I have definitely struggled with my demons, and used what I have learned, and my own transformational processes, as springboards for my connections, and work with others.
>
> I always got to this same, personal dead-end. This dead-end, despite my immense progress by external standards, is centered around not feeling capable of making that final step on this path, to create fundamental changes in an area of my life right now, that I know will lead to greater overall satisfaction and happiness. This internal re-arrangement is something I have worked tirelessly toward in the past years, only to hit this wall, over and over again.
>
> However, last night was different. The power went off in my apartment as of the late afternoon, and did not return for the remainder of the night. Everything slowed down, and I suppose I needed this to get to that place inside where I ended up. I decided to write by candlelight, and meditate longer than I might have done if there was electricity.
>
> I proceeded to write down every limiting belief that brings pain in life right now, and also ends up being used as a block toward taking that strongly yearned-for, step further.

> I reduced them down to a most common denominator: *"I don't have a right to exist."* As soon as I wrote it down, I began to cry. My whole body felt the "truth" of it in my cells. I knew immediately that this belief has been there in the background, gaining strength through my lack of conscious awareness of it, and wreaking havoc on my larger goals, and my efforts to create large-scale changes in my life.

Although her mother cared for her, Pommerenk felt like she was a burden to her parents. In her experience, her beingness had to be justified or earned. Her right to exist was not her birthright. When we miss a kind of confirmation that we are welcome *as a person* in this world, it can make it difficult to embrace ourselves as worthy human beings (Rogers, 1980). Pommerenk's blog illustrates how therapeutic work on the micro- and meso-dimension might fall short when this existential issue on the macro-dimension has not been addressed. More often, existential issues and questions are reduced to problems in emotion regulation, as problematic cognitions, or just as the consequences of one's history. However, existential concerns have to be attended to as they are. Our human condition and the questions of life exist beyond our ways of coping with our particular histories. In the case of Pommerenk, it was her lack of experiencing, allowing, and owning her right to exist that enabled all kind of other problems.

Lacking this right to exist might be accompanied by feelings of loneliness, worthlessness, inferiority, rejection, and *shame* (Wille, 2004). We could call it *existential shame* because this shame does not cover an aspect but rather the entirety of one's being in this world. Wille (2014) reminds us that early childhood experiences of being hated and rejected might contribute to this deep shame and the experience not to have the right to live.

Doubting one's right to exist also resonates with that inner critic voice, which we usually situate on the micro- and meso-dimension. The inner critic is that internal voice that criticizes and demoralizes us. It is a self-interrupter that stops us from opening up ourselves to the world (Stinckens, 2008). While many of us might suffer from that critical voice from time to time, in people who doubt their right to exist this voice might sound continuously and louder. More than that, people might not be able to distinguish themselves anymore from this inner critic. In essence, the inner critic is preoccupied with not wanting to be rejected and fights to be tolerated. However, this being tolerated is not the same as receiving and owning the confirmation that you have the right to be.

On the one hand, working with the inner critic without paying attention to the existential layer of this problem may bring little relief. On the other hand, only focusing on this confirmation that you have the right to be, without paying attention to the inner critic or other problems on the micro- or meso-dimension, might also not fully help this process unfold in a life-affirming way.

The lack of this existential affirmation combined with basic distrust can lead to destructive and self-destructive behavior (Wille, 2014). Early psychological injuries might lead to a deep distrust of oneself and others. Not being able to tolerate one's own vulnerability or the closeness of the other can result in harsh and hurtful ways of being. After being abused as a child, potential proximity and care by others in later life might be perceived as extremely threatening. This was the case with Bruno, who was referred to a colleague of mine whom I supervised (Gunst & Vanhooren, 2018). Bruno could erupt violently and aggressively during therapy. He would kick the low table that was standing between him and the therapist. At other times, he would start slamming the wall. In the beginning, it was not clear to us what caused these eruptions, which would happen suddenly and without a clear motive. It took a while before we came to understand that when the therapeutic relationship would start to convey something of closeness, psychological intimacy, or warmth, something in him would erupt. This also happened when the therapist got too close to his inner tender places. Having been sexually abused by his mother, experiencing vulnerability and receiving care was a potentially dangerous situation. This "maternal" comfort was often intertwined with transgressive sexual behavior in his past. Therefore, experiencing vulnerability (micro-dimension) was always followed by a protective but excessive aggression. Paradoxically, this protective secondary emotion that ensured the prevention of any transgression also prevented his need for basic safety and care from ever being met. Any therapist or counselor would immediately realize that it would take more than a short-term and solution-focused therapy to help Bruno find a new way of living. The American Psychological Association guidelines for complex trauma emphasize a humanistic and personalized approach that pays close attention to the therapeutic relationship, emotion regulation, and the existential layer of the client's suffering (Pappas, 2025).

It would take 123 sessions of hard work to build a safe therapeutic relationship through which Bruno would learn how to attend his almost intolerable pains and explore their meaning (micro-dimension). In the later stages of this therapy, Bruno came to realize that his anger was more than a protective reaction. During a moment of focusing, he came to understand that at the very core of his anger there was also something else. Behind that anger and the pain, there was a self-assertive sense that he had the right to exist in this world. One breath later he sensed a strong urge to make something of his existence, more concretely, to mean something and matter to another person. The work of Bruno and his therapist paid off: It turned a lifelong suffering into existential growth. It shifted a deep-anchored distrust of himself and others into a newly felt but still fragile sense of basic trust.

Finally, while some of us are struggling to experience this existential affirmation, others tend to dismiss or undermine the basic needs and wishes of others. This can take the shape of denying the mere existence of others. Some of the offenders I met as a therapist over the years experienced others as not really existing. They tended to have I–it relationships without being aware of it. This did not arise from being "evil" or from an active wish to harm others. Others were just more like things. They did not really exist, meaning that others were not recognized as having their own personal needs and wishes that were different from the offender's beliefs about these others. Interestingly, these offenders would feel misunderstood when others did not act as they had expected or wished. Paradoxically, the otherness of the other felt like a threat to the offender's own existence because the otherness seemed to threaten the meaning system of the offender (meso-dimension; see Chapter 2). This eventually led to anger and aggression in order to get the other back into line, control the other, and get control over one's life again.

We do not need to work with prisoners to recognize this dynamic. In history and in our current times, there are always dictators in different sizes, ranging from violent husbands to presidents and kings who feel the need to get control over other people's lives in order to preserve their own fragile existence. By building walls, real walls and symbolic ones, they try to lock the otherness of the other out of their lives, deny the other person's right to exist, and kill them if needed. But it stretches even further. While we are curious to know if there are other living species in the universe, we might forget that we are not alone on this very planet. Our planet is filled with other species who cannot stand up for themselves. What would it take to affirm the existential rights of all these species, human and non-human, that are our brothers and our sisters? How would it be to grant existential affirmation not only to ourselves but also to others? Would it help us to find our righteous place, in the spirit of anavah?

Growth and Basic Trust

When life circumstances undermine our basic trust and when we experience ontological insecurity or a persistent doubt about our right to exist, the path to a new horizon is often long and steep. This does not mean, however, that growth is impossible. Bruno's story clearly shows the opposite. Growth is a force, visible in all living beings. In Dutch, growth ("groeien") is etymologically close to the word green ("groen") and grass ("gras"; van Veen & van der Sijs, 1997). To grow means at a minimum to stay green, or to be alive. Even in the darkest hours, there is usually still something—however small—that wants to live and grow. People with suicidal thoughts do not necessarily want to die or be dead. They might feel hopeless because they feel persistently stuck in a situation that no longer offers them any perspective for change or growth. Nevertheless, and especially when they seek help, there is often something that still hopes for change and the possibility to live differently (Verdegem et al., 2025).

A Seaworthy Hull and Wind in the Sails

Obviously, growth is easier when our living conditions are cooperative. Rich or poor soil makes the effort to grow quite different. This applies not only to plants but symbolically also to people (Afschrift, 2018). This is where the importance of basic trust, the experience of ontological security, and the right to exist come into play again. In his reading of Maslow's entire works, Kaufman (2020) uses a powerful metaphor for our need for basic trust to spur growth. Instead of Maslow's pyramid of needs—which Maslow never drew or used—Kaufman uses the image of a sailboat at sea. The hull of the ship represents our basic trust, our sense of security, which is nurtured by biological, psychological, and physical safety, a sense of connection, and a healthy dose of self-confidence. The mast and sail of the ship represent what drives us forward. In the sail, Kaufman pictures our need for growth. This need shows itself, among other things, in our need for exploration and our need to matter. Also, our love for others is a powerful drive that might make us grow and move forward. The sea, in turn, represents the existential layer of life, with its storms, its tides, and its mysteries. Finally, Kaufman situates in the sky our possibility for self-transcendence.

In reality, our need for safety and growth are very often intertwined. However, the metaphor helps us to see that we ultimately need a boat whose planks are sufficiently seaworthy. Even though we might want to matter and leave a mark, a lack of basic safety will make it difficult for us to reach our promised land. Without sufficiently trusting ourselves and others and the sea itself, we might feel discouraged when the first storm comes up. So even though we have colorful sails and know where our destination might be, without a solid hull sailing will be difficult. Our trip might become unintentionally heroic. However, the need to give our lives meaning and the urge to connect with others might help us cope with the damage we have previously experienced in terms of basic trust. After all, growing does not always mean getting somewhere. Growth also lies in learning how to cope with life or understanding ourselves much better. *Proactive* growth, or reaching new destinations, can thus be distinguished from *reactive* growth. The latter shows itself in understanding what happened to us in the past, over and over, in order to liberate ourselves from sailing in circles.

Therapy and Counseling as a Growth Process

In terms of Kaufman's metaphor, therapy can be understood as repairing the planks of our boat, setting out a new course, learning more accurate ways to navigate, finding new clues to learn if something is going right or wrong, and taking steps in going into the water again. Before we take the step to counseling, we might have discovered that our lives were not going the way we wanted, our rudder was faltering, our compass was not showing the right direction, or we found ourselves unexpectedly in choppy waters. In experiential–existential therapy, we do not only pay attention to the existential sea and our aspirations. All the aspects of our sailboat are important, from the crow's nest to the planks or foundations of our boat. Understanding our foundations, our fragilities, and vulnerabilities better is part of our reactive growth. We can situate this understanding on our meso-dimension. Learning to trust our boat and daring to take the helm—our ownership of our journey—is part of this growth process. We can situate our learning on how to read our inner compass and the complexity of our situation as a sign of growth on the micro-dimension. We are on the macro-dimension when we learn to understand ourselves as a small but significant sailboat on that vast and ever-moving ocean, and when we commit to take on that great adventure of living our existence in full awareness.

This type of therapy is essentially growth oriented in the sense of sailing with an openness of heart and mind while recognizing our limitations (Rogers, 1942). Taft (1962) describes the therapeutic process as a condensed growth experience. Repairing a hull or habituating to the water again is only part of the work. Setting sail on a sea that completely transcends us and will remain unpredictable is part of an experiential–existential therapy process. It is not measured by how far or where we get. How we experience our journey is more important. It is no coincidence that the effect of this type of therapy increases even after the therapy itself has ended (Angus et al., 2015). After all, once we have found a way to deal with our situation differently, we move and grow again as our journey continues. Rogers (1961) observed how his clients' growth usually pointed in the same direction.

Common Growth Directions

Rogers (1961) describes how clients often experience growth in terms of a change in relationship with themselves, others, and life itself. For many, an important shift lies in experiencing the possibility of *allowing oneself to be*. Through the therapist's empathy and acceptance, clients might experience for the first time that they have the right to exist (Rogers, 1980). Buber (1997) notes that once we have the feeling that our right to exist is confirmed by the other, a next important step or challenge unfolds: Can I affirm my own being, my own sense of self, now that I have felt completely affirmed by a trustworthy living being? Once we have felt our right to breathe and once we have affirmed ourselves as living beings, we might experience a shift that is sensible through our deepest fibers. It increases our existential strength (Depoorter, 2022) and it will help us cope or just to be with the small and bigger storms of life.

This kind of growth often runs simultaneously with an expanded openness toward our inner experiences, whether we understand them or not (Rogers, 1961, 1980). While experiencing this richer inner life, clients might also grow in listening more attentively to the different layers and nuances of their experiencing. From there, they might expand their use of language or other kinds of symbolizations to express and understand these embodied meanings. This increasing awareness is accompanied by insight and a more realistic view of one's own functioning. Interestingly, people might also become more sharply aware of an incongruence between this enlarged embodied awareness (micro-dimension) and former self-descriptions such as one's self-image and narrative (meso-dimension). These inner frictions also might be understood as growth, as they are invitations to alter our understanding of who we are. By opening up to the world inside us and around us, Rogers notes how people start to feel more in sync with themselves and also more connected to others (see Chapter 2). In existential terms, we could speak of a shift from an I–me and I–it to an I–I and I–Thou relationship. Indeed, there is also a growth experience in feeling more connected to others, in having more empathy for others, and in accepting the uniqueness of the other. When we are more in touch with ourselves and more aware of our own needs and limitations, the color of our relationship with the other changes fundamentally. Only now can we face the other as being "not–I" or not as the person who needs to fill in our gaps or shortages. The gained self-affirmation allows the other to be different. The other becomes a "Thou." In the other, we might sense a "more." And we might sense this difference and this more in our encounters with many others, such as with a tree, distant planet, or dewdrop on an early blossom in spring. Indeed, Rogers notes how clients begin to live a richer existential life. There is a growing appreciation for life as it is (macro-dimension). He sees how clients—aware of the fragility of existence—feel more engaged in being alive and less guided by preconceived answers; instead they begin trusting their inner intuition and embodied knowing to a larger degree.

Timulak and Creaner (2010) and Elliott and colleagues (2021) also discuss clients' reported changes and growth at the end of their therapies. Based on different qualitative studies, Timulak and Creaner report eleven broad categories of change, which are largely in line with Rogers' description. They distinguish a healthier emotional experience, an appreciation of vulnerability, increased self-compassion, resilience, autonomy, symptom reduction, less suffering, an increased appreciation of changed life circumstances, greater insight and self-awareness, and, finally, an altered experience of the other.

Schneider (2009) adds awe and wonder as tangible signs of an increased openness toward the mystery of life. Research shows how awe corresponds with being aware of one's place in the whole. The realization that we are just a speck of dust in that endless universe, surprisingly also diminishes our fear of death (Stellar et al., 2018). Awe clearly aligns with spirituality. In research, spirituality is understood as being different from religion. De Jager Meezenbroek and colleagues (2012) define spirituality as "the pursuit and the experience of connection with oneself, with others and nature, and with the transcendent" (p. 338). There is a striking similarity between spirituality and the process of growth as described by Rogers (1961) and Gendlin (1962, 1973), as Leijssen (2009, 2021) suggests. There is that recurring theme of a growing openness in the experience of ourselves, the other, and the larger whole.

Wisdom as a Result of a Deeply Rooted Growth

Finally, we should not forget growth in terms of wisdom. Although some people demonstrate wisdom from an early age, it is often very hard earned (Weststrate & Glück, 2017). We could argue that for many people, wisdom might come as a result of posttraumatic growth (Blevins & Tedeschi, 2022). Recurring characteristics of wisdom are insight and continuous introspection, especially when it comes to one's own emotional life, a deeper empathy for others, the recognition and ability to be with the ambivalence of life, and the ability to choose a direction while having a nuanced view of the situation (Glück et al., 2019). That wisdom can have its roots in suffering, at least when that suffering has been worked through to a certain extent, offering a hopeful perspective. If Rogers (1961) had read the contemporary studies on wisdom, he probably would have recognized it as a recurring theme of growth in therapy. Wisdom implies that our wounds are sufficiently healed so that they do not cloud our view but also that we remain in touch with something of the fragility of our woundedness as an expression of the vulnerability of existence itself. It is this being in touch with the fullness of life, both the joy and the pain, that can make us wise people. It teaches us to understand that there is a universe of shades and colors between black and white. Nevertheless, we also realize that despite all possible outcomes, we often must choose a direction. And this, at its best, is a direction that is life affirming.

Let it Grow

It is important to realize that we cannot have control over life-affirming growth either in ourselves or in others. We cannot force any living organism to grow without running the risk of harming it. When we grow tomatoes, we cannot force the sprouts to grow faster. By getting impatient, touching the sprout might force it out of the dirt. That would be the end of the tomato plant (and you can tell that I am a tomato lover). Fortunately, there is a growing awareness that quality of life is worth the investment. Ironically, this shows itself most explicitly in palliative units and hospices or in the care of patients suffering from chronic diseases such as cancer. The closer to death, the more attention to life. Specific existential therapies that include meaning-centered therapy (Breitbart & Poppito, 2014), supportive–expressive group therapy (Classen & Spiegel, 2011), dignity therapy (Martinez et al., 2017) and experiential–existential group therapy for cancer patients (Verdegem et al., 2022) focus on being with those facing such existential concerns. Therapy often focuses on meaning, values, and mourning over the unlived life. But even close to death, growth is sometimes possible, and these existential therapies support this kind of growth in the latest hour. The ability to share one's legacy in terms of values and other lived experiences with others can be powerful and joyful. Luckily, we do not need to wait until this last moment to share what is most precious to us.

The stories of Annable, Gunther, Ayla, Aisha, Marie, and Bruno have shown that existential and experiential therapies can bring important shifts throughout life. They also showed that existential concerns and dynamics are part of the therapeutic process itself. In the next chapter, we will explore in detail how the therapy process and existential dynamics are deeply intertwined. We will be accompanied by Thomas, a 64-year-old man who suffered from panic attacks, depression, suicidal thoughts, and a deep sense of meaninglessness.

Chapter 4

A Therapeutic Process

"Therapy is a process in which a person who has been unable to go on with living without more fear or guilt than he [she/they] is willing or able to bear, somehow gains courage to live again..."
(Jessie Taft, 1962, p. 283).

In the Beginning There is a Client and a Therapist

What is a process? Etymologically, the word "process" can be traced to the Latin *prōcessus*, with *prō* meaning "before" and *cēdere* meaning "going" (van Veen & van der Sijs, 1997). We can understand a process as a transition, a development, or a progressive movement. Etymologically, a process always implies some form of change, but the word leaves open the question of whether the change is constructive or destructive. In psychotherapy and counseling, we hope for a constructive change, starting from a state of being stuck and/or suffering and moving to a different way of living. According to Rogers (1961), this moving process is characterized by an increasing openness in wideness and depth toward ourselves, others, and life. It is a way of living in which we are less defined by unprocessed life experiences, stuck patterns, and unrealistic expectations. There is a larger sense of freedom, a realizing that life is just life and at the same time that life is an opportunity to temporarily help shape and color what we call existence (Rogers, 1980).

In the footsteps of Rank, Taft, Rogers and Gendlin, we can understand psychotherapy and counseling as a crystallized form of living. Psychotherapy is therefore a process in which we taste and live through the ontic and the ontological dimensions of life. However, the psychotherapeutic process is not a random interaction between two people. As everyone is well aware, just putting two human beings together does not always guarantee a positive change. Although the therapeutic process, like any life process, is to a certain degree unpredictable, we can identify some characteristics that make this process therapeutic.

Taking a closer look, we can understand psychotherapy, counseling, or any form of psychological assistance as a coming together of at least two people who interact with each other in a specific way. Inspired by Rogers (1957) and Gendlin (1997), we can say that one of these two people is asking for help because their living process, or certain aspects of it, is hindered or blocked at the moment. Even before this first person (whom we call the client) knocks on the door of the second person (whom we call the therapist or counselor), both persons have already completed a long journey. The client has already tried to do something in various ways to unblock their life situation with no, little, or only partial success. Often it is not clear to the client what is going on. Sometimes there is even no clear demand for help, only a vague suspicion that something is wrong. There might be a general or a vague sense of suffering without knowing what it might mean or be related to (Pascual-Leone, 2017). Some clients also doubt whether they want to be helped. As a consequence, they might start therapy with a lot of ambivalence: They are not sure whether they actually want to see something changed about their current situation. Perhaps they took the step to therapy because others insisted. Then again, other clients might have a clear view of what is going wrong, how they want to be helped, and how their future should look like. Some others might only want a safe space in order to engage in self-exploration.

All characteristics and dimensions of this first person play an extremely important role in the process of therapy. The (dis-)ability to tune in to one's own experiences (micro), to feel safe enough to explore one's own story and significant life events (meso), and to face one's deeper existential concerns (macro) will steer the interaction into a particular direction. Taking all research on psychotherapy together, the client has indeed the largest impact on the therapeutic process and its outcome (Cain, 2016; Wampold, 2015).

The other person—the therapist—commits to interact with the first person in a well-defined manner so that the life process of the client might eventually move again. Rogers notes that for the process to move in the desired direction, this second person must be *congruent*. By this he means that the therapist is in touch with their embodied life process. The therapist is aware of what is intra-personally and interpersonally happening in the here-and-now (micro), and how their own narrative, self-image, opinions, and training colors the experience of the client's situation and the therapeutic relationship (meso). Finally, the therapist is also aware which and how existential challenges are currently shaping the client's experience and the relationship, including those that are currently the counselor's concern (macro). When we are aware of this macro dimension, we are also *ontologically congruent* (Vaidya, 2013).

How the therapist interacts with the client to help set their life process back in motion depends on a multitude of factors. The therapist's person clearly plays a role (Norcross & Lambert, 2018). One's own emotion regulation, one's sensitivity and ability to pick up on small changes or disruptions in the therapeutic process, one's life history, basic trust, one's relation with the challenges of being, and one's current personal situation all play a role in how the therapist might meet this particular client (Frediani et al., 2025; Pellens, 2025).

In addition, the therapist is expected to help shape and maintain the therapeutic relationship in a specific way (Norcross & Lambert, 2018). Obviously, but not always guaranteed, Rogers (1957) notes that the client and therapist must be in contact with each other. Although this is often taken for granted, it is not always evident. For example, when clients experience ontological uncertainty, making contact might be a challenge; therefore being in contact may be the goal of therapy itself (Prouty, 1994). Also, basic distrust might complicate contact between client and therapist. In addition, clients can also lose contact when they re-experience traumatic experiences. As a therapist, it is important to ensure that the client is in contact. After all, without contact or connection there will be no movement or meaning-making (see Chapter 2). Rogers (1961) further formulates how the therapist can help shape a safe therapeutic relationship through an ongoing genuine, accepting, and empathetic attunement to the client's felt experiences. This therapeutic relationship manifests itself through multiple layers, ranging from the constant exchange of pre-verbal signals that we often only register through our bodily senses, through words that do not always capture what is intended to be said, through an amalgam of expectations and experiences and a mutual search of how the other one feels, and through a formative story about the therapeutic process itself. There is no technology available that can register all layers of this ongoing interaction between the client and therapist. Artificial intelligence might go a long way, but organismic or *embodied intelligence* goes further.

In optimal conditions, the embodied therapist succeeds in registering all these layers. We call this high quality of awareness about the therapeutic process *presence* (Bugental, 1978; Geller & Greenberg,

2012). The therapist obviously not only listens to what is said but also to what is *not* said. In order to listen so closely, therapists attend not only to their thoughts and feelings, but also to their *felt sense* about this process in the here-and-now. It provides them with pre-conceptual sensory information that would be overlooked if we only listen to the spoken words (Gendlin, 1996). Bugental (1978) further notes how presence not only includes receptivity but also expressiveness. The therapist or counselor is not only a sensitive receiver but also makes this presence known to the other through attuned silences, empathetic reflections, questions, and non-verbal communication.

Tracking, Following, and Directing the Process

Client and therapist shape the process together through a myriad of interactions, or by "just" being together. The therapist tries to contribute consciously and conscientiously. After every sentence spoken by the client, the therapist needs to decide how to respond to what is happening in the here-and-now. Indeed, the existential challenge of freedom, choice, and responsibility literally enters as an existential dynamic after the client speaks their first sentence (see chapter 2). The therapist has a large responsibility in terms of presence and how to facilitate the unfolding therapeutic process. There are fundamentally two options. The therapist could decide to give the client and the ongoing process their maximum space by keeping the directive contribution of the therapist to a minimum. We call this *following* the client or the process. However, the therapist can also decide to direct the process in a different direction by, for example, asking the client an exploratory question. We call this being directive or directing the process. Both following and directing are ways of responding to the ongoing process. The extent to which we follow or direct might depend on how we are generally present in relationships and how we have been trained as a therapist or counselor.

In experiential–existential psychotherapy, it depends on the process itself: Does the process need something now in order to move in a more life-affirming direction? Being excessively or unnecessarily directive can disrupt the process, while being directive can be important when the process is lingering. The therapist might be more directive if what is currently happening does not contribute to the process. Here again, the therapist is faced with several options. Which intervention to use and how to intervene depend not only on the problem; it certainly also depends on what the client can take right now and how safe and sturdy the therapeutic relationship currently is. It demands a close reading of what is currently happening in the different registers of the ongoing process. It also demands a sharp attunement to the implicitly felt direction of this process and what it needs right now in order unfold in a life-affirming way. Further, the therapist should also keep the timing and the stage of therapy in mind. The reading of the process and the question of what it needs is called *process diagnosis*.

The more attentive the therapist is to all these aspects of the process, the more precise the process diagnosis and the more attuned the intervention will be. Research shows that interventions that are not attuned to the ongoing process are not very helpful (Harrington et al., 2021). Attuned therapists can choose from their accumulated repertoire to respond to what the process needs. Humanistic and experiential interventions are designed to help the client deepen and broaden their experiential awareness and foster self-exploration, meaning-making, and life-affirming engagement. These interventions align with the overall goal of helping the client to be more present in their lives. However, the presence of a genuine, empathic, and accepting therapist is already an intervention. This way of being already directs the process in a certain direction that is usually different from what the client is experiencing in daily life.

The therapeutic process and the attunement start as early as when the client and therapist first hear from each other. The sense of the other, and all that it sets in motion regarding expectations, start when a first meeting is planned. The therapeutic process is also still active after the therapy has been finished. Sometimes the therapist notices after the very last conversation the need to write something down in order for the process to be completed. In essence, also at this moment the therapist responds to what the process needs. For the client, the process might continue long after the concluding session. The internalized therapist might remain a companion for many years and help the client attune to their own process, or the *client's client*, in order to make the next choices in life (Gendlin, 1984).

This short introduction might illustrate the complexity of the therapeutic process. It is practically impossible to depict the intricate dance between client and therapist. When we describe the therapeutic process technically, we often do not succeed in picturing the wildness of the process, with its unpredictable twists and turns. Therefore, in order to paint a picture of what an experiential–existential process might look like, we choose to discuss one case study in detail. The word "case" is actually misleading and disrespectful. After all, the therapeutic process is not only about the client but equally about the therapist and their fluctuating therapeutic relationship. What follows here is a description of the therapeutic process that includes both the client and therapist and their accounts of this particular process.

Not our First Journey Ever

The more layered our experiences are, the harder it gets to convey their meanings in conceptual language. This also seems to be the case when we try to describe what the therapeutic process and personal change entail. In these instances, metaphors might be more useful because they succeed in capturing the whole of the experience, including those implicit meanings that we find hard to verbalize. When we try to explain the different aspects of a phenomenon, we run the risk of losing touch with this whole and its essence. In a metaphor there is room both for the essence, the implicit coherence of the phenomenon and also for the direction in which the phenomenon may or may not be moving (Ellis, 2020). In order to describe the therapeutic process, many have used the metaphor of an epic journey (Bugental, 1978). The client and the therapist can be understood as *companions de route* or travel companions. The therapist is sometimes described as a blind but experienced traveler who needs the client to describe the exact landscape or obstacle that is in front of them. The client has a better view of their inner environment but does not know how to proceed in this landscape. In a sense, both therapist and client are blind, but differently. And even when the travel plan seems to be clear, it is an illusion to know how this journey will unfold. It is through the process itself that the path unfolds. It is, as Gendlin (1996) refers to Kierkegaard, that life has to be lived forward but can only be understood in hindsight. Only afterward can we understand which steps have been decisive.

The fact that the client and therapist are forming a new reality together makes the process rather unpredictable. Their encounter creates unforeseen impasses and opportunities. Although we might sense the possible direction of this process, we do not know what is exactly waiting for us. The realization that we do not know does not necessarily mean that we should not trust the process. Here we might realize again how thoroughly our existential concerns are intertwined with the dynamics of therapy. For the therapist, a basic trust in life processes might play a major role in allowing themself not to be overly directive; with a lack of basic trust, the therapist might restrain the therapeutic process and its possibilities. Embarking on a therapeutic journey requires something of a surrendering to life. It is reminiscent of Kierkegaard's (2013) leap of trust, where we take a leap or step that we cannot always back up with rational arguments. This does not mean that science and principles of evidence-based practice should be denied; on the contrary (Zegers & Vanhooren, 2026). However, we do not have the means or measures yet to fully comprehend and explain the intricacies of living processes such as therapy. Maybe we never will, precisely because therapy is of life, and life remains mysterious at its core (Rank, 1936).

The question remains whether I, as a therapist, dare to engage with this client whom I do not know yet in a process that I cannot predict? This question is existential: Do I, as a human being, dare to enter into life once more and engage with and affirm life, not knowing what the outcome will be? It takes quite a lot of courage to start therapy this way, but it sets us up for the great unknown and a deep respect for the client who vulnerably enters this process. In the spirit of Kierkegaard and Tillich, we might say that we could use something encouraging from life itself to explore and face our *terra incognita*.

This is precisely why Bugental (1978) compares the therapeutic process to an epic journey. I was privileged to engage in such a journey with Thomas. The metaphor was also well chosen for our therapeutic process because it turned out that Thomas and I had made the long pilgrimage to Santiago de Compostela in Spain, albeit separately and at different times. Although we never went into the details of this pilgrimage—that would not have taken the therapeutic process any further—we had this experience in common. The metaphor of carrying the weight of our backpacks as a metaphor for what we were bringing to therapy was spot on.

This Therapist's Backpack

As for my backpack, I can say that I was feeling pretty good at the time of our first meeting. I remember that there was not a lot in the way of being fully present during our sessions. Before our first meeting, I had literally and metaphorically completed many journeys. With the help of good friends, introspection, and many hikes, I was experiencing posttraumatic growth after a brutal relationship break-up. I had been growing as a person in many ways. Challenged by life, I had been searching for new meaning. I took postgraduate trainings on person-centered, experiential, and existential psychotherapies. I explored religion and spirituality from different angles, delving deeper into existential philosophy, Taoism, Christianity, Judaism, and mysticism. I searched for their common ground and eventually found myself rooting into Judaism. This entire process made my life richer. Peering through my telescope would keep my field of vision sharp and wide. All of this grounding would give me courage to take some bold steps. I would remarry and become a father. I was playing in a music band and enjoyed our rehearsals and concerts. This joy and a good portion of hedonism balanced out my enduring existential search to comprehend more about life. I had the wind in my sails, but I was well aware that the weather could also suddenly turn against me. I had learned this lesson a few times already. My early childhood was filled with nightmares, night terrors, and death anxiety but also a with deep concern for the others around me and a sense of awe. From a very young age, night terrors had made me sensitive to human suffering, existential issues, and Das Ganze.

At the time that I met Thomas, there were no major obstacles. During the course of the therapy with Thomas, however, I would lose two special people. My mother passed away in a relatively short time from cancer. My dear friend Lukas died unexpectedly from heart failure. My father had a heart attack and had to have open-heart surgery just before the COVID-19 pandemic broke out. He was a high-risk patient for many months during this pandemic. Nevertheless, and thanks to my posttraumatic growth, I was able to remain present with Thomas. I could empathize with hope and despair. My basic trust had been enriched, and I felt open to whatever life had in store for us. As a clinical psychologist and psychotherapist, I could rely on many years of clinical experience. I experienced something during our first sessions that made me trust the journey that was ahead of us.

And the Backpack of Thomas

At the time of our first meeting, Thomas was a 64-year-old man who had recently retired from work. He was a sociologist and had worked as a bank clerk, a job he never loved. Thomas was bullied at work. He felt a physical aversion to his job, and the harassment became so severe that he dissociated from time to time. During those assaults, he felt like he was watching himself from above. Thomas was not able to resist these bullies. He considered himself weak. He experienced disgust and shame toward himself. For this and other reasons, Thomas previously had been in therapy with different therapists.

The inner peace he hoped to find since his retirement did not come. Paradoxically, he experienced an ongoing agitation or restlessness. Now that his two daughters had also left home, he felt lost in his empty house. He had trouble concentrating and mostly just walked back and forth like a restless man. He also experienced panic attacks that seemed to come out of nowhere. In addition, there was that omnipresent dark mood. He struggled with suicidal thoughts. Although he had friends, he experienced them as distant. In a sense, everything seemed distant. It was as if Thomas was not *in* his life. He felt isolated, hopeless, and lost. There was an overall sense that his life had no meaning as he was experiencing it at that time, and maybe it never had. The way of living he described was very like the phenomenological description of depression (Fuchs, 2019), and his symptoms met the criteria of a major depressive disorder according to the DSM-5 (American Psychiatric Association, 2013).

Although Thomas's previous therapies had been helpful, he had the sense that they never got to the heart of his problem. More than once he had mentioned how his life felt futile and that he experienced himself as a nobody. However, he never felt received or met when he raised his existential concerns. Thomas had heard about my explicit focus on the existential dimension in therapy. He hoped he would find that therapist in me that could finally listen to his existential needs.

The Prologue to Our Journey

In Hohl's book *Ascent* (2014), two men prepare early in the morning for a trekking across the Alps. This trekking starts—to put it euphemistically—not very smoothly. The two men do not seem to get along. Also in therapy, things might not always go smoothly right from the start. First encounters with clients are often tense, and as with other first impressions, we risk judging our clients based on a just a few cues. Right away, an I–it relationship lurks around the corner. When we don't let ourselves get caught by our own judgements, we can catch a glimpse of how this new client relates to themself, to the other (ourself) and to life (therapy itself). It immediately sets the stage for an I–Thou encounter.

Cain (2016) points out that as much as we try to do our best not to be caught by our first impressions, mutual sympathy or the absence of it plays an important role in therapy. Clients and therapists who feel a natural click can have more of each other's presence. When something goes wrong, it is more easily and rapidly repaired. Overall, there seem fewer alliance ruptures in these therapeutic relationships. However, when there is no instant liking, more explicit empathic efforts are necessary to forge a therapeutic bond. Experiencing something of that liking or sympathy often lies in very small things. One of my clients came into therapy for committing criminal offenses. Despite his criminal history and my immediate distaste of working with this man, I also noticed in that first session that something made me curious about him. Later, when I was focusing on this something, I discovered that he made me think of my father. It was this element of sympathy or recognition that counterbalanced my immediate dislike and gave this encounter its full chance. I agree that this might sound rather unprofessional. However, all our human facets play a role in our therapeutic relationships. It seems wiser to recognize them instead of denying them. Moreover, curiosity is an important driver of therapy and most helpful when it is also attuned to the client and the overall process. Curiosity has served me well over the years, especially when I felt that spontaneous empathy was sometimes lacking during a first session with clients.

Although sympathy might be helpful (Cain, 2016), it can also set us up for an I–it relationship. Even having a good feeling about someone can make us not really see the person. As a result, we might not really meet clients in their otherness. From the first moment, I felt something of sympathy toward Thomas. I think this sympathy was also mutual. We were a step ahead of other counseling processes where therapist and client have to put in more effort in order to find each other. This does not mean that I understood Thomas right away. Initial conversations are usually a matter of mutual searching and probing. Who is this person in front of me? What is this person exactly asking for, and can I offer this person my genuine, accepting, and empathic presence?

First Impressions, Questions, and Answers

The first sessions taught me that Thomas was having a really hard time. His hopes to enjoy rest and quiet during his retirement seemed to be in vain. The freedom that the situation offered did not come with pleasure or joy. He felt completely lost at home, constantly walking up and down the stairs without knowing what he was looking for. There was a sense of emptiness but also a nervous tension. He could be overwhelmed by panic attacks but, above all, there was that dominating heavy mood looming in the background. Thomas had totally lost his zest for life. If his life had been taken away during his sleep, he would have been fine with it. It all felt so pointless. The word "depression" was appropriate. Thomas knew that therapy was no panacea, but he was at the end of his rope, and there was no way to fix things by himself.

As dark as his initial story sounded, it struck me that he also had some surprising resources and strengths. Noticing these strengths and little sparks of life is as important as noticing clients' structure-bound experiences. Although Thomas felt exhausted, he often found the courage to go running or swimming. He was also a painter. As a Catholic, he could feel inspired by his faith and Bible study. However rich these resources might seem, at the time of our first encounters he drew little vitality from them. They just seemed out of reach. Nonetheless, it was important to notice them as we would be able to draw from them later. Likewise, he had friends and acquaintances, but he felt rather disconnected from them. This distance was also noticeable in his marriage. Interestingly, during our first conversations, I noticed how he really tried to establish contact with me. He tried hard to show me who he was and how he felt inside. He tried to be as open, honest, and committed as possible.

What struck me was the very nuanced way he talked, as if he tried to avoid any possible conflict. He never took a stance. His reflections were so circumspect that it was no longer clear to me what he was actually trying to say. I could begin to imagine how his way of being with others might eventually get in the way of real contact. When I had him check inside how things felt in the here-and-now, Thomas could not answer. Although Thomas was fluent with words, when it came to descriptions of external situations he felt less comfortable or able to find words to describe what was going on inside. The inner voice seemed to be thin or just silent.

I did not go into his family background during our initial contacts, although this is what psychologists and therapists often do. I found myself more interested in noticing how he connected with me, with himself, and with those close to him. Asking about his life history would not have been of much help during those first moments. I probably would have heard a lot of stories and narratives. However, when they are told as fixed entities and not sensed in the here-and-now, they bring little movement or energy to the process (Gendlin, 1996). It also creates the false expectation that once these stories have been told, the problem will be solved. In addition, it sets up a dynamic in which the therapist or counselor becomes a witness–listener rather than an active listener. This does not mean that these stories would not be important at some point, as we will see further down. Similarly, just telling what happened since the last session is also often of little use unless it touches on a real lived experience or serves as an introduction. After all, we are then getting acquainted with only the meso-dimension. However, when people feel the urge to tell their story, and we listen carefully, we can invite them to the micro-dimension (how the story is told and what the client is experiencing while telling the story) and to the macro-dimension (what of the client's life wants to be listened to, what is at stake at this moment). Thomas noticed during these first sessions that I did not actively ask about his past:

> I was somewhat surprised that you did not ask about my family situation during our initial conversations. Your image of me was not colored and burdened by an image of my parents, what I appreciate in retrospect. The family in which I grew up was not addressed until over a year and a half later—and after both my parents had died. Then I was ready, you told me once. And then it never really disappeared.

During those first conversations, I had a sense that I was getting an initial picture of what was going on. In addition, I inquired about his two previous therapies and how they ended. He never felt fully received or understood. This gave me an important hint about what an important role this "feeling fully understood" might play during our process. It further struck me that Thomas did not have a sense of direction in life. There was no future, there was no tomorrow, and the past seemed like place to run from. This lack of a future perspective is a recurrent phenomenon in people who suffer from depression (Fuchs, 2019). While there is little access to the here-and-now, there is also more than this here-and-now. Yet dwelling on this here-and-now was just what brought movement.

With Thomas's motivation and resources in mind, I had an inkling that we would be able to engage in a process that would help him find direction and a new sense of meaning in life.

Regarding the Entire Voyage

Looking back, our journey ran through several stages. These stages could be distinguished by the challenges and obstacles we would be facing. Each stage had its own landscape and horizons. They followed each other chronologically, but the content of the therapy ran through a different temporal–spatial order. We often would re-encounter the same issues, but they would never be quite the same. It seemed as if we were at the same place again, however at a different level. In my experience, the therapeutic process seems to develop more like a spiral than as a curve.

In retrospect, the focus of the first stage of our journey was mainly on finding our way together. Thomas came to articulate his request for help, and we would discover the goal of our journey. The main challenge during this stage was for Thomas to learn how to make contact with himself and others in a more direct and authentic way. The therapeutic relationship would play a significant role in helping him to contact himself, his significant others, and life more openly. The therapeutic relationship would continue to play this fundamental role through the subsequent stages.

Six months after we finished our first stage, both his parents passed away. Thomas contacted me again, and we got ready for a second stage. Building on what we reached during the first stage, we were taking great leaps forward. We would dive into the darkness together and explore his meaninglessness. Movement would set in, keeping his dark heaviness company. Through experiential exploration, dreamwork, focusing, and chair dialogues, we would discover what was of essence to him. He would make new life choices, and so we thought we had written our story.

Then there was that world-wide COVID-19 pandemic. His initiated growth was flattened as a consequence of the lock-down measures taken by the government. Thomas sensed how his inner darkness was taking over again, but he did not want to end up in the same place as before. We would explore his existential concerns almost continuously during this third stage. Facing life and death now came with acceptance and a deep affirmation. Thomas had grown beyond himself. Neither of us could have predicted that we would reach this destination.

Unlike the short- or medium-term therapies we referred to in the previous chapters of this book, the overall therapeutic journey with Thomas took more than eighty sessions. Eighty sessions does not immediately fit the length of a protocolized therapy. However, to the best of my knowledge, there are no records of how many (protocolized or other) therapies and counseling sessions people have during their lifetime. Added up, the number of sessions the average client has had during their life might easily exceed these eighty sessions. In any case, this was the number of sessions Thomas needed to take him to that point where he could explore wider horizons without needing me. His inner therapist would become his truthful guide now.

The First Stage: In Search of Authentic Contact

Our initial sessions soon flowed into a series of intense conversations. During this initial phase, it is of special importance to build a trustworthy therapeutic relationship from where the therapeutic process might develop. Different than Rogers' description of this relationship with its genuine, accepting, and empathic qualities, Bordin (1979) interpreted the therapeutic relationship as a *working alliance.* He differentiated three important factors that would define this alliance: The *bond* between client and counselor (do I feel safe and understood by my counselor); the *goal* of the therapeutic process (what do we want to achieve); and, finally, the *task* of this therapy (how will we achieve this). Decades of research shows us that these three factors of the working alliance—as well as Rogers' empathy, acceptance, and the genuineness of the therapist—are robust predictors of therapeutic outcome (Elliott et al., 2018; Norcross & Lambert, 2018). Agreement between the client and therapist in terms of the working alliance are important and not only in the early phase of therapy. Disagreements, breaches, and ruptures in the working alliance can severely disrupt the therapeutic process. Not infrequently this leads to disengagement on the part of the client or therapist unless they find a way to learn from this disruption and deepen their connection and the process itself (Eubanks et al., 2018; Safran & Muran, 2003). From an experiential–existential point of view, the therapeutic process itself is a living process, and ruptures in the therapeutic alliance can be understood as missings in this process (Gendlin, 1997). When we attend to these missings and truly listen to them, the therapeutic process can be carried forward, enriched, and matured. It can grow significantly if the client is given an opportunity to understand themself better (including their relationships with others).

In this initial phase, but also further on, the formation of the bond and the formulation of the therapeutic goal and its tasks or paths require special attunement. When it comes to the goal, it is often a matter of balancing the client's wishes and possibilities with the obstacles and (temporary) limitations on the other. Although Thomas and I discussed a lot during those first conversations, there was indeed that implicit search to find each other (bond), to express the desired outcome (goal) and to develop a common understanding of how we would reach our destination (task).

Searching for Our Destination

Many therapeutic approaches offer models that help describe the goals and tasks based on their understanding of the client's problems and goals. Bugental (1999) emphasizes how important it is also to include the client's ultimate concern from the beginning of therapy. He argues that when clients make contact with their ultimate concerns it not only deepens the understanding of the problem and goal of therapy, it also gives us the mandate to explore the existential layer of the problem further. In addition, it often marks the start of the change process itself. As soon as it is clear to the client what their problem really is about, an engaged search process unfolds in which the client is maximally involved (Bugental, 1999). The question "What is this really about?" triggers a deeper reflection. It is the start of a profound exploratory process that brings us to the core of this type of psychotherapy, counseling, or care.

Asking Thomas what he actually hoped for (goal) was, in a sense, offering a new perspective. I remember his deep sigh. There was no immediate answer. It took a lot of courage to even look at this question. This question was not only an implicit demand for reflection but also a request to establish contact with something that was hardly there: hope. Tapping into hope is somehow linked to the change process itself (Wampold, 2015). It fuels the idea that change is possible. It also pushes mildly against the stalled life process. Contacting hope might be tricky if it is not properly attuned to the client and the therapeutic process. After all, every growth movement involves some kind of suffering in one way or another (Taft,1962). Asking clients what they are hoping for might also bring their lack of experiential freedom and structure-bound experiencing to the surface. Hope and despair are often simultaneously experienced at those moments. Unrealistic expectations on the part of the client or counselor might quickly nip this hope in the bud. However, not daring to hope might also fuel despair. By exploring possible goals, we are rubbing against existential concerns and processes such as death and limitations (not everything is possible); vitality (nurturing change and growth); freedom, choice, and responsibility (helplessness, despair, but also choosing a goal); isolation and connection (feeling perhaps misunderstood or experiencing hope through the therapeutic relationship); meaninglessness and meaning (the goal setting itself); and basic trust (we will not be able to reach this goal, will we be able to reach this goal, or something different that will also be worth the effort). This a great example of how existential dynamics are deeply interwoven from the first sessions.

In seeking and articulating goals, it is important to reflect upon the following questions: To what extent do we take into account the client's limitations, and to what extent do we leave room for the growth zone? What is our assessment of the client capacities: Does the client mainly need to achieve intermediate milestones in a relatively short time, or is the formulation of intermediate goals a distraction from the actual mountain to be climbed? Does pointing out intermediate successes feel infantilizing or motivating? To what extent is achieving or not achieving the goal a problem for the client? How can the client's vitality and life force be supported and strengthened? Have not only the obstacles but the strengths been taken into account? Formulating the goal should thus take death and life and limitation and vitality into account, along with a large dosage of not-knowing. In the end, it might not be the goal that matters the most. Having a first sense of direction might instill confidence to embark on this journey. Later on we might wander off the path into the wild if this feels like the right thing to do.

I Wanna Dare to Live

Thinking about what we were hoping for and wanted to achieve through this psychotherapy, Thomas noticed a warm feeling when he formulated his goal: "I want to become an old wise and mild man." This goal sounds much deeper and broader than "I want to get rid of those depressed and anxious feelings." Obviously, Thomas also wanted to get rid of his panic attacks and his depression. However, if we are to explore the client's existential concern in our therapy sessions, it is important that we include this layer immediately in our therapeutic goal. I remember another client who suffered from an obsessive–compulsive disorder. In this case, the goal of therapy was not limited to no longer checking whether he had locked his front door but also how to be more trusting in life. There is a special task here for the therapist to help deepen the therapeutic goal and to include the hopes of the client in terms of life with respect to the limitations of life. Once therapist and client have found a way to formulate this existential goal, they might find it easier to explore this existential space together.

The goal of therapy is not a fixed concept even when it has been clearly formulated. Goals are part of the process and often change along the way. Fixed goals might leave little room for growth. All too often goals are limited to fixing the problem instead of helping the client live their life differently. The inner search for existential goals goes far beyond a barometer reading of our symptoms, thoughts, and emotions. To be clear, improved emotion regulation and the reduction of psychological suffering are important. However, the growth process aspires to not only less suffering but also a deeper rooting in life.

As we move along and the process unfolds, the goal also tends to be refined. It reminds me of how a mountain changes shape and shows more details when we get closer. It gets sharper and, paradoxically, sometimes bigger and further. With Thomas, the goal of therapy gradually shifted from "becoming an old wise and mild man" to "I wanna dare to live." It could hardly be more existential. With this goal in mind, we could certainly get started. We regularly checked to ensure we were still on track. Are our conversations currently helping us to reach our goal? What should be addressed today in order to get closer to our goal? It makes the therapeutic process a meaningful endeavor even when only little change is noticeable. In addition, it is important to realize that it is not the goal that brings change. Even though the goal offers a certain perspective, it is ultimately what we are experiencing along the way that makes us move along. Or to quote a saying attributed to the Chinese philosopher Confucius: "The way is the goal."

An Experiential–Existential Case Formulation

Having a destination is one thing; getting there is another. This applies not only to any kind of traveling but especially also to counseling. In order to know what to do (task) and to get there, knowing the goal is insufficient. We also need an understanding of what exactly is stuck in the client's life situation. Psychotherapeutic models, including experiential and existential, increasingly emphasize the need to compile a case formulation in order to comprehend the problem of the client more systematically and delineate the therapeutic tasks from there (Temple & Gall, 2018; Timulak & Keogh, 2020). A case formulation is a construction or a hypothesis of how the therapist understands the client's situation based on a pre-existing theoretical model. It is an act of meaning-making in itself. Different sources of information are combined to draw a coherent sketch of what caused the problem, which characteristics or events enabled the current situation, and what should be done to change the situation. The case formulation also incorporates the therapeutic task in order to achieve the therapeutic goal. In some therapeutic approaches, it is discussed with the client. Because the case formulation basically offers an alternative interpretation or framework on the meso-dimension, it might bring hope, relief, and reassurance. However...

Although changes on the meso-dimension can have an effect on the other dimensions, this is often not the case. Many people know what caused their problem, but knowing as such does not alter it (Gendlin, 1996). A change in how we think about our situation does not always result in how we experience it. In addition, a case formulation might create the impression that the therapist is the all-knowing expert who will change the client. Depending on how the case formulation is presented, it might immobilize the client's self-exploration process.

From an experiential–existential view, the question of if and how to discuss a case formulation depends on whether it would be process enhancing. Would it be helpful for this particular client to share our understandings at this point? Would it give the client some reassurance to know how we will try to help them? Would it be clarifying and help the process forward? Would it be life affirming? Therapists who do not write down the case formulation might have implicit ideas about what may be going on. Making this more explicit might be helpful to disclose the gaps in our understanding.

Experiential therapists might add to their case formulation their felt sense of how the client's situation presents itself in therapy. This might symbolize the whole of the process rather than a conceptualized understanding that might only speak to reason but not to the soul. Using Kaufman's (2020) metaphor of the sailboat might help to portray the client's strengths as well. In addition, small trial interventions during the first sessions can give a clue about which interventions might be helpful in bringing some movement in the client's stuck situation.

In the case of Thomas, we not only explored what he desired as an outcome (goal), but I also tried to notice how he reacted to exploratory questions and small experiential and interpersonal interventions. It helped me to notice how difficult it was for Thomas to attune to his inner experiences. I also learned through observation how cautious he was while he was reflecting on his situation. He did not want to step on anyone's toes, although those people were not physically present. I also learned how devoted he was to this therapy. He really wanted to be as open as possible and took the therapy seriously. It gave me an indication of what could work here, or which intermediate steps we needed to take in order for these interventions to work (task). It also gave me a glimpse of which existential challenges we might meet or which dynamics might play out along the way.

In order not to violate reality here, it is important to note that not everything was crystal clear to me from the beginning. In principle, it never is. An initial view of a case formulation is more like having a few puzzle pieces rather than seeing the full picture. Some people might want to fill in the blanks because it might feel better to them. However, by doing so they might mistake their imagined coherence for reality. Patience and tolerance for the *not-knowing* is crucial here. "Knowing" only arrives afterward. It reminds me of the ancient wisdom of Lao Tzu (2000), who states that we cannot see the bottom of a puddle until the mud has sunk. It needs the time it needs, and stirring the puddle to speed up the pace will only create more turbidity. So what follows here only appeared with patience.

Seeing the Forest Through the Trees

There is a real art to seeing "the forest through the trees." This Flemish expression means that we might feel lost by being occupied with the details and forget about the bigger picture. In this case formulation, we will try to sketch the forest and the trees. When you start to feel lost, it might be helpful to reconnect with the forest. In order to keep the forest in mind, we will explore what happens when we order our first impressions of Thomas on the micro-, meso-, and macro-dimension (see Chapter 1).

Let's start on the micro-dimension. Here we zoom in on how Thomas's structure-bound experience appeared on the immediate intrapersonal and interpersonal level. This involves dipping into the lived experience, how life is actually lived in relation to ourselves and to others. On this dimension, in the here-and-now experience, we sense what our existence actually feels like and how it is to be alive right now (Gendlin, 1973). The micro-dimension also helps us to notice if the therapeutic process is unfolding or not.

On this micro-dimension, things did not go smoothly for Thomas. Although he had a rich vocabulary, it was particularly difficult for him to articulate his inner experiences. His self-reflections were initially rather intellectual. His here-and-now experiencing of his being seemed inaccessible. Measured with the Experiencing Scale (Klein et al., 1969), his level of experiencing was rather low during these first sessions. When he was talking and I asked him to notice how that felt inside, he would pause shortly and then go on with a rational answer or an anecdote.

It felt to me as if something was missing there. I was left with the question of whether there was too much distance from his bodily sensations or whether there was something absent in there. It would have been fruitless to ask him something about this absence. He would not be able to answer, and so I kept these thoughts and questions to myself for the time being. The ability to keep thoughts and hypotheses to oneself until the moment is right is called the *negative capacity* of the therapist.

Something of this distance or absence was also noticeable on an interpersonal level. Thomas seemed neither present in his friendships nor in his marriage. It was as if Thomas was miles away from himself and from others. When I asked him to notice what he was experiencing while he was talking, he observed a kind of inner censorship that distorted his message completely. He would eventually forget what he really wanted to say. If he did formulate an opinion, he would come up with counterarguments at the end of his sentence to weaken his statement. As a result, what he ended up communicating was quite cryptic. While he was speaking, Thomas would disappear and lose contact. Much later, when he found a way to describe his experiences, he would describe these moments as being in dense fog, separated from his surroundings—outside and inside. Later, we would be able to link this fog with his early experiences with significant others (meso-dimension). Also, he would start to realize that there was a connection between this *being absent* on the micro-dimension and a state of *absent being* on the macro-dimension. However, all these links were not obvious in the early stages of therapy.

What was palpable was a vague feeling of fatigue and exhaustion. In addition, there was also something of an agitation. What was remarkable was that these experiences did not seem to be related to his personal story or have any personal significance. These experiences once again reminded me of the phenomenology of depression. Fuchs (2019) describes how people with depression seem to be remote from time and space. The distance to others, to the world of objects as well as to the life within, felt unbridgeable. The connection with his body seemed to be paused. The bottom-up meaning-making from his immediate bodily experiences became extremely difficult. Connection, as an essential ingredient of meaning-making, was impoverished. His temporary inability to connect with his body, with himself, and others was probably one of the sources of his experienced meaninglessness.

All these micro-dimensional experiences would have their influence on how he experienced his existence (macro-dimension). Although we will discuss the macro-dimension a little later, with the micro-dimension fresh in mind, it does not take a lot of effort to see how problems on the micro-dimension would color his experience of the major existential givens such as meaning and meaninglessness and isolation and connectedness. It is clear that Thomas would feel rather isolated rather than connected. Furthermore, the limited experiential space would reflect his experience of freedom. All paths seemed to be blocked, which opened all doors for despair. There was no space for the future, and the past seemed to be frozen in time. There was restriction over expansion. Invisible threads seemed to constrain every step he would take. He was tied to his current immovable situation.

On the meso-dimension, we could discover problems but also identify important resources. For example, Thomas appeared to struggle with low self-esteem and said he did not know who he really was. He no longer had any personal goals. He also lacked the energy to realize them. Above all, he was searching. Interestingly, there was not a lot of a narrative or a story in the beginning. It made me think of what Angus and Greenberg (2011) call the *empty story* or the generalized *same old story*. There also was not a lot to talk about because nothing really happened in between sessions. Being retired, he did not know what to do with himself. Although work might be an important source of meaning and identity for many people (Delle Fave, 2020), this was not the case for Thomas. However, retirement caused a loss of structure. Hours, days, and weeks lost their function. The cadence of week and weekend, work time and vacation was broken. The meaning of time was possibly lost.

During our first series of conversations, there were signs of unresolved experiences from his past. Thomas would lie awake at night and worry about the many things that could go wrong. He always thought he would get into trouble. Something from there-and-then seemed to be undermining him. Since Thomas seemed to disappear when in contact with others, it was important to me that he would experience therapy primarily as a place of his own without significant others immediately taking up too much imaginary space. Consequently, there would be more space for something like his autonomy to grow. Interestingly, and contrary to his feeling of being a nobody, Thomas secretly hoped that others would discover his greatness. As a result, Thomas took a wait-and-see approach toward life's opportunities. He hoped to be discovered and invited as a speaker or artist but did not take steps to be more visible. In hoping to be discovered, he kind of outsourced his responsibility for his life to others.

Fortunately, we discovered some important resources and strengths during these first sessions. Thomas has been able to draw meaning from his faith. Although he had difficulties with the Catholic Church as an institution, something would revive in him when we started talking about the spiritual or the religious, even when he was arguing against the conservativism of the church. Thomas also drew meaning from his role as a father, although this role also came under pressure now that his children had left the house. He was looking for a way to redefine his fatherhood, but there was a warm smile when he remembered how he told stories to his children when they were little.

On the macro-dimension, we probably met all the existential themes that you could imagine. The most prominent issue during these initial conversations was that of meaninglessness and missing a sense of purpose or mattering. Thomas was carrying a massive sense of meaninglessness. He felt caught in Frankl's existential vacuum. Later he would call it a sucking void. As we have already indicated, on the micro-dimension Thomas had a hard time generating meaning through contact with himself or others. Along with the problems of meaning on the meso-dimension, there was little supply from the ontic layer. Combined with his sensitivity for the macrocosm, he felt confronted with his human condition and had nowhere to go or hide. There was no shelter or home to in which to rest. There only was Thomas and his existence.

In my experience, when we as therapists are open to the ontological layer of being, clients are also fairly quick to share their existential issues in therapy. Thomas shared his most pertinent existential questions early on: "Who am I?" "Did my life serve any purpose?" "Does my life matter?" All of these questions conveyed a grim feeling of being *existentially insignificant*, fueled by his *existential guilt*. He felt like he only made a mess. Luckily, he could cling to his role as a father. He tried really hard to be there for his daughters. But his overall feeling of existential guilt was not separate from the realization that he was getting older. There was that impending death. Time was ticking. Later on, he would admit that he had moments when he was looking forward to his ending. Then all of his misery would be over.

Thomas was struggling with feelings of hopelessness and helplessness at that time, showing how he experienced the existential givens of freedom and responsibility. There was little experiential freedom. There was nothing to choose from as he lacked the energy to take steps in life. Thomas could not imagine a future that would be any different. In terms of isolation and connectedness, there was a striking ambivalence. On the one hand, he wanted to feel connected to others, but, on the other, he was so afraid of any possible conflict that it made an authentic connection impossible. Between the lines, I could read how he wanted to be seen, appreciated, and loved. His need to be recognized as a person felt duplicitous and childish to him, as if this need or desire was a taboo. There was also the spiritual search for a deeper connection with the Divine. He could experience awe and was humbled, imagining to be in front of the All. During our last stage of therapy, when I suggested praying directly to God and ask for what he deeply needed, he resisted this kind of direct praying. However, when he studied the Bible, he could sense a kind of spiritual connection.

As far as I could see, there were no extreme problems in terms of ontological security, but there were traces of a battered basic trust. For example, when something changed for the better, he would expect that something would go terribly wrong soon. This negative expectation fueled his fear of life, which was all around. This lack of basic trust further showed itself in a fear of authorities. There was that apprehension that "they" would come after him. It more or less resonated with his censored speech. In sum and in terms of Kaufman's (2020) sailboat, his boat seemed seaworthy but battered by life (see Chapter 3). Thomas lacked drive or wind in his sails. His boat was stationary, and he must have lost his compass along the way. Yet there was something in Thomas that didn't give up. There was that precious spark of life. Although he was totally out of sorts, he still came for help.

How to be of Help

Our case formulation helped to understand that helping Thomas would not be a matter of simply pushing a button. It showed how his experience of meaninglessness covered all three dimensions. It was intertwined with many other existential concerns as well. Thomas's living process seemed to be blocked at many levels. We could call it a structure-bound experience of life itself (Missiaen & Vanhooren, 2021). Our overall task would be to bring some movement to each ontic and ontological dimension with respect to Thomas's *draagkracht* (a Dutch word that means the capacity to carry the weight of one's own existence), the therapeutic relationship, and the unfolding process itself.

There is empirical evidence that psychological methods are only truly effective when they take the therapeutic process and the client's readiness to take a particular step into account (Krebs et al., 2018). It shows that process diagnosis precedes any step-by-step therapeutic plan, even if it was specifically designed for this particular client. However, process diagnosis, meaning the continuous attunement to what the client and the process need to unfold, does not preclude the therapist from having a sense of a plan. Having the case formulation and the general therapy goals in mind ("I want to become a gentle wise mild old man" and "I wanna dare to live") is one thing. Attuning to how the client's living process is currently showing itself during the interpersonal encounter is another. In any case, the counselor and the client are faced with the choice of where to go to next. For the therapist, this choice might be informed by the case formulation and goals, but foremost by this constant attunement, including their felt sense of what's the next step. The client might choose which direction to take based on their sense of safety and trust, their curiosity to know more, and their stream of felt senses and consciousness.

During the first stage of our conversations, I was faced with the choice of how I would be present with Thomas's inner and interpersonal existential absence. There was little or no movement on the micro-dimension, and this would require attention. I was aware that this would take many sessions, and I did not expect any quick changes. In this context, Hoffman (2021) speaks of long-term interventions, meaning that they might take a longer time to be effective but also that they would serve the client for life. After all, phenomenologically speaking, this being out of touch with existence goes to the heart of what depression might be (Fuchs, 2019). Depression might be the opposite of being present in one's life—the overall goal of existential psychotherapy (Bugental, 1978). We also know that helping clients to make contact with their immediate felt experiences is an important catalyst of change (Peluso & Freund, 2018; Pinheiro et al., 2021). According to Rogers (1957), next to the formation of an empathic and genuine therapeutic relationship, exploring one's felt experiences is a prerequisite for facilitating therapeutic change. In addition, making contact is also an essential element of any meaning-making process (see Chapter 2). Helping Thomas to be more in touch with himself and the other (meaning me as a therapist during therapy) would be one of our primary tasks. We would pay explicit attention to this task during every session.

On the meso-dimension, there was a search for a new or a different sense of self, identity, and a meaningful occupation now Thomas had retired. I also noticed signs of unprocessed experiences that may have played a role in how he experienced his existence. Not only the fact that Thomas had dissociated in the past reminded me of this; there was something else I could not put my finger on. However, it was clear to me that we would not be able to work with these unprocessed experiences until there was also more experiential freedom and safety at the micro-dimension. Of course, there was probably an interplay between these unprocessed experiences and the absence or silence at the micro-dimension. Nonetheless, I decided to focus on cultivating a sufficiently secure relationship with his embodied experiences (the hull of the boat) before we would engage with the stormy seas again (unprocessed negative life experiences).

On the macro-dimension, there was that looming darkness, that deep despondency, that massive existential vacuum, existential guilt, life anxiety, and pervasive existential loneliness. But that was not the entire story. There was also awe, a sense of spirituality, and a search for connection with the Divine. Eventually we would visit, meet, and explore all these existential challenges using a number of interventions to build a living and ongoing relationship with his experience of what it means to be alive. We would use interventions such as focusing, dreamwork, empty-chair and two-chair dialogues as well as writing and homework assignments. We ended each session by checking in and asking Thomas what he would take home or try out this week. These smaller ontic goals, which emerged each time from our sessions, would add up to the ontological goal. In hindsight, the assignments did not evoke change itself. They functioned as forms of deliberate practice (Goldman et al., 2021), helping to anchor or root the changes that were experienced during the session itself.

Although we used all those interventions and assignments, they were but a small part of the therapeutic process. The process was unfolding through the therapeutic relationship in the shape of an authentic, empathic, and accepting attunement from person to person and the ongoing facilitation of experiential self-exploration. According to Rank (1936) and Rogers (1942), we can consider relationship and experiential self-exploration as the main ingredients of the therapeutic process. Relationship and exploration—or contact and meaning-making—would be the essence of this therapy. Experiential interventions such as focusing and chair work were implicitly at the service of this dual task: making contact and engaging with the other, oneself, and life in a more profound way in the here-and-now and discovering meaning and making sense of oneself and life.

During our sessions, I would help Thomas to make contact at least with myself as a therapist in the here-and-now (I–Thou) and with himself (I–I). It was my hope that by emphasizing this empathic here-and-now attunement, Thomas would eventually be able to reconnect with himself, with others, and with life. Through this succession of empathic reflections and questions, I invited him to be more present rather than absent. I also hoped that the created safety would help him to look at his unprocessed life experiences. I hoped we would engage in getting to know his old wounds, core pains, or missings as important—but still unknown—characters in this life. Finally, I cherished the hope that meeting these old wounds would eventually help him understand what was essential to him in life and to choose this essence. The therapeutic relationship was not the only factor that would bring change, but perhaps it was the most fundamental one throughout our entire journey.

On Holy Ground

Although the therapeutic relationship is sometimes narrowed down to the working alliance in research literature, this relationship is far more than that. It is the ongoing exchange between therapist and client that develops over time. It is this constant, authentic resonating and searching to understand that facilitates the client's self-exploration process. It is the ongoing exchange of non-verbal and verbal communications, a fine-tuning of meanings that changes while this fine-tuning is happening. The extent to which the therapist can tune into the client's level of experience and help the client explore the topic just a little deeper is predictive of the therapy progress and outcome (Krycka & Ikemi, 2016; Singh et al., 2021).

The therapeutic relationship is about making contact and deepening this contact. It is an ongoing invitation to go deeper into this awareness of being oneself at this very moment. It is also an invitation for those aspects of oneself that are scared or scary to join this living conversation, to make themselves known, heard, and seen. We could metaphorically picture the client and therapist descending together into the client's inner world, trying to understand what is going on there. The therapist is a respectful, cautious, and curious guest who tries to understand this inner landscape. As they descend further, they come to the most tender places, at least if the client allows the therapist into these rooms. They might enter the most vulnerable and uncharted sacred grounds of the client, where it is better for the therapist to take off their shoes. Unlike the client, who knows what it feels like to be there, the therapist may notice elements that the client ignores out of habit. Therapy not only takes place when we enter difficult places or explore holy grounds. Although these are landmark experiences in therapy, therapy is also at its best when we explore those ignored rooms that do not look so special at a first glimpse. During this intimate search, the therapist helps the client learn to understand themself differently. The client might enter into a renewed I–I relationship with themself, making them curious to explore their next rooms or new paths.

Searching for Wisdom

Thomas's learning how to connect with himself, others, and life in a more direct way would be the mountain we had to climb during this first therapy stage. I remember how Thomas started to realize that he could not become an old wise man without establishing a more authentic connection with himself and others. Becoming aware of how he clouded his communication by a complex process of inner censorship was a first step to take. Thomas was hardly aware of this self-censorship. I often invited Thomas to be more aware of what he actually wanted to say. I helped him notice what was happening inside while he was forming a statement. Thomas gradually became aware of how he lost contact with his actual message or need while he was anticipating the other person's reaction. This recurrent pattern created a kind of vacuum in which he kept drifting away from himself and the others as well. Learning how to make contact with what was happening in the here-and-now was extremely important.

By dwelling on this dynamic of his self-censorship and his alienation and absence from life, the feedback his partner gave him repeatedly also started to make more sense: "I don't know what you feel or think." or "Don't fill in what I would think. You don't know if this or that would make me angry." Taking steps toward more authenticity in connection to others and himself, both during and outside therapy, became a central theme in this first series of conversations. It became an important intermediate goal toward eventually becoming wise and mild. Within the safe space of the therapeutic relationship, Thomas took the risk to let go of self-censorship:

> **Thomas**: I really don't want to censor what I'm saying here. But I do think it's important what I say here, or how I use words. Searching for the right words seems to be an important part of what we're doing here....
> **Siebrecht**: Help me out... Can you tell me why it's important for you to find the right words here?
> **Thomas**: When we find the right words, the sense or image gets sharper of what I feel. And not only that. I also feel that you really understand me and understand what we are talking about....

In this small excerpt, Thomas brings several lines of the therapeutic process together. He makes the implicit link to focusing, which we had been using in very small portions. The search for the right words refers directly to making contact with his felt sense in the here-and-now. In focusing, we search for words or other symbolizations that fit closely with what is directly experienced (Gendlin, 1962). This process of searching for the right words presupposes a noticing of what we are sensing. In Gendlin's theory, this "what we are directly sensing," with its characteristics and implicit meaning that we are trying to express through these right words, is called the *direct referent*. Through this process of sensing, expressing, and meaning-making, the immediate contact and connection to ourselves become firmer and more quickly accessible (see Chapter 2). Thomas notes in this therapy excerpt how there is an implicit link between him getting closer to himself and me understanding him better. Session by session, our efforts to grow toward a more authentic intrapersonal (I–I) and interpersonal contact (I–Thou) were paying off.

Feeling at Home and Fully Accepted

Shortly after Thomas let go of his self-censorship in therapy, he expressed his desire to have a more open and authentic relationship with his children, partner, and friends. Inspired by the therapeutic relationship, Thomas expresses his new desire as follows:

> You are about twenty years younger than me. You could have been one of my children. That idea crossed my mind several times. I wonder... Talking as openly as we do in these sessions here, and talking about the things that matter, and finding each other in this talking... I wish I could do the same with my daughters. Our sessions could be an exercise in talking to the people who are important to me.

We started to explore very specific situations in which his connection with others and himself got lost. It would help us to get more clarity on what exactly was holding him back from being more present. For example, there was a friend who expressed having more than ordinary feelings of friendship for him. Thomas felt that he did not share these feelings or desires but could not get this past his lips. The desire for more authenticity was there but the fear of conflict was bigger in this concrete situation. The contrast between what he could experience in our therapeutic relationship and express in his own environments was growing:

Thomas: It's weird to say, but I feel at home here (sigh).

Siebrecht: "I feel at home here" and there comes a deep sigh....
Thomas: Yes...
Siebrecht: Thomas, that feeling of being at home here, what is that exactly?
Thomas: I don't know... I feel fully understood here. And also really accepted.
Siebrecht: Feeling fully understood and accepted, that's really coming home for you.
Thomas: Yes... [silence]. It's that acceptance... I feel completely accepted here, just the way I am. And it's terrible to say, but elsewhere I don't have that feeling... I even don't have that feeling at home.

This is a great example of how growth also often means becoming more aware of our incongruences and pains (Rogers, 1961). Noticing what is possible can be accompanied by sadness and suffering because it immediately means that one has not been allowed or has not been able to experience this possibility before. The client becomes aware that their reality does not need to be as it was, and that another reality might indeed be possible. This kind of realization is often accompanied by an experience of mourning for what has not been, might be, or might never be. It is often initiated by the therapist's accepting empathic understanding and the growing self-insight in the client. It challenges the client's former self-image and worldview (Rogers, 1942). This has been called the *deconstructive function* of empathy (Watson, 2016). Although this comes with mixed feelings, it is above all a sign that the therapeutic process and the structure-bound experience of the client is in motion.

In the short excerpt above, we could read how the therapeutic relationship is setting some of the fundamental existential experiences of Thomas into motion. To feel fully accepted and to realize that he did not feel this anywhere else touches directly on Thomas's need for existential affirmation. It resonates with pains regarding his right to exist. In our second stage of therapy, we visited this place again, albeit more informed by content from his meso-dimension. Therapy often spirals. We wrestle with the same existential challenges time after time but sometimes wider and deeper. At this point in therapy, however, Thomas feels through this empathic acceptance that his existence has been confirmed and accepted for the first time. Rogers (1980) emphasizes that therapy is the place where clients often feel fully seen and heard for the first time. To know that someone might understand you to a higher degree and also—or still—accept you fully can be a powerful confirmation of being. Buber (1997) adds that this process is only complete when we also grant ourselves the right to exist, affirm ourselves, and affirm life as such. We were not ready to take this leap yet, but we were on our way.

Moments of affirmation are special and precious. They are corrective experiences and have the power to recalibrate our basic existential experience. It is also a layered experience, not necessarily only a joyful one. We might become painfully aware of our otherness compared to significant people in our lives. Therefore, this affirming I–Thou encounter does not exclude experiences of existential isolation with others. This moment of meeting entails a feeling of connectedness and acceptance but also difference. Maybe, as Rank explained, it is precisely this succession of feelings of connection and difference that makes this moment truly corrective (Kramer, 2019).

Feeling Carried by Existence

I also hoped that we would be able to strengthen Thomas's *draagkracht* and basic trust during therapy. I do not think that there are specific single interventions capable of shifting basic existential experiences such as basic trust or one's right to exist. These kind of changes are rather a development, a result of a succession of long-term interventions such as the therapeutic relationship or experiencing the therapeutic process as a whole (Rank, 1936). Next to the therapeutic relationship, establishing an ongoing inner experiential relationship through focusing can also help to feel more carried and supported by life (Vanhooren, Grosemans, et al., 2022). Developing a stronger connection to our physical and spiritual reality also nurtures our basic trust and *draagkracht* (Dana, 2020; Leijssen, 2013). Fuchs (2019) recommends that people with depression also physically exercise. Exercising helps us get back in motion in other ways. Walking in nature specifically helps to nurture our basic trust (Dana, 2020). Being in nature appears to help us safely reconnect or reaffirm our contact with the ground of our existence (Anderson et al., 2018; Dana, 2020).

During the first stage, I advised Thomas to walk every day. I had the intuitive feeling that running was rather exhausting him. I asked him to be mindful of the landscape that gradually changed while he was walking. It also helped him to reconnect with his former pilgrimage to Santiago de Compostela in Spain, which had been helpful to him. Later it turned out that swimming worked better for Thomas:

> I discovered the joy of swimming during our summer holidays. Feeling being carried by the water, moving freely with arms and legs, breathing regularly, and taking up space... But now that I'm back home, it is difficult for me to allow myself the time or space to swim weekly. Afterward, when I uttered those negative comments: "Isn't that a luxury? Consuming so much water and heating energy for only two euros? you replied: "Yes, it is a luxury yes, but what you experience in this swimming doesn't seem like a luxury to me." It was as if you were giving me a free pass. And I have to confess that I used your statement to say to my wife: "Siebrecht said that swimming is good for me." However, she did not oppose or need your authority to have me swim; I apparently did.

The last two sentences show how the therapeutic process had not helped Thomas to take full responsibility for his choices yet. Nevertheless, by swimming, Thomas felt increasingly included in something larger than himself. It beautifully shows how a microcosmic physical activity can help us to experience our macrocosmic or spiritual realms. As Leijssen (2013) notes, this spiritual reality can take different forms or shapes, but a recurring element is indeed that we feel a part of something larger. For some of us, this connection between our physical and spiritual realities might express itself in the form of rituals, dancing, playing music, gardening, or in Thomas's case, bathing and swimming.

It was remarkable how he could enjoy the water and entrust his body to the water. These, too, were signs that something was moving. There was a growing openness to the world around and in him. Thomas explained how swimming gave him ground under his feet, like something of a trustworthy bottom was forming itself. He felt truly carried by this something. It struck me how existential confirmation and *draagkracht* only seem to develop when we feel sufficiently carried. Meanwhile, his depression and panic attacks were diminishing and disappearing.

It was probably not a coincidence, rather something of synchronicity, that while his life started to move and flow again, he was invited to collaborate on an art exhibition. Although the practical side of things would cause some frustration, Thomas was able to enjoy the exhibition. He experienced his days to be more meaningful. Thomas felt ready to finish our therapy, although I was less convinced that it was time to end our quest. It seemed to me that we had not yet touched on many aspects of his existence. Although Thomas was more present in his life, something about taking responsibility and autonomy felt unaddressed. The therapy clearly had its effects regarding his depression and panics, but I had my doubts whether we had really achieved our larger goals. It often happens that we, as human beings, are getting close but have not really reached our promised land. I told myself that therapy was only one way to get there. Maybe life was just good enough. I could certainly live with his decision, but I deliberately left the door open.

The Second Stage: Death, Meaninglessness, and Responsibility

Six months later, I received a message from Thomas asking if he could come back to therapy. I was worried by his situation. Not only had both of his parents died over the course of just a few months, his depression—whether or not mixed with mourning for his loss—had returned in full force. Depression and grief reactions are often hard to tell apart, but for Thomas this mood was very familiar. Nevertheless, death immediately set the tone. During the first conversation of our second stage, Thomas immediately told me that it was really high time for him to live. There was no more time to waste. Thomas encountered what Rank (1936) would call the intersection of death anxiety and life anxiety. At this crossroad, the combination of realizing one is running out of time while being afraid of living to the fullest can have a paralyzing effect. Thomas seemed to have slipped into this abyss. "Keep me being grounded and help me to live," he literally asked me. Since we had already been traveling together, this stage did not need long introductions. We just would go straight ahead into his Himalayas and plunge into his fearsome gorges.

Thomas was filled with existential guilt and wondered what his life had meant so far. While I could imagine that many people were grateful to him for one reason or another, I decided not to ease his questioning. After all, there was a certain power emanating from this question. It was a mobilizing call to go to the heart of the matter. At the same time, I was aware that we would be walking on a tightrope. There was that looming abyss, and over the course of our conversations the darkness would be so encompassing that I was genuinely worried. I made my concern known, but he reassured me. He would not actively seek death, but he did indicate that it would feel like a relief if everything should be over. "I already feel death in my body," Thomas told me more than once. Metaphorically, we sat flat on the floor of our shared existential space. The air was dark and dense. It felt like I also could touch it.

The Courage to be Existentially Empathetic

What makes existential work different is that we engage with the ultimate concerns or the human condition without taking many detours. We make no attempts to avoid them, although we do try to keep it safe for our clients and for ourselves. Knowing ourselves existentially and feeling thoroughly grounded or rooted in life and—I would say—the universe, is essential. Though heightened existential awareness ultimately leads us to appreciate the deeper layers of our own existence; it can also overwhelm and crush us. Therefore, although we might be eager to dive in and explore our deeper existence, attention to our basic trust and grounding in life is as important (Depoorter, 2022; Missiaen & Vanhooren, 2021).

Here we can distinguish existential empathy from what we might call ontic or general empathy (Vanhooren, Conrado Veiga Bosquetti, et al., 2022). Where the ontic differences between client and therapist still allow us to maintain the "as if" character of empathy, differences between client and therapist might evaporate when we move into the existential space. By the "as if quality" of empathy, Rogers (1957) originally meant that it is important that we not identify with the other person's feelings:

> The therapist is experiencing an accurate, empathic understanding of the client's awareness of his own experience. To sense the client's private world as if it were your own, but without ever losing the "as if" quality—this is empathy, and this seems essential to therapy. To sense the client's anger, fear, or confusion as if it were your own, yet without your own anger, fear, or confusion getting bound up on it, is the condition you are endeavoring to describe. (p. 99)

The "as if" character has several functions. It ensures that we, as listeners, make the effort to understand the client's experience from their framework, not from ours. In addition, it also helps to distinguish our feelings from those of our clients and vice versa. The fact that this is not an easy task is evidenced by how some caregivers distance themselves too much out of for fear of being contaminated by the client's emotions, while others become emotionally drained by constantly allowing themselves to descend into the other people's inner worlds (Arnold et al., 2005; Geuzinge, 2015). Neuropsychology shows us that there is only a very thin line between what we perceive to be our own experiences and what we perceive to be the other's (Cuff et al.,

2016). After all, when we are trying to understand the other, our nervous system and mirror neurons ensure that we also physically experience the experience of the other person to some extent. That "as if" quality of empathy, or the difference between the other and ourselves. is really only a matter of intensity and the cognitive awareness that we have not experienced it ourselves (although in this sense, the latter is very relative). Empathy seems to occur through a process of temporal fusion and differentiation. In a later description, Rogers (1980) places less emphasis on this "as if" quality and more on the need for a kind of thread of Ariadne in order to find our way back to home. Just as in that Greek myth, in which Ariadne gave Theseus a thread so he could return from the labyrinth in which he had to face the tormented Minotaur, we also need something to find our way back when we venture deeply in our client's existence. Or as Rogers describes it:

> It means entering the private perceptual world of the other and becoming thoroughly at home in it. It involves being sensitive, moment to moment, to the changed felt meanings which flow in this other person... It means temporarily living in the other's life... In some sense it means that you lay aside your self; this can only be done by persons who are secure enough in themselves that they know they will not get lost in what may turn out to be the strange or bizarre world of the other, and that they can comfortably return to their own world when they wish. (pp. 142–143)

This dynamic of descending into the world of the other and returning to our own place gets more difficult when our own experiences turn out to be not so different from those of the client (Vanhooren, 2022b). When we only engage with the ontic layer, the differences are usually clear enough to maintain the distinction between ourselves and the other. Once we move into a more existential space, we are on common ground. After all, by traveling to the client's existential layer we find ourselves not only in the client's most intimate world but also in the lived experience of what it means to be human. For this very reason, during our existential empathy, we not only resonate with this particular client but also with humankind, and from this we often experience compassion for humanity.

We know by now that empathy is one of the most studied and robust factors that predicts psychotherapy outcome (Elliott et al.,

2018). Through our empathic attunement and our empathic communication, we help make overwhelming experiences digestible. Within neuropsychology, this is referred to as *co-regulation* (Lux, 2021). But there is more. When we succeed in helping our clients find words for what is experienced, as was the case early on with Aisha (Chapter 2), we also help to establish a sense of safety in that existential space. This is particularly important given the fact that existential concerns have a certain potential to be highly overwhelming (Bugental, 1978). By doing so, we not only create the possibility to meet our core pains without having to overly fear them but we also create the possibility to meet ourselves authentically and foster new or core growth.

Our own research shows that not every counselor or therapist shows the same degree of existential empathy. There are significant differences between therapists with different therapeutic backgrounds when they assess their own existential empathy (Vanhooren, Conrado Veiga Bosquetti, et al., 2022). Furthermore, existential empathy in action seems to cover a set of different therapeutic skills, such as maintaining a sense of being grounded in one's own existence, feeling sufficiently at ease with existential challenges, being able to maintain a stance of not-knowing and openness for the client's experiences, and being present with the process (Frediani et al., 2025).

For Thomas and myself, this meant that we could not get around the looming abyss of meaninglessness and death. I could notice that I felt resistance to explore that full darkness in the here-and-now. However, the real psychotherapeutic work is there where the client is (Gendlin, 1990). During our last sessions, the whole therapeutic process seemed to have slowed down. Nothing was moving at all. Our explorations of Thomas's life story did not produce any shifts (meso-dimension). There was no way around it but to be where that blockage was.

Silently, we spent more time with the feeling of being stuck. We took our time just to be with that meaninglessness. I tried to parcel out these moments because I feared they would become too much for Thomas. But it was clear that we had to be there; otherwise, I just would have left Thomas alone in the dark, all by himself. Interestingly, when I started thinking that we needed at least a small thing to keep our hopes up, Thomas told me how he lately was awakened by nightmares or very poignant dreams. There, too, death and meaninglessness were omnipresent.

The Dream Shows Possibilities

One of the recurring dreams Thomas had was of his youngest daughter being buried. Thomas found himself howling in these dreams. Another dream was about his daughter committing suicide. Thomas recounted this dream and how he saw himself listening to her while she was telling him that she could not bear life any longer. Her life felt completely meaningless, and she felt like she was suffering without any perspective. She came to the conclusion that she wanted to end her life. He told her that he could truly understand her death wish. An hour passed in the dream, and Thomas suddenly wondered where his daughter had gone. He ran to her room and discovered that she had locked herself in. He started panicking. He rammed into the door and found her lying on the floor and had overdosed on medication. He rushed her to the hospital, where she was rescued.

Dreams not only refer only to day remnants. Dreams can be understood as symbolizations of the felt sense of our situation (Gendlin, 1986) or, put in different words, as metaphors for our current lived existence (Ellis, 2020). They are full of meaning even if the images we produce at night seem all too crazy. Whatever metaphors our dreams use, they show us the implicit meanings of our life process. That Thomas dreamed about death and meaninglessness was no surprise. Mostly, dreams do not just sketch our challenges but also solutions. Or they share at least some helpful life-affirming elements that we can use in order to take our process one step forward (Gendlin, 1986). From an existential perspective, particular attention has been paid to the dream as a possibility (Moustakas, 1994). The dream might reveal something of a possible direction (Gendlin, 1986). In this sense, the dream is sometimes ahead of our waking reality (Moss, 1996). It gives us a taste of what might come.

Thomas's dream was based on a difficult period that had occurred with his daughter years ago. When we were exploring the dream in the here-and-now, Thomas was surprised by how calm he remained while he was listening to her death wish in the dream. This troubled him. It felt like he was giving her permission to commit suicide or that he just resigned from this conversation. What also surprised him was how quickly he acted in the second part of the dream, and how he managed to save her from death. This movement was indeed remarkable. During the conversation, we explored this movement in more detail.

> **Siebrecht**: So there is something in you that really can understand her heaviness and her meaninglessness, but there

also seems to be something in you that, regardless of the fact that you might recognize that heaviness, says to your daughter: "You should continue to live." You break down the door. You take her to the hospital. What is that—that thing that takes immediate action even though life feels like a burden?

Thomas: Yes... Now that I'm thinking about it... Yes... There is something that wants to live and feel. And indeed, it is noticeable in that desire, that urge to move, to walk, to swim, to feel that you have a body. Maybe this is something completely different, but this week I was aware that I got irritated more quickly than usual and that I didn't want to get rid of it immediately. I also noticed the opposite. Last week we went to a concert. Bach's Magnificat... I felt really moved. I could almost weep—but I can't weep. That's joy! I felt it opening up when I heard the phrase sung: "He has seen me."

Siebrecht: Feeling irritated more quickly. You also feel more quickly affected, both negatively and positively. What does that do to you?

Thomas: In that moment, this gives me energy. It really makes me happy. But then during the week I feel that burden again, that hopelessness, and being out of energy.

Siebrecht: And talking about this also gives you energy, I notice.

Thomas: Yes!

Siebrecht: So where do you feel that when you notice "this gives me joy"? Where do you feel that energy in your body?

Thomas: It feels like I can breathe again.

Siebrecht: And where do you sense that hopelessness?

Thomas: That's a shrinking...

Siebrecht: That is a shrinking movement.

Thomas: Yes, and that is a feeling of having no breath. Breathlessness. And not wanting to do anything anymore. The things that have to be done, they feel heavy, heavy, pounds of weight...

Siebrecht: You say a shrinking, breathlessness. Heavy pounds... It reminds me again of your dreams. There is that heavy burden of life, the meaninglessness of life, and then something that comes to the rescue, being rescued, getting new energy....

This therapy excerpt is interesting for several reasons. I could have addressed the meaningful "He has seen me," but I made the choice to give more space to the movements of the dream. The dream beautifully reflects where Thomas is at this point in his life. By moving back and forth between the dream images and the felt sense of these images, we get in touch with the implicit meanings of the dream (Ellis, 2020). The two episodes in the dream represent two different experiences. There is the being tired of life, on the one hand, and something that "wants to live and feel," on the other. Thomas recognizes himself in the two dream scenes. The connection to the goal of this therapy "I wanna dare to live" is also obvious. The possibility that shows itself powerfully here in the dream—that something of himself comes to the rescue and wants to live—also showed itself during the week. Thomas notices that he feels more and decides not to deny these experiences or put them away. There is already something that peeks out like an early flower in spring while it is still cold—something that dares to live. As we can read in the transcript, I try to help Thomas experience both movements in the here-and-now. We use elements of focusing to experience both sides of his dream in the here-and-now. We recognized the heavy burden of life as well as the new, that something that wants to be alive.

Focusing on Meaninglessness

Although Thomas started to notice that something was moving or shifting, this early change was easily overruled by that recurrent tsunami of meaninglessness. The fact that he started to sense something different, that new openness to life, gave me the courage to explore his darkness more thoroughly. There was that rescuing living quality, this life force, we could eventually return to. I assumed that by listening carefully to his deep sense of meaninglessness—his core pain, his missing—we would be able to facilitate that carrying forward of energy, his living process, letting his core growth unfold. While I was aware that it would be important to spend explicit time and space with his dark feeling during the upcoming session, the therapeutic process gave us a pass.

> **Siebrecht**: What would you like to do with your time today, Thomas?
> **Thomas**: I would like to use it well. But I'm not sure how...
> **Siebrecht**: Aha. You would like to use it well, but how...
> **Thomas**: How should I put this... Last week it was about that dynamic between that life-giving quality and that other side that is pulling me down...
> **Siebrecht**: Hmm.

Thomas: That pulling down is... has been strong the past few weeks. And I can't grasp that side, I have no grasp on it. I only know that thing as something that... yes, that has been there all my life. It is a sucking force, something that literally takes me down.
Siebrecht: Something that really sucks you down.
Thomas: Yes, it's quicksand; that's the feeling of sinking... Yes. It is really powerful. It takes everything down. Like "What am I actually doing here today?"
Siebrecht: Like wanting to make use of your time but not knowing how to.
Thomas: Yes, but even more. Does this, what we are doing here, make any sense? I want to, it runs away with all my energy. So...
Siebrecht: What would you say if we would get a very close look today at that feeling that pulls you down... Because it seems crucial.
Thomas: Yes. Yes.

It was perhaps the first time that the meaninglessness manifested itself so directly in therapy. His meaninglessness was no longer present as a content but also as a dynamic of our therapeutic process. It was no longer about meaninglessness. Therapy itself started to feel like a meaningless endeavor, at least at this moment. There was a stark contrast between this overwhelming feeling of meaninglessness and his growing sense of responsibility. He really wanted to use his time well, knowing that the session—and maybe in between the lines, life as such—was limited. The opening sentences show how the existential concern of death and also the will to take responsibility over his life were present as dynamics during our sessions.

Trying to minimize this ubiquitous meaninglessness by highlighting the small positive changes he sensed over the last few weeks probably would have intensified this dark force that pulled him down. Instead, it was wiser to give this meaninglessness our full attention. It would be important to approach this darkness without getting completely paralyzed by it. In order to support my existential empathy for this dynamic that pulled him down, I tried to ground myself by keeping my thread of Ariadne close to me. I felt supported at this moment by the living force of nature, my spirituality and basic trust, and by what my teachers taught me about the therapeutic process. Structure-bound processes and negative life experiences would only transform and start to make sense when they were listened to respectfully, patiently, and sufficiently (Gendlin, 1996). I kept this knowing close to me as I tried to give this part of his being-in-the-world its full voice so it could really feel it was listened to. Through focusing and experiential language ("something," "it," "this," or "that") I would help to dis-identify this pulling-down experience while giving it our full attention (see Chapter 2). It would help Thomas relate to it rather than coincide with it:

> **Siebrecht**: So *something* runs away with all your energy, you say. That sucking down, pulling you down, that swamp or quicksand... What strikes me when I hear this, is that you have no control over *it*.
> **Thomas**: Nothing.
> **Siebrecht**: *It* pulls you down. *It* makes you... powerless. I don't know if that's right, if this describes what is happening to you.
> **Thomas**: It's all pretty vague, I know.
> **Siebrecht**: How does *this* actually feel here *right now*?
> **Thomas**: Yes, *that* pulling me down... It seems like I have heavy blood actually.
> **Siebrecht**: Heavy blood... and where exactly do you feel *that* Thomas?
> **Thomas**: Physically, you mean?
> **Siebrecht**: Yes, where do you feel this heavy blood now?
> **Thomas**: That's everywhere, my body all around. Like carrying a heavy weight constantly.
> **Siebrecht**: Like walking around with a heaviness through your life.
> **Thomas**: Yes, and right now that's... having no breath, having a thin head. And it's very heavy...
> **Siebrecht**: Having no breath, a thin head, and it's weighing heavily. That heaviness. Heavy blood.
> **Thomas**: Heavy blood. It's like lead. It is circulating through my body. It pulls me down [makes a pushing down movement with his arms and hands].
> **Siebrecht**: Circulating lead that runs through your body, and it pulls you down like this [making the same gesture].
> **Thomas**: Yes, and… That's that thing... Fatalism is a weird word. Yes, it's a surrendering. A surrender to… Because there is no energy to go against it.
> **Siebrecht**: Yes...
> **Thomas**: [Long silence]... And, on the other hand. there is… the despair and, on the other hand, the anger. Yes! Anger! And I

haven't been angry in years. At others, but now, at myself. Man! You won't have lived.

Siebrecht: Yes, there is now something that's really starts to worry and gets really angry?

Thomas: Yes! That's actually... I can curse myself, man. What have you actually been doing here? That's not living. That's waiting for it to be over! Until the light goes out!

Siebrecht: Yes! So there's something in you that feels like heavy blood, that pulls away your energy, that feels like lead and takes your courage away. And there is also another side, that says: "Hey you there, you won't have lived!"

This condensed transcript shows how we stayed very close to the felt sense of meaninglessness. We did not get into a discussion of what is meaningful or meaningless in life. Instead, we went straight to the felt sense or the embodied lived experience of meaninglessness (micro-dimension) with all its macro-dimensional aspects and connections to other existential challenges such as death, life, and responsibility. The symbolization of the current felt sense shifted during the focusing from a "pulling down" to "quicksand," "heavy blood," "no breath," "thin head," "heavy weight" to "circulating lead." Following this experiential exploration closely, the living process of meaninglessness of Thomas finally arrived with the words "fatalism," "despair," and "a surrendering." It is a process of meaning-making in action, making all the implicit bodily felt meanings explicit until its meaning was complete. In terms of the therapeutic process, what follows next is quite spectacular. This is exactly what Gendlin means by *carrying forward*. By listening to the felt sense of the situation and symbolizing this experience, there was a shift or a transformation of the situation itself. Our therapeutic process had carried Thomas's existence forward.

What showed itself in his dream occurred to Thomas here in vivo. Once we fully attend to our living process without imposing anything or wanting to change it and just try to understand it by searching for words or symbols that could capture its embodied, implicit meanings, the process shifts and further unfolds. It is fascinating how Thomas moves from that fatalistic experience into something completely different. There is a palpable change or a felt shift (Gendlin, 1996). The experience of being pulled down and powerlessness makes way for anger. This anger was new. Adaptive anger is a mobilizing emotion that emerges when we have reached a limit. Here, as in the dream, something sets itself in motion, rams into the door at the very moment of death ("...waiting for it to be over, until the light goes out"). The quality that wants to live takes control of the steering wheel. It is that life force, that living-forward energy, that self-healing capacity of the therapeutic process that comes into action.

This important tipping point makes me think of what both Kierkegaard (1978) and Jaspers (2003) write about hitting our limits. According to Kierkegaard, we find our essence when we fully experience despair or, as Jaspers puts it, when we fail. According to Tillich (2000), we experience courage only when we can embrace both non-being and being. And this is precisely what happened during this process. Without thinking or talking about meaninglessness, something arose from the realm of death. What wanted to live gained strength and space during our conversation.

Resisting the Authorities

This session had important consequences. Thomas surprised himself by taking small and larger steps. For example, at the local supermarket, he got involved in a discussion over the price of a jar of yogurt. A few weeks ago, he would have paid too much, but now he calmly stood up for himself. He also walked into the city hall. Years ago, he had donated some paintings to the municipality, which had been on display since then. However, he had not put his name underneath these paintings. He now kindly insisted that his name appear under the paintings. It was remarkable how Thomas took his rightful place in the world. Interestingly, it also felt to him like an act of resistance against the "authorities." After wondering in therapy who these authorities might have been in his life, it made him think of his late father. It was remarkable how Thomas seemed to physically shrink in his chair when we started talking about his father (meso-dimension). The feeling of the heavy blood came instantly back (micro-dimension), showing us a possible source of this experienced meaninglessness in life (macro-dimension).

Over the sessions, Thomas had cultivated a firm connection with his here-and-now inner experiences. As a result, self-explorations on the meso-dimension were not just thinking or talking about the past. When he was exploring, he could also directly sense and experience what these authorities and his father meant to him. While we were exploring his life story in an experiential way, Thomas came to realize that his father had strongly determined his life. All his life choices had been made or at least had been strongly influenced by his father. Therefore, the life Thomas had lived did not feel like his own. Acknowledging this was confrontational. His resistance to the "authorities" now made sense, as a rebellion against something that was steering, determining, or even stealing his life.

In recent years, Thomas had been very caring toward his elderly father. Nevertheless, his father had left him with much unprocessed pain and unspoken words. In the past, Thomas had made frantic attempts to talk to his father. He had organized birthday parties and anniversaries to celebrate him in the hope to experience approval and connection. He had written him cards and letters. However, it was all in vain. His attempts to have a real conversation were rejected time after time.

Through this experiential exploration of his experiences with his father, Thomas was able to talk about these adverse life experiences that had a hold on his life for far too long. During these sessions, Thomas oscillated between loyalty toward his parents and a growing awareness of what he had been denied: unconditional love and his right to exist. Experiential therapeutic approaches such as emotion-focused therapy have elaborated powerful ways to work with unprocessed experiences such as unfinished business with significant others (Elliott et al., 2004). Through an empty-chair dialogue, we would invite his father to join us.

An Appointment with His Father

In handbooks, therapeutic interventions always seem to have an immediate success. I can reassure you that this usually is not the case. Quite often clients need to feel comfortable enough to go along with certain interventions that feel out of the ordinary. Sometimes the client's structure-bound experiences, unattended layers of the process, or problems with the therapeutic relationship might be in the way of using interventions or assigned deliberate practices successfully. For example, early on during our first stage, I suggested that Thomas have a look at whether he would like to do any volunteering. I thought it might help him to get more structure and meaning during the week. However, it did not take off. The problem was that this idea was not aligned with the process itself. Thomas was not to blame. During the previous sessions, we had tried experiential interventions such as two-chair dialogues, but these were not really transformative (Elliott et al., 2004). Thomas became somewhat familiar with this kind of experiential work, but not much more. However, the fact that Thomas already tried some chair work would come in handy very soon.

Thomas's birthday was approaching, and he had decided to visit his parents at the graveyard that day. I was curious to hear if there was anything he wanted to say to his parents. He said he did not really need anything from them now. They would not be able to help make his future. I asked him if it would not be a good idea to use this session as a practice or a rehearsal for the conversation he wanted to have at the graveyard. Thomas liked the idea and we gave it a try.

Siebrecht: So imagine that your father would come into this room here. How would that be for you?
Thomas: [Breathes very deeply].
Siebrecht: Hm ... that sounds as if he's already here. [Thomas nods]. How would he sit there?
Thomas: [Thomas looks and points at the empty chair]. He would say: "Yes." He sinks down into his chair here because his father sinks down into his chair when he sits ...
Siebrecht: "Yes."
Thomas: Yes, and he would say: "Wouldn't you offer me anything to drink?"
Siebrecht: "Wouldn't you offer me anything?"
Thomas: I don't know. He wouldn't stay very long ...
Siebrecht: Aha.
Thomas: He never stayed anywhere very long....
Siebrecht: Your father comes in, he sinks into his chair and asks: "Don't you have anything to drink?"
Thomas: Yes... Yes, yes.
Siebrecht: How would you start the conversation now that he's here? What would you want to say to him?
Thomas: I don't know. He wouldn't be interested.
Siebrecht: He wouldn't be interested..., but you look interested to me.
Thomas: Yes. I actually wonder what it was like for him to be my father.
Siebrecht: Yes, ask him now that he's here. He's sitting here; you can ask it directly to him [looking and pointing at the empty chair].
Thomas: [Hesitating and asking timidly]. What was it like to be my father, Dad?
Siebrecht: Can you switch seats? Let's see how he would answer
Thomas: Really? [Thomas changes chairs and now sits in the father's place; he sinks into this chair]. How was it like to be his father... Great expectations... Great expectations.

Siebrecht: Great expectations.
Thomas: [Father's chair] And big arguments... Well. It's up to him now. Go ahead. I'm not interested.
Siebrecht: Can you say this to Thomas directly [points at the client's chair]?
Thomas: [Father's chair] Go ahead. I'm not interested in what you're doing! You're stupid. It's your life. You're free.
Siebrecht: Let's switch seats [Thomas returns to his own seat]. Your father says: "I had great expectations. But I'm not interested in what you do. You're stupid. It's your life. You're free." What happens to you when you hear this?
Thomas: [Sighs]
Siebrecht: A deep sigh... What do you want to say to him?
Thomas: [Talking to his father] Did you really set me free, or are you so disappointed that you gave up on me?
Siebrecht: Let's switch seats and see how your father reacts.
Thomas: [Father's chair] Disappointed of course. You wasted your talents!
Siebrecht: Change seats.
Thomas: [Client's chair] Talents? What kind of talents are you talking about [stamps on the floor]? Because regarding my talents, you have never been able to see or value them!

What takes place here is not just role play. There is a taking of deep breaths, sighing, sinking down in chairs, and stamping on the floor. It all indicates how involved Thomas is in this event. For his body, it is real, and it is happening right now. Just like dreams are real to the body, so is this empty-chair dialogue. For the first time in his life, Thomas can speak his truth in front of his father. Although his father died, the process between father and son is fully alive. It is a carrying forward "was" situation. Thomas marvels afterward that he had the courage to speak here out loud to his father in ways that he never did before. Giving words and speaking out loud brings our process into motion. His father looked down on Thomas and was never able to see Thomas as he was. His father was not able to see how talented Thomas was. He only saw what he was not. In the chair dialogue, which went on a little longer, Thomas claimed his right to exist. Instead of being pushed or pulled down, he chose having and living his own life. He chose to be autonomous from his father's will (Chapter 2).

One week later, Thomas celebrated his birthday with his wife and children in a very intense and intimate way. Thomas told me how healing the embrace of his children felt. Where there is room for autonomy, there is also often room for deeper connection.

What Ultimately Matters

Unpredictable as life is, Thomas received a letter from a man claiming to be his cousin. Thomas sent me an e-mail between sessions in which he explained the situation. He hoped it would help our coming session so that we would not have to spend too much time telling that story. Indeed, time or rather how to spend time became important to him. Briefly, the cousin revealed that during World War I his grandfather was engaged to a young French lady. Although she was pregnant, she broke off the engagement. She forbade the grandfather to visit his French son but he kept sending his son letters and postcards for years, it turned out. The cordiality toward this unknown son was in stark contrast to the emotional distance that he kept toward his Belgian children. The grandfather kept this history secret. When the man grew old and was in need of care, he ended up staying with Thomas's parents. Thomas remembered painfully how his grandfather was bedridden and completely neglected. Thomas also remembered how as a child he was angry with his parents for taking such poor care of his grandfather. At the same time, he also felt guilty, although there was only so much he could do as a child. After Thomas vented his anger, the following happened.

> **Siebrecht**: Thomas... this story. What are you actually facing here? What is of essence here?
> **Thomas**: [Silence]. This means being there for my children, being there for my wife... [silence]. Taking care of the relationships I have with my family..., regardless of what I think of them.
> **Siebrecht**: It shows what ultimately matters to you? What really matters? Or it is one of the things that really matters...
> **Thomas**: [Silence]. It is *the only thing* that matters... [Silently and softly]. It is the only thing... It's the only thing...
> **Siebrecht**: How does that feel to say this out loud Thomas?
> **Thomas**: I'm getting emotional, yes...
> **Siebrecht**: It is the only thing.
> **Thomas**: It's the only thing... And it's ultimately the only thing a human being can desire. Connection. And all the rest... That manuscript I'm working on... It has its relative value... But actually.

Siebrecht: Actually...
Thomas: If you really can be there for people... Being more considerate toward the other person... Visiting people that I really should be visiting but that I'm looking up against...
Siebrecht: It's becoming clear and obvious now. This is what ultimately matters. Nothing more and nothing less.
Thomas: Nothing more and nothing less.
Siebrecht: And that's the goal in your life?
Thomas: The only ... [silence]. And about religion, what difference does it make whether I die as a believer or an atheist? It doesn't make any difference. It doesn't make any difference! But being a father, being a husband, being a friend...
Siebrecht: Being yourself ...
Thomas: Being yourself by being with others... That's the only thing.

Building on the work of the previous sessions, and with a larger degree of experiential freedom, we were clearly moving on the macro-dimension. Thomas did not need a lot more than that one question, "What is of essence here?" to move into this existential space. Resonating with his whole being, he comes to express what is essential and ultimately meaningful to him. The process seems to unfold itself by itself. The letter of his cousin and our therapy session carried forward his existence once again—deeper and clearer. Over the next few weeks, we see Thomas taking conscious steps toward people. He makes the choice to life more fully. He is fully engaged in life. He visits relatives and settles old family arguments. He also takes up volunteering for the first time. Thomas becomes a palliative care worker in a hospice. He will spend many hours with people who are on the verge of life and death. These people, as well as their families and the hospital staff, are extremely grateful.

These new steps are the result of his conscious choice to connect more authentically with the other. At this point we have clearly achieved our therapy goals: to become an old wise and mild man and dare to be really alive. And Thomas dares to live. The way he lives his life gives his life meaning. For Thomas, this does not mean that life is inherently meaningful or not. What he discovered was a solid ground from where he could face the meaninglessness that often occurs in life. He experiences the courage to live. He concludes his therapy by stating that he can call himself a happy man.

The Third Stage: Living the Full Life

And then suddenly, out of nowhere, there was a pandemic. The COVID-19 virus would set the existential situation of many people on the edge. Not only did the pandemic cause heightened anxiety, it sharpened the awareness of death and the fragility of existence in a collective way. With the lockdown measures and insistence on vaccination by the government, existential concerns such as freedom, choice, and responsibility were hot topics on social media and in political debates. Inside our houses, lockdown measures put relationships under pressure or, in the opposite way, created more connectedness. Where some couples and families grew closer because of the lockdown, others would leave each other as soon as they could. For some people, it was also a period of awakening and setting new priorities. In the United States, many people resigned from their jobs and were looking for new and more meaningful horizons.

During this time, Thomas e-mailed me to reconnect. However, I found myself in a different place. COVID-19 had made my backpack heavier. Navigating between the new needs of my work situation, our family, and my deathly ill father, I did not find the time, energy, and mental space to take care of others. I left Thomas's e-mail unanswered for some time. It was not an example of good care toward him, but I seemed to struggle with the limitations of existence myself. I could have let him know something, but I did not get around to doing it. It was not clear how things were evolving during that early stage of the pandemic. We were taking it week by week, and we did not know if things would rapidly turn back to normal or not. However, Thomas felt disillusioned and angry because my response was delayed. Given his conflict avoidance in the past, the fact that he was angry was a sign of his growth and acquired autonomy. I could only be pleased with this. Eventually, we started seeing each other online.

Thomas described his situation as feeling fragmented. There were moments of having a sense of deep peace but they were becoming increasingly rare. He felt discouraged when he saw how work accumulated in the house or in the garden. He did not manage to focus on these chores. There were also quite a few family problems that demanded his attention. There were problems in one of his daughter's marriage, unemployment, and a new partner relationship in another daughter's life. Because of pandemic measures, it became impossible for him to continue his volunteering, which had become so meaningful to him. He felt a lot of compassion for those lonely people in the retirement home and hospice, some of them dying all by themselves. He also felt strongly emotionally involved with his daughters' situations. Overall, he felt quite powerless. It felt like he had lost control over his life. He was no longer at the helm of this sailboat. Rather, he seemed to be rolling on the bottom of the ship. He called it his "waiting mode." He seemed to be in a place that was neither life nor death. It was a state of being, he told me, in which he could no longer stand to be with himself. And just because it was so hard to endure, he didn't want to run away from it. By running away from this awareness, he thought he would slip straight back into a depression. He was alarmed by the situation. This too—this sense of being alarmed—was a result of our work in the past.

A Different Therapy

The third stage of our journey would be considerably shorter but also particularly intense. By now we were experienced travel companions, and Thomas was also no longer the man I once got to know. There was no longer something like self-censorship when he was speaking to other people, and even in these challenging times he still had a sense of connection with himself. This situation would have made him feel lonely and lost in the past. However, now, it was his involvement with others that knocked him down. He was trying to be helpful in this extraordinary situation, and the fact that he could not help others made him feel helpless. By being so concerned about others and not knowing how to handle these concerns, he started to neglect his own needs. What previously had given him vitality and meaning just vanished because of the circumstances. Thomas found himself in a situation of mental anemia.

Consequently, the case formulation looked substantially different now. Unlike in the previous stages, there was no longer a general structure-bound experiencing of life. Thomas was not facing any structural problems when he tried to access his here-and-now experiences. Overall, the way he was self-exploring showed—technically speaking—a high level of experiencing (Klein et al., 1969). In sum, on the micro-dimension, there was little in the way. Thomas could sense his bodily felt existence without many obstacles or hindrances. There was no longer a structural incongruence between his embodied sense of self and his self-image or narrative. There were no significant unprocessed life events of the past that were standing in the way of being fully present (meso-dimension). We also had worked hard on the macro-dimension during the previous stages. We met and explored his existential core pains, such as his feeling of meaninglessness, his lack of existential confirmation, his existential guilt, and his life anxiety. By attending and exploring his core pains experientially and patiently, we witnessed how his living process unfolded in unpredictable ways. We could summarize his core growths in terms of his will to live and an awareness of what would make life worth living. Thomas found his meaning in life in being consciously and authentically there with others, precisely there at that intersection between life and death. This made life significant for Thomas and made Thomas significant for life.

What Thomas experienced now no longer had anything to do with being structurally stuck in certain life patterns. Rather, he had run up against the limitations of the circumstances. It seemed that his growth process had slowed down. Thomas described it as being everywhere and nowhere and therefore being lost in a no man's land. This non-growth showed itself especially on the macro-dimension. It had something to do with a waning vitality (death and life), a neglect of what gave him meaning (meaninglessness and purpose), a growing concern for the other but at the expense of himself (isolation and connection), and an increasing lack of agency over his situation (freedom, choice, and responsibility). On the positive side, Thomas had moments where "life felt good," but they were rapidly getting scarce. Overall, his being-in-the-world was subject to these exceptional circumstances. He suffered from not growing, which could, over time, lead to a more structural stagnation. Thomas had noticed this negative direction and was right to call for help.

Given that we were dealing with non-growth rather than with old patterns blocking his living processes, we needed something different. Although experiential–existential psychotherapy is implicitly growth directed, we had to switch our focus from clearing old obstacles to a more explicit facilitation of his growth process during these exceptional circumstances. Although we would re-encounter familiar obstacles and revisit old places, we would need something different to fuel his growth. Inspiration would become an important resource to get him out of his current turmoil.

Inspiration as an Intervention

Etymologically, to inspire means to breathe in, or to breathe in the spirit (van Veen & van der Sijs, 1997). Inspiration is not recognized as an intervention in psychotherapy or counseling. However, in sports psychology, there is an interest in how inspiration might help athletes perform better (Klein et al., 2017). The fact that inspiration is not recognized as an intervention does not mean that psychologists, psychotherapists, and social workers cannot inspire their clients. Whereas self-exploration focuses on an understanding based on the past or in the here-and-now, inspiration is rather future-oriented. Inspiration does not unlock what is structurally stuck. Instead, it deepens or broaden what is already available. It helps to realize newly felt possibilities. It is sometimes experienced as an enthusiastic leap. It takes us to a new version of what is on our minds.

Psychological research shows how inspiration is intrinsically linked to growth (Thrash et al., 2014). It is associated with creativity, purpose, meaning, well-being, and self-transcendence (Belzak et al., 2017). People who feel inspired also succeed better in performing difficult tasks (Klein et al., 2017). Translating this into therapy and counseling might mean that when we feel inspired, we might find the courage to get through our growing pains more easily. In their attempt to capture the phenomenon of inspiration, Thrash and colleagues (2014) arrived at the following description. According to them, inspiration has at least three core characteristics that distinguish it from similar concepts. First, inspiration starts from an external source. We get inspired because something from the outside appeals to us. That external source of inspiration evokes something within us. We are also receptive to it at that moment. Second, inspiration has a transcendent quality. The inspired person experiences something new or experiences possibilities. It opens new avenues. Inspiration holds a promise of something different. Third, inspiration calls to us. It has a motivational quality. The inspired person wants to turn the new insight or experience into action, such as writing down one's thoughts, making and executing a plan, or making a commitment.

Regarding the first characteristic, Belzak and colleagues (2017) indicate that the external source of inspiration can be anything—music, prose, and poetry or a physical experience (think of Newton's apple or Archimedes' bath) as well as an I–Thou encounter. In the context of therapy, we could speak of implicit and explicit sources of inspiration. The *implicit sources* of inspiration in therapy and counseling are almost inexhaustible. They are implicit because the therapist does not consciously use them to inspire. With *explicit inspiration*, the therapist seeks specific sources of inspiration to help the client's process unfold.

Implicit Sources of Inspiration

The therapeutic relationship, the person of the therapist, and the entire therapeutic process are implicitly inspiring to many clients. For example, Thomas felt inspired by the therapeutic relationship and our conversations, which helped him to engage with others more intensely and authentically. Thomas also felt inspired by smaller therapeutic interventions. As he reflected on what was helpful in therapy, he emphasized language and metaphors, among other things:

> I found the way language was used particularly helpful. It made me feel understood and it often opened up new ways or ways of looking at things. When you asked me what my core was, I had to search for a long time and just couldn't put my finger onto it. But when you asked what my ground was, I was able to answer. And this proved to be fruitful. The image of the therapy as a spiral was also helpful: If you climb up a mountain, you do not circle around it but rather make a spiral movement; you seem to keep coming back to the same point, but you are actually at a higher, different place. This was enlightening and encouraging.

In this sense, we can understand re-experiencing and crossing as inspiring paths (see Chapter 2). Unlike with empathy, in re-experiencing the therapist also explicitly brings in something of their own experience (Ikemi, 2017), although in practice the difference between re-experiencing and highly accurate empathy is not always clear. Probably there is a continuum between the two because in empathy we ultimately also reach out to what we experience in ourselves while trying to understand the client's lifeworld. In any case, in re-experiencing the therapist is consciously aware of what the client's experience evokes in themself. When the therapist communicates how they experience the client's experiences, this might influence or cross the client's initial experience. This might evoke a micro-movement. In other words, the therapist's experience of the client is at that moment an external source of inspiration that might put the client's experience in motion. The therapist's experience helps the client discover new aspects or layers of their own experiencing.

During our third stage, there would be quite a lot of re-experiencing and crossing. In one of the first sessions of this third stage, Thomas talks about how he can feel really happy at certain moments while feeling totally out of sorts at others. He wanted to kneel during a recent abbey visit, which was a moment of deeply experiencing and appreciating life. But at other times, there was that despair again.

> **Siebrecht**: When I hear you talking about these experiences, there seem to be moments where you are really absorbed in your experience of life. Your description of wanting to kneel *reminds me of experiencing something like adoration, of a surrendering actually, of being in contact with what is bigger than ourselves...* And in those moments, you seem to be completely "in" your life. In touch with that existential layer. Those seem to be the moments where you say you feel deeply happy.
> **Thomas**: Yes! That's right! [Thomas responds enthusiastically to this crossing, moves his arms and body, laughs]. Yes, it certainly is!
> **Siebrecht**: Whereas in those other moments, it strikes me that you are not "in" your life, not "in" that fully living. And then there is something like "I need life energy; I kind of lost it along the way." So at one moment you are really in touch with everything..., and at the other moment you are a... [takes a pause to search for the right words]... a *spectator* almost... I don't know if this feels right for you?
> **Thomas**: Yes, that image of *spectator*... That's right... [deep sigh]. That evokes a lot...

Thomas explores what the image of the spectator means to him. The image of the spectator speaks to him, and it helps him to recognize situations in which he feels like an absent spectator. My re-experiencing of his situation ("a surrendering actually, of being in contact with what is bigger than ourselves" and "spectator") crosses his experiences ("Yes! That's right! Yes, it certainly is!"; his bodily reaction such as moving and laughing), which enriches his experiencing and helps it to move forward ("that image of a spectator... That's right... [deep sigh]. That evokes a lot..."). It helps him to identify moments when he feels totally empty and powerless. It helps him to be aware of these situations, and he wonders how he could act differently.

The first characteristic of inspiration—getting and being inspired—immediately reveals its Achilles heel. For inspiration to be evocative, the person must be receptive to it (Thash et al., 2014). This receptivity presupposes a certain degree of openness to one's own experiencing. Structure-bound experiences on the micro-, meso-, or macro-dimension could prevent this necessary experiential freedom from being received (see Chapter 2). In addition, it seems necessary to me that what seeks to be inspirational also sufficiently aligns with the client's process. What is inspiring—from a simple gesture to a whole story—implicitly connects to the client's growth edge, to that point where growth and change are about to happen. It plays into the carrying forward of the process itself.

Moreover, when Thomas read the manuscript of this chapter, he explained how inspiration and crossing, in particular, helped to strengthen the therapeutic relationship and carried the therapeutic process forward.

> An important element in crossing, which I clearly experienced during our sessions, is that the therapist not only offers inspiration by telling something from their own experience (the right thing at the right moment) but that this crossing also strengthens the relationship. As a client, you experience that the therapist has similar experiences and shares them with you. It strengthens the interaction in the relationship and that is a beneficial and inspiring experience. As a client you experience how openness on the part of the therapist is revealing and liberating. It inspires you to be more open too.

It sometimes happens that the therapeutic process also inspires the therapist. The therapist's level of receptivity and attunement to existential processes plays a significant role here. Rank (1996) explains how *Das Ganze* becomes palpable at these moments in therapy. Although this living existential dimension might feel palpable, it also stretches itself beyond what can be expressed in words. It moves beyond the concrete ontic lives of the particular client and therapist, although it flows through their concrete togetherness and separateness. What the therapist and client experience is not just theirs. They are the expression of the dynamics of life itself. These moments are inspiring and invigorating. This is no longer just a crossing between therapist and client but also a crossing with the existential transcendent itself. Rogers (1980) describes it as follows:

> I described earlier those characteristics of a growth-promoting relationship that have been investigated and supported by research. But recently, my view has broadened [...]. When I am at my best, as a group facilitator or as a therapist, I discover

> another characteristic. I find that when I am closest to my inner, intuitive self, when I am somehow in touch with the unknown in me, when perhaps I am in a slightly altered state of consciousness, then whatever I do seems to be full of healing. Then, simply my presence is releasing and helpful to the other [...] which have nothing to do with my thought process [...]. It seems that my inner spirit has reached out and touched the inner spirit of the other. Our relationship transcends itself and becomes part of something larger. Profound growth and healing and energy are present. (p. 129)

There is clearly an I–Thou encounter in these moments. The existential living process or dimension, or whatever we call it, is prominently present. There is a distinctive clarity. It touches both client and therapist. I have had the opportunity to experience this with my clients more than once. Hitching on to Buber, Rank, and Rogers, we could call these events transcendent.

Close, and on the edge between implicit and explicit sources of inspiration, we find the use of poetry in therapy. Hoffman (2014) describes how therapists can transform their experience of therapy into poetry. Through poems, they can convey their deeper understanding of the client's situation, the therapeutic relationship, and the process. In his experience, using poetry can be growth-enhancing and deepening. Hoffman furthers explains how poetic language has some similarities with dream language. Both are symbolic languages, which means that they can communicate aspects of the process that are hard to put into words. However, symbolic languages are also open to many interpretations. The therapist should be aware of the fact that the client might understand the poem quite differently than it was intended. Therefore, therapists should be careful in using poetry, especially when the therapeutic relationship feels fragile and when the client (and/or when the therapist) is struggling with boundaries.

Explicit Sources of Inspiration

The active use of inspiration in therapy could be called explicit inspiration. Here the therapist searches, with or without the client, for sources that could inspire the client. This involves resources such as music, texts, books, videos, pictures, and other media that could resonate with the current therapeutic process. What might be inspiring is often noticeable during therapy itself. In one of our previous sessions during stage two, Thomas explained how he felt touched by the music of Johann Sebastian Bach. This kind of music clearly evoked something in Thomas. By dwelling on this experience, Thomas felt inspired and motivated to go back to music school, this time together with his wife. He studied music history and took singing classes. This boosted his openness to his emotional world and created new possibilities and opportunities to express himself and be heard and seen. It demonstrates how inspiration can facilitate new possibilities and engagements.

Thomas sometimes asked for literature that connected to the issues we were exploring during our sessions. However, existing literature, podcasts, or videos are often not fully aligned with what the client needs. It can confuse the client or even undermine the ongoing process. Literature on existential, therapeutic, or emotional matters can sometimes be too matter of fact or far too theoretical. Sometimes literature or other material can be very discouraging. Existential literature, for example, often tends to emphasize the tragedy of life without showing encouraging possibilities. In turn, positive psychology literature sometimes treats existential obstacles too lightly, and pop psychology misses all the nuances that are characteristic of human processes. Sources that are written in an inspired way are more likely to inspire. Still, there is no way to predict whether this book or that video will be inspiring. The extent to which the resource matches the growth edge might be more predictive. For Thomas it was Bach; for Newton it was an apple.

In keeping with Thomas's therapeutic process and his specific preferences, I eventually recommended some books and videos. *The Courage to Be* by Tillich (2000) dovetailed nicely with his request for help in daring to be alive. I recommended the book only at a later point of our sessions. In the earlier stages, when we were primarily seeking to connect more authentically with himself or the others or when we were fully engaged in processing painful experiences of the past, this book would not have been helpful. At a later moment, when he was exploring himself being a spectator of his own existence, I recommended he read Buber's *The Way of Man* (2010) as a counter-balance. Another time, I forwarded him a link to a poetic video that reminded me of our last therapeutic session. At some point, I also passed him material about *anavah*, which particularly inspired him.

> You suggested Paul Tillich's *The Courage to Be.* I read that book and got a lot out of it. It was comforting and encouraging: Life *is*

> not evident; it has to be conquered against the negative force of non-being. It aligned with my question to you, the question which I expressed several times: Help me live, that I dare to be alive. And when you saw that television show with Willem Vermandere [a Flemish poet and folk musician], you thought of me and sent it to me. Those were real encouragements; they helped me to keep going. They also made me feel really seen and heard. The book by Martin Buber, where he writes about God's question—"Adam, where are you?"—was very inviting and fruitful. There was one moment when, it has become even clearer to me in retrospect than in the moment itself, the important insight came to me to take my own space and also to take care of it. This was when you gave me literature about *anavah* and the Jewish thinking around it. I quote: "When we say that this seat is mine, we are saying that the other seat is not mine. [...] Anavah means taking the appropriate space and stepping up when called. [...] It implies being fully present (Morinis, 2007 p. 49)." This is where the connection between spiritually and concrete action became clear to me. This gave me a frame of reference, *ground* under my feet, grounding my daily concrete decisions and actions.

The Prophet and the Angel

When we are inspired, we feel engaged. We feel motivated and we want to express the new ways we are experiencing life. Thomas would take very concrete steps. As soon as possible, he took up his volunteering again. It was like he had to be reminded of what had proved to be helpful earlier.

One of Thomas's own sources of inspiration turned out to be very helpful during this third stage. We noticed earlier how he could get energized when he was immersed in unraveling the deeper meaning of the Bible. Then he really felt fully alive. He told me how he felt drawn these days to the story of the prophet Elijah, who was about to give up his life and mission. The prophet sinks down by the side of the road and prays that he could die. An angel appears and gives Elijah food. Up to three times the angel comes by with water and bread. Finally, the angel puts Elijah back on the road in order to fulfill his mission. Thomas recognized how Elijah felt overwhelmed by his mission and how he lacked the courage to go on. Or to put it differently, Thomas recognized himself in that moment in Elijah's life: The discouragement and reaching that moment when one is about to give up everything. The story is inspirational because it succeeds in symbolizing the client's felt sense of their situation (Vanhooren, 1997). It manages to capture the implicit meanings of one's own process, including something of the possible direction of one's own process. Fairy tales, myths, and dreams that speak to us can be understood as symbolizations of our own felt senses (Vanhooren, 1997). They can help us to unfold our living process by teaching us metaphors that symbolize our felt directions in life, as well as the helpful elements that are part of our process, too (Gendlin, 1986). Clearly, in this story, the helpful element is the angel, but in dreams that could be anything that is extraordinary, different, odd, or life affirming (Gendlin, 1986). Therefore, Ellis (2020) suggests that we pay special attention to the helpful elements in our dreams and sense them in the here-and-now before we start exploring other elements in the dream. It is clear that this counts for other inspiring resources such as Bible stories, myths, and fairy tales.

It is no coincidence that Thomas felt inspired by this story of Elijah. You might already have noticed that there are strong similarities between Thomas's dream about his daughter committing suicide, the focusing session about his heavy blood, and the story of Elijah. The dream, the focusing, and the story had a common dynamic. First, there is an exhaustion, a giving up, something that wants to die. Then there is a counterreaction: The father saving the daughter in the dream, something of himself getting angry and wanting to be alive in the focusing session, and now a nurturing angel that puts Elijah back on track. Because this movement had proven to be helpful before, I asked Thomas to reread the story frequently. And so, once again, our sessions were about life and death.

The Ethics of Inspiring

Before we go on, let's address some topics concerning the ethics of inspiring as a possible therapeutic intervention. There is an important difference between inspiration and indoctrination. As we indicated early on, addressing the existential dimension of the client's problem is different from "philosophizing" together. Theoretical exchanges do not create change in a therapeutic setting. On the contrary, they can be alienating and make the client feel even more alone and demoralized than before. This also counts for sharing one's life's wisdom or sources of inspiration that are not meant to help the therapeutic process or do not connect to this process. Cooper (2015) argues that we must respect the client's meaning system and world assumptions of their existence (meso-dimension), even if it is contrary to our own beliefs.

Clearly, the therapist or counselor is not a guru or a spiritual teacher. However, they might feel eager to share their own beliefs and convictions, as clients are often searching for answers. Out of despair, some clients are eager to take on new beliefs and to adopt a therapist's meaning system. Although it might help them to shelter for a while, it probably will not last for a long time. Posttraumatic growth, which can result in setting new life priorities and a new philosophy of life, only comes by wrestling with one's lost meanings and the existential dimension of the experienced adversities (Tedeschi & Calhoun, 2004). Spiritual bypassing or other kinds of bypassing will not help the client in the long run. They also might feel betrayed when quick fixes like adopting a new ideology or a new religion does not seem to deliver the promised land. What can help us as therapists and counselors is to be aware of our own cultural and ideological framework and its limitations and cultivate an awareness of the mystery and the great unknown in our lives.

Instead of putting our own frame of reference at the front, we would do better to draw on inspirational resources that match the client's cultural and spiritual lifeworld (Cleare-Hoffman et al., 2020). As the American Psychological Association points out, it is critical to respect our clients' meaning system (Abrams, 2023). When clients find courage and inspiration from their religion or other ideological framework, we should use this resource in therapy as well. It places the client's experience into a broader perspective and opens the door to explore the client's concerns existentially. The existential dimension does not have a name, image, sound, or language by itself. However, in every culture we find expressions of this macrocosmic layer (Rank, 1932). We not only find language for the macro-dimension in religions and philosophy (Hoffman et al., 2009; Yang, 2017) but also in myths and the epic stories of today (May, 1991). People who excel at sports or science might also inspire because they show us how to live our lives with regard to the existential challenges of today. For some people, Stephen Hawkin might be inspirational—the brilliant mind who tried to unravel the universe despite his ALS disease. For others, this might be Nirmal Purja, the Nepali climber who turned the climbers' world upside down by climbing all fourteen peaks above 8,000 meters in seven months. And there is Greta Thunberg, who called for climate action around the world.

For Thomas, the language of the Bible and its stories were most helpful because they resonated with how he was experiencing existence. They resonated with how he was sensing himself, the world, and the Unspeakable. This language was his thread of Ariadne that helped him to explore his existential space. Therefore, it was crucial for him that this language could be used in therapy. The fact that I was familiar with his resources was helpful and important. Thomas picked this up early on.

> The fact that religion could be explicitly discussed during our sessions played an important role in me feeling safe and trusting you. Before our therapy started, I heard that you had hiked to Santiago de Compostela, and I suspected that you had a feeling for philosophical questions and spirituality. That helped me decide to contact you. In previous therapies, the spiritual and religious was something like a taboo; I was knocking on the door, but nobody answered. What I considered an important part of who I am stayed out of the picture. In our first sessions, when you asked me how I would call by demons, and I said "Legion," you knew what I was talking about. I thought: "Hey, you know the Bible!" And you understand it, you know that name and it helps me to understand my situation.

Jacking-up Existential Awareness

The story of the prophet and the angel served as a metaphor to help Thomas reflect on what kept him leaning away from his path and what put him back on track. When Thomas noticed that he sometimes slipped into being a spectator of his own life, he experienced that "lying by the side of the road" was a "safe, but deadly place." As a spectator, he was watching his life going by instead of living this existence. It was like living in a bunker: It was safe there, but it was not a place to live.

> **Thomas**: That bunker, that's a waiting room. You can keep waiting there.
> **Siebrecht**: Once you are in that bunker, what signal are *you waiting* for in order to come out?
> **Thomas**: Right... Yes...
> **Siebrecht**: In seems like a grim place to be. It also might be confronting to realize that *you* keep going back to that place.
> **Thomas**: Yes... Yes... [Smiles].
> **Siebrecht**: You're smiling?
> **Thomas**: Yes man, where am I? I'm 67 years old. And to discover that I'm still...... [sighs].
> **Siebrecht**: That's confronting....

Thomas: That is confrontational, yes.
Siebrecht: Yes, isn't it.
Thomas: It's confrontational and on the other hand ... *I am* that old now; surely I won't have to wait that long in my bunker anymore until it's all completely... over.
Siebrecht: But, Thomas. This is not the place in which *you* want to die, is it?
Thomas: Yes... no, of course not!

Although this last intervention, "This is not the place in which *you* want to die," might sound odd, it was characteristic of this third stage. Whereas in the previous stages we would experientially explore both sides of the movement—something that wanted to resign and something that wanted to live to the fullest—here I consciously addressed Thomas's choice and responsibility. I consciously did not use the word "something," which is often used in focusing language to point at parts of oneself, but used "You" and "I." We had experientially explored inner parts or this dynamic before. We were familiar with them, and because of our former therapeutic work, Thomas had grown in experiential freedom. Now, however, was the time to help him make choices (Gundrum, 2007). This does not mean that I forced him to make a decision. We would further explore what he (rather than it) would need in order to get out of his bunker—or in other words, how the angel could put the prophet back on track. And that angel, it would appear—as in that dream or in that focusing session—was something of himself or of his beingness. Thomas kind of knew what would be helpful or what would save him. By making space for himself and doing the things that were essential to him, he would naturally come out of this bunker. This answer came fairly quickly and, as a result, Thomas would visit his aunt who was dying. For him, this visit was more important and essential than working in his garden. Not long after this session, he would also resume his volunteering again. He would also start working on a book. It felt to him that his life would not be complete if he did not finish this book.

Existential Boosters

In addition to these types of interventions and inspirational resources, we also used other existential boosters during this final stage to remedy Thomas's growth process. In order to help clients experience the felt sense of their existential space, we developed specific experiential–existential exercises over the years (Missiaen & Vanhooren, 2021;

Vanhooren, 2016a). It might help clients to become more aware of the ontological layer of their life situation. In its simplest form, the client is asked to bring their attention to what is noticeable in their body in the here-and-now (Gendlin, 1978). We then use very simple phrases and invite the client to repeat these sentences one at a time and experience what they do to them. Originally, we used the following phrases, which basically reflect Heidegger's *Dasein* or the Hebrew tradition of *hineini* (here I am): "I am, I am here, here I am" (Vanhooren, 2016a). These simplest of words seem to resonate deeply with people's most basic dimension of being. We start with "I am" and pause sufficiently, letting the client repeat this sentence to let it cross with the client's felt sense of being. It usually takes the client directly to their current existential concern. The other short sentences, "I am here" and "here I am" might be helpful too. Although quite simple, these sentences can have a confronting effect. Clients might experience a lack of existential confirmation or an experience of lacking the right to exist. They might experience emptiness, nothingness, or their mortality but also connectedness, harmony, or relief. These *hineini* exercises hold up an existential mirror. In experiential–existential group therapy for cancer patients, we have used these exercises to help evoke existential and experiential depth across the sessions (Verdegem et al., 2022).

In this third stage, we also used these *hineini* exercises. It took Thomas straight to his current challenge: to take in his place in life and to self-confirm his existence:

> Although this therapy was about life and death, *space* might have even been more present as a theme throughout our sessions. And maybe this was indeed the most central theme. Now that I think about it, it makes everything possible or impossible. For me, it was the biggest challenge as well: daring or not daring to take in space, not daring to live. Waiting to take a seat until everyone has taken their place... Waiting until others have set their agendas... I will see how much time there is left to speak... That's the waiting mode I was talking about; that's the hesitation, the hesitation to say: "I will go swimming this afternoon." That is the waiting for death, and by doing so, I was on my path of dying already. For me, it was also the result of my conflict avoidance. By taking up your space you also might provoke tensions, conflicts about who does what and when. You repeatedly reminded me of the importance of having my own space and taking my own place... When we redecorated our

house, the room that was to become my office was used as a repository of furniture for months, and everything was covered under a thick layer of dust. Therapy also pointed out the importance of my own *time*. The book materials around anavah, combined with that hineini exercise, helped me to get clarity. It encouraged me to take in my place in life, in a very concrete way.

Beyond Dualism

This last stage had something of Homer's *Odyssey* (2012). In this ancient Greek story, King Odysseus, the war veteran, seeks his way back home after the Trojan War. It becomes a true quest, full of temptations and dangerous situations. Passing the seductive Calypso, the sirens, and a Cyclops, Odysseus ends up in the realm of the dead. The confrontation with his deceased mother and the shadows of the fallen heroes finally sets him on the right course. He reaches his homeland, the island of Ithaca, but another bloody battle awaits him before he can reclaim his own place and space. You would think that the story would be over now. However, this story, written 2,700 years ago, takes a different turn. It does not follow the script of a happy ending; nor does it end in a disaster. Odysseus no longer feels at home in his house. Coming home in the Odyssey means going further. His home from before the Trojan War no longer fits him. Odysseus, the famous sailor, now travels over land. The oracle prompts him to stay where they do not know what an oar is. Only in this new place—a dimension where the sea no longer matters—can he truly live (Vanhooren, 2016b).

Therapy with Thomas would take a somewhat similar turn. In the third stage, Thomas not only resumed his growth also but grew beyond what or where he had been before. He no longer found himself in one of two poles of his recurrent pattern—being either in a place of death or in a place of life. In our final sessions, he came to realize that in the end it was not about being in the one or in the other. It was not about death or life, meaninglessness or meaning, isolation or connection, freedom or being stuck:

Siebrecht: Maybe we could just reflect on how it feels to be alive today? Take a moment and check how it currently feels inside there... Maybe there are some words or images that resonate with how it feels over there at this moment?
Thomas: [Long silence. Thomas looks down and is in the now. He turns his attention to his bodily experience and takes his

time to search for words]. My life feels uncomplicated...and good ... And the clock is ticking.
Siebrecht: It feels uncomplicated and the clock is ticking...It is not a "but," but an "and"...
Thomas: Yes, my life feels uncomplicated and I am getting old. And all the concerns that would arise around aging... and as a volunteer in the retirement home, I see what aging can do, but when I sense inside here, there is none of that...
Siebrecht: My life feels uncomplicated and the clock is ticking. I'm getting old.
Thomas: And to be able to say this, does not feel like a sign of resignation. It feels surprising to me. It feels powerful!
Siebrecht: There's a smile there, I see. And you say this with vigor.
Thomas: Yes, I could also put it this way: I feel good. I feel uncomplicatedly good—period. And this does not mean that there are no tensions. There are. But to be able to say this, I haven't been able to experience this very often.
Siebrecht: Surely this is something very special and something very powerful. Getting old, being able to face death and fragility, and still feeling basically good. The clock is ticking, and I know this, and yet I have an uncomplicated feeling. Things are allowed to be there or are there right now.
Thomas: They are there.
Siebrecht: As if this all forms a whole, and you feel good about it. Something of an acceptance perhaps. Or maybe something else. Is there an image that would capture this whole: I feel uncomplicated *and* the clock is ticking?
Thomas: [Searching] It reminds me of those walks we are taking now together in the morning, and how the winter sun casts long shadows... The light is beautiful. And that existential question, it doesn't feel like threatening now or being oppressive. It is there. And... this is me too. And to realize this and to feel it's good ... yes.

This therapy excerpt speaks volumes. Thomas's life at the beginning of therapy was marked by depression, panic attacks, meaninglessness, existential guilt, and difficulties in terms of experiencing contact and his right to exist but feels uncomplicated and good now. His relationship with his life has fundamentally changed. Life is now uncomplicated because both poles—life and death—can be experienced at the same moment. It is good and the clock is ticking. There is no life anxiety, death anxiety, or any existential guilt. Living and dying now belong together. Thomas not only owned his own existence but also the human condition and the existential question—the ultimate concern (Tillich, 2000)—as such.

Three Stages and a Quantum Leap

What Thomas was able to accomplish during these three stages is not for everyone at any moment. Nor does it have to be that way. There is no standard when it comes to living. This particular therapeutic process shows what is possible, although it does not mean that Thomas's embodied insights are an eternal achievement. Nor did the final quantum leap—his ability to accept, affirm, and own not only his existence but also the human condition as such—come out of nowhere. This kind of leap, a qualitative change that makes us move from one dimension into another, is only possible when everything is ready. The step in this final therapy excerpt seems small, but it is the result of a long struggle and hard work. It reminds us of how Tedeschi and Calhoun (2004) describe posttraumatic growth. It is the result of wrestling with our existential concerns. This kind of growth takes work and effort.

Loveling (2021) describes in her novel *A Gunshot* how preparing the field was exuberantly celebrated among farmers decades ago. In industrial agriculture in Western countries, where manual labor is minimized and where fewer people are involved than before, the various steps of weeding, feeding the soil, plowing the field, sowing, and harvesting are not celebrated anymore. In our times, where natural processes are pushed to their limits when it comes to quantities and speed, I can imagine that the hurried therapist would want to have the equally hurried client experience existential quantum leaps in a minimum of sessions. There is also the societal expectation that we should always achieve the highest goal and achieve this as soon as possible. I do not think it works like this. Regardless of what we reach or achieve, it seems important to celebrate whatever we harvest and celebrate the steps in between as well.

Although we are gaining a deeper understanding of how psychotherapy might work, we are still dealing with a process that incorporates all the elements of life. Just as medication can support or adjust our biochemical processes or just as surgery can remove a melanoma, the healing and recovery ultimately remains a matter of the body. Our living processes incorporate our entire situation, including the existential reality that runs through us as living beings. The therapeutic process as it developed here with Thomas had its own logic (Gendlin, 1996). It developed itself through three stages ,and there was nothing we could skip. As Gendlin explains, the process itself carries its next implicit step. One flows out of the other. In the end, everything seems to have contributed to the outcome.

As we might describe it in terms of Greening (1992), Thomas was able to leave behind his one-sided positive or negative answers to his existential challenges (see Chapter 3). His new relationship with his existence embraced life and death, meaninglessness and meaningfulness, isolation and connectedness, and freedom and powerlessness. This did not mean that from now on life would be free of distress and limitations. Thomas was well aware of it. But something had fundamentally changed. Living felt different now. Beyond the daily noise, life felt good and uncomplicated. The final shift of this therapy had been transcendent. Just like Odysseus, Thomas had carried forward existence, and existence had carried him forward to a new place of living.

At this point, didactic models lose their value. It would not make sense anymore to sum up the changes made on the micro-, meso-, and macro-dimension. When our life processes are faltering, models might help to identify problems at different levels. It might help us to understand what might be going wrong or what needs our attention to support this process of being and becoming. But now at the end of this therapeutic process, everything was functioning as one. There was *ontological congruence*: This existential dimension (macro) was tangible in Thomas's daily experiencing (micro) as well as in his view on life (meso), and vice versa.

As it goes with I–Thou encounters (Buber, 1998), and especially when we open up to the existential of transcendent dimensions of these encounters (Rogers, 1980), we rarely walk back home unchanged (Frediani et al., 2023). This was not only true for Thomas but also for myself. Our shared existential time had enriched me as a therapist and a human being. Although therapy is finite, we might carry this experience with us until the end of our days.

Saying Goodbye, Over and Over Again

There is that moment when we get up, put on our coats, and say goodbye. Leijssen (2001) emphasizes how the very last stage of therapy has a character of its own. The final conversations are clearly related to existential concerns about the finitude of our existence. Rank emphasized the importance of picturing therapy as a finite story (Kramer, 2019). This does not mean that the therapeutic process is over when the last session has come to a close. Just as we somehow retain a bond with our deceased family members or friends, clients often retain an imaginary bond with their therapist as a supportive character. In other words, the client might have integrated their therapist, which shows itself in how they attend to their "inner client" (Gendlin, 1984) or the people around them. What Rank is getting at is that an endless therapy might undermine the vitality of the process. By denying its finite character, we might harvest that kind of energy that only reveals itself when we are getting near the end.

We almost forget that every session in itself is finite as well. How does the client cope with the fact that time is limited in this concrete situation? Can the client say goodbye at the end of each session? Does the client struggle with leaving the therapy room? Does the client tend to continue talking despite the fact that the time is up? Or does the client keep an eye on the clock time anxiously? And how does the therapist cope with a client who denies the limitations of time or is so preoccupied with time that they do not really live during their therapy sessions? All these questions foreshadow how the client might experience the ending stage of therapy and, obviously, the existential challenges of death and the limitations of our existence. This not only is true for the client but for the therapist too. How do you as a therapist or counselor say goodbye to your clients? How do you experience final farewells?

I have learned to consciously mark the end of each session in one way or another depending on the client and the process we are involved in. I discovered that it is helpful to round up a session by reflecting on the session itself. We might reflect on what the client and the therapist experienced as important during the session, on what has been missing and what the client wants to take home for now. Although clients often find it difficult to reflect on their sessions, these questions ritualize the wrapping up. There are surely other ways of doing it, but rituals like asking the same questions might create safety. They give us a structure, a marked space or a "house" in which we might wander or help us relate to the challenge of our finitude. As clients, reflective questions at the end of our sessions might also help to make sense of our experiences. It might help us to experience our sessions as meaningful and to let them further unfold during our daily experiences. It might help us learn how to complete our lives in a meaningful way.

Spreading Our Wings, Flying into the Sky

It is told that therapists can only accompany their clients so far, which is up to the point where they have been (Bugental, 1978). Although a client can also take the therapist further than they have been, there is some truth to this idea. Therapists' blind spots or unfinished business can hinder the therapeutic process. Exploring one's own existential challenges is crucial when we want to engage in existential processes with our clients (Bugental, 1978; Frediani et al., 2023; Hill, 2017). It seems obvious that our blind spots around dying and the limitations of life might be in the way of finishing our sessions and therapies in a fruitful way. So what is the place of death in our own existence? How do we say goodbye to our family members, pets, colleagues, or friends on a daily base? How do we deal with our own experiences of loss? And finally, how do we experience the end of a session and the wrapping up of an entire therapeutic process with our clients?

Very often, finishing therapies with clients reminds me of how we used to take care of injured birds at our home. With my father having a heart for birds and with my two older sisters being biologists, people used to bring injured birds to our home. We had a spacious bird cage at the end of our garden where these injured birds could find some rest. I remember a time when a friend brought us a screech owl that we named Marcel. He had flown against her car, and he was quite dizzy. After a couple of days, he seemed to be doing well, and we opened the door of our cage. But Marcel did not move. He was watching us carefully, and it was clear that he did not want to fly away as long as we were looking. It was quite a process. We went back inside, peeking through the curtains, but still he was watching us. He just did not move. It was only when we got distracted that he spread his wings and disappeared. He chose his moment carefully, and we missed it. Like those others countless blackbirds, redwings, or sparrows, we never saw "our Marcel" again. Those goodbyes were always bittersweet. It was a layered experience, colored by love, warmth, and some sadness. There is the joy in noticing how the bird is ready to fly off into the sky, and there is the pain of the parting. I have the exact same felt sense at the end of successful therapeutic process. It's not a bad thing. It feels right to me. It means that we have developed an authentic bond within the restrictions of the therapy setting. It means that this life experience was significant.

How we part obviously depends on the therapy itself. Therapeutic trajectories that have a bumpier ending also require more of an after-process. Clients who fly away without saying goodbye leave us with some unfinished business. They did not do anything wrong; neither did we. It only means that this was the only way the client could leave. Maybe there was too much pain involved, or there was too much (death) anxiety. Depending on the client's and therapist's existential capacities, we get different endings. With Thomas, every stage was finished differently.

Ways to Complete the Process

There are countless ways to complete processes, and the most common ones are not the best. It is sobering to learn that a lot of counseling processes are abruptly aborted (Leijssen, 2025). The client does not show up at the next appointment, and so the process comes to an end. As therapists, we usually do not have a clue what triggered this sudden end. Often this absence of the client is understood as a therapeutic failure. Whatever it means, at the very least it means that the client did not get around to consciously saying goodbye. For clients who struggle with traumatic losses and attachment issues, finishing the process consciously can be a real challenge (Leijssen, 2025). However, in those instances, therapy could offer a corrective experience by helping the client to complete this process and to part in a constructive way.

As we already mentioned, rituals might help to mark and seal this ending. These rituals do not have to be big, complicated, or dramatic. It might simply mean that we announce the last session to be different and help our clients to prepare for this last session with some questions: What have we reached together, what has been helpful, what did we miss, and what was hindering? This immediately makes this session different, and it also feels different. I remember how Gunther, Annabel, and Marie, reflected on what had been helpful or what had been hindering during our journey together. What should have been different in order to have reached their goal more fully? Dwelling on what went well and what was helpful helps the client to internalize the therapy. In turn, dwelling on its deficits has another function.

First, it stimulates the autonomy of the client, who now has to continue their journey by themself (Rank, 1936). The imperfectness and fallibility of the therapist and therapy might help the client realize that failure and the imperfect are part of life. The imperfect is one of the many options of the possible. It is part of the whole, although this might be a hard thing to accept for some of us. Second, the ability to express what had been missing and the acceptance of this expression by an empathic therapist might be a corrective experience in itself. As Rank (1936) would say, by empathizing with the missing, the difference and autonomy of the client is fully confirmed and validated. Although this is not always the case, the quality of the final conversation might make up for what has been missing and help reach the client's goal *in extremis*. In order to harvest these special fruits of our hard labor together, the final conversation requires some preparation, also on the side of the therapist. It is helpful to reflect beforehand on the remarkable moments that happened during these therapies.

With Thomas, I completed our therapy three times, and each time it was quite different. The first time, we reflected during the sessions leading to our final appointment on how Thomas had completed his therapies with his previous therapists. This prompted him to write a farewell letter to one of his previous therapists. In this letter, Thomas articulated some unfinished experiences with this therapist, who took advantage of the opportunity to respond in an authentic and very empathic way. By doing so, a therapeutic process from more than a decade ago was rounded out beautifully. Further, I asked Thomas what he would need in order to conclude our sessions. Thomas wanted to read some psalms with me, and so we did.

The ending of the second stage was less marked or ritualized. Although we reflected on this second stage, Thomas's heart and mind were already set on the future and his new commitments. Closing one door often means opening another, and Thomas had already opened the next door with his new job as a volunteer.

The last stage was again different. This farewell reminded us both of an ancient Jewish ritual in which a field is allowed to rest after several decades of hard labor. The seeds that come to fruit during that year are the result of the work of the previous years. The idea of taking a sabbatical is derived from this ritual. This time of rest is also a time when things can return to their rightful place. We shared the thought that after our diligent work, it was time to trust the ground itself. It was a beautiful metaphor to conclude a rich and deep therapeutic experience.

An Afterword by Thomas

The process with its three stages was, like any therapeutic process, unique and unrepeatable. To conclude this chapter, we give the final word to Thomas:

> Dear Siebrecht, we both have grown older, each in our own way, since our therapy sessions started. "Growing old" has actually been a theme throughout our conversations, sometimes

dormant, sometimes explicit. In the very first session, my question was: "How can I become a wise and gentle old man?" Our conversations were about death and life, in many different forms and shapes. Life for me was living with a narrow breath, never full, never free, always with a certain suspicion. Death was literally present during the course of therapy: My parents died, my aunt, my old uncle. As a volunteer in the hospice of the retirement home, I have been present during the process of dying with several people. Each time these moments were very intense, and there was a strong presence. Perhaps this is what helped me to live. It makes me grateful. And being grateful is a sign of life, isn't it?

There is, however, the realization of getting older. And this realization comes along with certain questions around family and friends. Our children are getting older. It has become really important to me to have a sincere relationship with them. Also with family members with whom there had been a break-up for years, I'm happy and proud that these relationships have been restored. But there are also disappointments around some old friendships, about the depth and relative importance of those ties... All of these too where part of our sessions.

At the beginning of our therapy, I wrote in my notebook: "My only fear when I think of my dying is the thought that I would have lived a lost life. That I didn't make anything of it." This fear is gone now. The thought has completely disappeared. I am at peace with the past. And I consider this time to be the most beautiful time of my life so far. Also the most beautiful time of our marriage. Therapy has guided this process, all of this.

Chapter 5

Some Encouragement from a Fellow Traveler

"Within experiencing lie the mysteries of all that we are...
From out of it we create what we create."
(Gendlin, 1962, p. 15)

With Thomas's final words, we are coming to the end of this book as well. The book is the end of a long and creative process, and it has been waiting to be picked up by you. Maybe the reading felt like an adventure. It might have been too lighthearted or too heavy handed, too colorful or too neutral, too detailed or too vague. Who knows? Maybe this book offered you just what you needed. Maybe it carried something of your existence forward. Maybe it has been a source of inspiration, an invitation, or a little encouragement on your journey through life.

Courage is something we certainly can use when we take the existential path. When we are open to the mystery of our existence, regardless of what it might mean, we might feel overwhelmed by fear or by beauty or both. There is nothing that can fully explain how and why we got here, but life is ours to live together with the many creatures on this planet (and, who knows, beyond). But what we do know is that sharing and deepening our lived experiences makes us live more consciously and fully. There is evidence that we can help those people who suffer psychologically appreciate their life more deeply. Humanistic, experiential, and existential therapies are indeed evidence based (Elliott et al., 2021; Vos & Vitali, 2018; Zegers & Vanhooren, 2026). They can alleviate our suffering while supporting our growth and existential well-being. However, this does not mean that every session will immediately lead to a success. The therapeutic process still needs to be lived and experienced. On the side of the therapist, working with existential concerns implies encountering our own existential challenges, developing existential empathy, and learning how to navigate the therapeutic relationship together with facilitating the micro-, meso-, and macro-dimension of the therapeutic process (Frediani et al., 2023, 2025). As a bonus, we might learn more about living and what gives meaning to our own lives while also appreciating that life itself is fragile and unique.

Growing Continuously

Searching for the essence of life is a full-time job. It takes us a lifetime, I guess. The fact that the epic story of Gilgamesh still resonates with us speaks volumes (see Chapter 1). Regardless of the many cultural, industrial, and technological revolutions we have been through, the 4,000-year-old questions of Gilgamesh are still ours. Although religious, cultural, and ideological frameworks can help us navigate through our existential challenges (Abrams, 2023), they also come and go. The existential questions remain.

Our personal answers also shift regularly. New situations challenge us to relate differently to existence. Perhaps, as Tedeschi and Calhoun (2012) tell us, our answers might become somewhat more robust over time. Or rather, our responses have something more of an open quality. The more open we become, the less shattered we might feel by the unexpected (Rogers, 1961).

With that many questions and only a few answers, there will always be a need for existential counseling or therapy, although its shape and name might change over the ages. It also means that for us, as therapists, there will always be more to learn. Our growth edge is expanding and moving forward with us. So what is next, or rather what is on your existential agenda right now? What do you need in order to continue your existential adventure?

Working Existentially in Your Setting

Being present with existential concerns in therapy makes our lives rich and intense. When we embark on this journey with our clients, it might feel good to share it with our colleagues. The dark and the bright sides of our existential encounters often require sharing afterward. In sharing our experiences, we are not only sharing what we experienced but sharing our existence with another human being. We are connecting and reconnecting. We are helping ourselves to make sense of this new client–therapist encounter. We are helping each other to unfold its implicit meanings. We carry this experience forward, making us ready to encounter this client again. In sharing with our colleagues, we also enter into the implicit next step of our own growth process, which was addressed through our encounter with our client.

The characteristics of our work setting may or may not allow us the time and space to engage in this kind of sharing and subsequent growth. Our work context can be facilitative or rather constricting. Is there space and safety to talk about existential concerns during team meetings? Does the staff acknowledge that existential concerns matter? Does the mission statement of your clinic include existential care? Does your monitoring system include measures that also assess existential concerns, life satisfaction, meaning, and growth? Policymakers and staff members have a responsibility here, but you also have a voice. *Anavah*, remember? Even when your setting is not facilitative, it is remarkable how sharing existential concerns and growth can deepen and widen relationships, including at work. After all, beyond our ontic differences, we share existence. This is our common ground, wherever we are.

Closing with Gratitude

I recently learned that the Gilgamesh epic was given a different ending a thousand years after it was first written. At some point, somebody added a twelfth clay tablet to the story (de Feyter, 2002). Maybe the ending of the original story no longer fit the cultural context of the next millennium. The added clay tablet is still about mortality, loss, and the search for connection. However, the poet gives Gilgamesh the opportunity to meet his deceased friend Enkidu one last time:

> Shamash made a hole in the underworld and the spirit of Enkidu escaped. They embraced and kissed each other. They talked to each other and had an exciting conversation: "Tell me, my friend, tell me what the underworld is like. What did you see there?" "I cannot tell you, my friend, I cannot tell you (de Feyter, 2002, p. 134).

What follows is Enkidu's flawed attempt to describe what he has seen, but the text has no real ending. There is something that escapes us when we try describe what we are experiencing. Life itself is beyond our comprehension—not only metaphorically or philosophically. There is something that we find difficult or impossible to put into words. When we feel existentially touched by an encounter or see something beautiful, it often happens that we feel speechless, out of words.

Breaking that silence might also feel disrespectful. The meager words would take away the experience itself. We are engaged in an I–Thou encounter then. In awe, we might be realizing that we are small, fragile, and temporary. And at the same time, we might taste something that fully transcends us. We might be something that fully transcends us.

I wrote down some words. Now there is silence.

References

Abeyta, A. A., Routlegde, C., Juhl, J., & Robinson, M. D. (2015). Finding meaning through emotional understanding: Emotional clarity predicts meaning in life and adjustment to existential threat. *Motivation and Emotion, 39,* 973–983. https://doi.org/10.1007/s500-3

Abrams, Z. (2023). Can religion and spirituality have a place in therapy? Experts say yes. APA Monitor on Psychology, *54(8),* 67. https://www.apa.org/monitor/2023/11/incorporating-religion-spirituality-therapy

Afschrift, M. (2018). Wat ik beteken voor de ander ontstaat uit verbinding met mezelf. [What I mean to the other arises from connection with myself]. *Tijdschrift Persoonsgerichte Experiëntiële Psychotherapie, 56*(1), 3–18.

American Psychiatric Association (2013). *Diagnostic and statistical manual of mental disorders* (5th ed). American Psychiatric Publishing.

Anderson, C. L., Monroy, & M., Keltner, D. (2018). Awe in nature heals: Evidence from military veterans, at-risk youth, and college students. *Emotion, 18,* 1195–1202. https://doi.org/ 10.1037/emo0000442.

Anderson, R., & Cissna, K. N. (1997). *The Martin Buber–Carl Rogers dialogue: A new transcript with commentary.* State University of New York Press.

Andrews, M. (2016). The existential crisis. *Behavioral Development Bulletin, 21*(1), 104–109. https://doi.org/10.1037/bdb0000014

Angus, L. E., & Greenberg, L. S. (2011). *Working with narrative in emotion-focused therapy: Changing stories, healing lives.* American Psychological Association.

Angus, L. E., Watson, J. C., Elliott, R., Schneider, K., & Timulak, L. (2015). Humanistic psychotherapy research 1990–2015: From methodological innovation to evidence-supported treatment outcomes and beyond. *Psychotherapy Research, 25*(3), 330–347. https://doi.org/10.1080/10503307.2014.989290

Arendt, H. (2018). *The human condition: Second edition.* The University of Chicago Press. (Originally published in 1958)

Arendt, H. (2019). *De vrijheid om vrij te zijn* [*The freedom to be*]. Uitgeverij Atlas Contact.

Arnold, D., Calhoun, L. G., Tedeschi, R., & Cann, A. (2005). Vicarious posttraumatic growth in psychotherapy. *Journal of Humanistic Psychology, 45,* 239–263. https://doi.org/ 10.1177/0022167805274729

Arredondo, A. Y., & Caparrós, B. (2019). Associations between existential concerns and adverse experiences: A systematic review. *Journal of*

Humanistic Psychology. Advance online publication. https://doi.org/10.1177/0022167819846284

Barret-Lennard, G. T. (1990). The therapy pathway reformulated. In G. Lietaer, J. Rombouts, & R. Van Balen (Eds.), *Client-centered and experiential psychotherapy in the nineties* (pp. 123–153). University Press Leuven.

Becchetti, L., Bachelet, M., & Pisani, F. (2019). Poor eudaimonic subjective well-being as a mortality risk factor. *Economica Politica, 36*, 245–272. https://doi.org/10.1007/s40888-018-0134-2

Becker, E. (2011). *The denial of death*. Souvenir Press. (Originally published in 1973)

Belzak, W. C. M., Thrash, T. M., Sim. Y. Y., & Wadsworth, L. (2017). Beyond hedonic and eudaimonic well-being: Inspiration and the self-transcendence tradition. In M. D. Robinson & M. Eid (Eds.), *The happy mind: Cognitive contributions to well-being* (pp. 117–138). Springer.

Bi, S., Maes, M., Stevens, G. W. J. M., de Heer, C., Li, J.-B., Sun, Y, & Finenauer, C. (2025). Trust and subjective well-being across the lifespan: A multilevel meta-analysis of cross-sectional and longitudinal associations. *Psychological Bulletin, 151*(6), 737–766. https://doi.org/10.1037/bul0000480

Blevins, C. L., & Tedeschi, R. G. (2022). Posttraumatic growth and wisdom: Processes and clinical applications. In M. Ferrari & M. Munroe (Eds.). *Post-traumatic growth to psychological well-being: Coping wisely with adversity* (pp. 11–26). Springer.

Bordin, E. S. (1979). The generalizability of the psychoanalytic concept of the working alliance. *Psychotherapy, 16*(3), 252-260. https://doi.org/10.1037/h0085885

Breitbart & Poppito (2014). *Meaning-centered group psychotherapy for patients with advanced cancer: A treatment manual*. Oxford University Press.

Buber, M. (1997). *Good and evil*. Prentice-Hall Inc. (Originally published in 1952)

Buber, M. (1998). *Ik en Jij [I and Thou]*. Bijleveld. (Originally published in 1923)

Buber, M. (1991). *Tales of the Hasidim*. Schocken. (Originally published in 1946).

Buber, M. (2010). *De weg van de mens.* [*The way of man*]. Felix Publishing bv. (Originally published in 1947)

Bugental, J. F. T. (1978). *Psychotherapy and process: The fundamentals of an existential-humanistic approach*. Zeig, Tucker & Theisen.

Bugental, J. F. T. (1999). *Psychotherapy isn't what you think: Bringing the psychotherapeutic engagement into the living moment.* Zeig, Tucker & Co.

Cain, D. J. (2016). Toward a research-based integration of optimal practices of humanistic psychotherapies. In D. J. Cain, K. Keenan, and S. Rubin (Eds.),

Humanistic psychotherapies: Handbook of research and practice. Second Edition (pp. 485–535). American Psychological Association.

Calhoun, L. G. & Tedeschi, R. G. (2013). *Posttraumatic growth in clinical practice.* Routledge.

Camus, A. (1975). *De mythe van Sisyfus* [*The myth of Sisyphus*]. The Bezige Bij. (Originally published in 1942)

Cassiba, R., Granqvist, P., & Costantini, A. (2013). Mothers' attachment security predicts their children's sense of God's closeness. *Attachment & Human Development, 15* (1), 51–64. https://doi.org/10.1080/14616734.2013.743253

Castonguay, L. G., & Hill, C. E. (2017). *How and why are some therapists better than others? Understanding therapist effects.* American Psychological Association.

Cheng, C., Cheung, S., Chio, J. H., & Chan, M. S. (2013). Cultural meaning of perceived control: A meta-analysis of locus of control and psychological symptoms across 18 cultural regions. *Psychological Bulletin, 139*(1), 152–188.

Christian, B. J. (2020). Attachment, nature, and the young child's felt sense of God. Journal of *Research on Christian Education, 29* (1), 47–60. https://doi.org/10.1080/10656219.2020.1731031

Classen, C.C. & Spiegel, D. (2011). Supportive-expressive group psychotherapy. In M. Watson & D. Kissane (Eds.), *Handbook of psychotherapy in cancer care* (pp.107–117). John Wiley & Sons Inc.

Clayton, S., & Crandon, T. (2024). Climate distress among young people: An overview. In E. Haase, & K. Hudson (Eds.), *Climate change and youth mental health: Multidisciplinary perspectives* (pp. 3–20). Cambridge University Press.

Cleare-Hoffman, H., Hoffman, L., & Perlstein, J. (2020). Cultural myths, rituals, and festivals. In L. Hoffman, H. Cleare-Hoffman, N. Granger Jr., & D. St. John (Eds.), *Humanistic approaches to multiculturalism and diversity: Perspectives on existence and dissonances* (pp. 117–127). Routledge.

Constantino, M. J., Pinel, E. C., Sommer, R. K., Goodwin, B. J., & Coyne, A. (2019). Existential isolation as a correlate of clinical distress, beliefs about psychotherapy, and experiences with mental health treatment. *Journal of Psychotherapy Integration, 29*(4), 389–399. http://dx.doi.org/10.1037/int0000172

Cooper, M. (2015). *Existential psychotherapy and counselling. Contributions to a pluralistic practice.* Sage.

Coppens, T. (2024). De vijf-sessiestherapie: Over knopen ontwarren en knopen zoeken [The five sessions therapy: Searching for and untying knots]. *Tijdschrift Persoonsgerichte Experiëntiële Psychotherapie, 62*(3), 174–185.

Cottyn, H. (2022, November 5). Forest. *The Standaard.* https://www.standaard.be/cnt/dmf20221104_98264512

Coyne, A. E., Gaines, A. N., DeFontes, C. G., Constantino, M. J., Barcala-Delgado, D. I., Boswell, J. F., & Kraus, D. R. (2025). Parsing the existential isolation–outcome association into its within- and between-patient components in naturalistic psychotherapy. *Psychotherapy, 62(2)*, 235–242. https://doi.org/10.1037/pst0000564

Cruciani, G., Liotti, M., & Lingiardi, V., (2024). Motivations to become psychotherapists: Beyond the concept of the wounded healer. *Research in Psychotherapy: Psychopathology, Process and Outcome, 27*(2), 808. https://doi.org/10.4081/ripppo.2024.808

Cuff, B. M. P., Brown, S. J., Taylor, L., & Howat, D. J. (2016). Empathy: A review of the concept. *Emotion Review, 8*, 144–153. https://doi.org/10.1177/1754073914558466

Dabrowski, K. (2015). *Personality shaping through positive disintegration*. Red Pill Press.

Dana, D. (2020). *Polyvagal exercises for safety and connection*. W. W. Norton & Company.

De Feyter, T. (2002). *The Gilgamesh epic. Translated, introduced and annotated by Theo de Feyter*. Ambo.

de Jager Meezenbroek, E., Garssen, B., van den Berg, M., van Dierendonck, D., Visser, A., & Schaufeli, W. B. (2012). Measuring spirituality as a universal human experience: A review of spirituality questionnaires. *Journal of Religion and Health, 51*(2), 336–354. https://doi.org/10.1007/s10943-010-9376-1

De Meulemeester, C., Lowyck, B., & Luyten, P. (2021). The role of impairments in self–other distinction in borderline personality disorder: A narrative review of recent evidence. *Neuroscience & Biobehavioral Reviews, 127*, 242–254. https://doi.org/10.1016/j.neubiorev.2021.04.022.

de Montaigne, M. (2006). *Over de ervaring.* [About the experience]. Cossee. (Originally published in 1580)

Delle Fave, A. (2020). Meaning in life: Structure, sources and relations with mental and physical health. *Acta Philosophica, 29*(1), 19–32.

Depoorter, T. (2022). I am large, I contain multitudes: Ambivalence and existential bearing in psychotherapy from an experiential-existential perspective. *Tijdschrit Persoonsgerichte Experiëntiële Psychotherapie, 60*(1), 5–18.

Dewitte, L., Granqvist, P., & Dezutter, J. (2018). Meaning through attachment: An integrative framework. *Psychological Reports*. Advance online publication. https: doi.org/10.1177/0033294118799739

Dewitte, L., Schellekens, T., Steger, M.F., Martela, F., Vanhooren, S., Vandenbulcke, M., & Dezutter, J. (2021). What can we learn about the concept of meaning in life from older adults with Alzheimer's disease? A directed content analysis study. *Journal of Happiness Studies, 22*, 2845–2871. https://doi.org/10.1007/s10902-020-00351-4

Dezutter, J., & Dewitte, L. (2019). "What good is life anymore, ma'am?" On meaning and sense-making in old age. *Journal of Positive Psychology, 2,* 10–15.

Edberg, A. K., Trogu, G., Manattini, A., Renn-Żurek, A., Modrzejewska, D. M., Woźnicka, E.B., Popovici, S., Pintilie, L., Beck, I., Virbalienė, A., & Šiurienė, A. (2023). Existential loneliness among older people from the perspective of health care professionals: A –European multicenter study. *Psychology Research and Behavior Management, 16,* 2241–2252. https://doi.org/10.2147/PRBM.S408547

Eliach, Y. (1989). *Chassidic tales of the Holocaust.* BZZTôH Publishing House.

Elliott, R., Bohart, A. C., Watson, J. C., & Murphy, D. (2018). Therapist empathy and client outcome: An updated meta-analysis. *Psychotherapy, 55*(4), 399–410. http://dx.doi.org/10.1037/pst0000175

Elliott, R., Watson, J. C., Goldman, R. N., & Greenberg, L. S. (2004). *Learning emotion-focused therapy: The process-experiential approach to change.* American Psychological Association.

Elliott, R., Watson, J.C., Timulak, L., & Sharbanee. J. (2021). Research on humanistic-experiential psychotherapies: Updated review. In M. Barkham, W. Lutz, & L. G. Castonguay (Eds.), *Bergin and Garfield's handbook of psychotherapy and behavior change* (7th ed; pp. 421–467). Wiley.

Ellis, L. (2020). *A clinician's guide to dream therapy: Implementing simple and effective dreamwork.* Routledge.

Eneman, M., & Vanhee, L. (2011). Verlies, herstel en zin bij het lijden onder schizofrenie [Loss, recovery, and meaning in suffering schizophrenia]. In H. Zock & W. Krikillion (Eds.), *Eindigheid in de geestelijke gezondheidszorg [Finality in mental health care]* (pp. 18–35). KSGV.

Erikson, E. H. (1962). *Young man Luther: A study in psychoanalysis and history.* Norton.

Ernst, J., Northoff, G., Böker, H., Seifritz, E., Grimm, S. (2012). Interoceptive awareness enhances neural activity during empathy. *Human Brain Mapping, 34*(7), 1615–1624. https://doi.org/10.1002/hbm.22014

Eubanks, C. F., Muran, J. C., & Safran, J. D. (2018). Alliance rupture repair: A meta-analysis. *Psychotherapy, 55*(4), 508–519. http://dx.doi.org/10.1037/pst0000185

Flückiger, C., Del Re, A. C., Wampold, B. E., & Horvath, A. O. (2018). The alliance in adult psychotherapy: A meta-analytic synthesis. *Psychotherapy, 55*(4), 316–340. https://doi.org/10.1037/pst0000172

Fortems, C., Dezutter, J., Dewitte, L., & Vanhooren, S. (2022). The mediating role of meaning in life between the therapeutic relationship and therapy outcome in person-centered and experiential psychotherapies. *Person-Centered & Experiential Psychotherapies, 21*(1), 73–93. https://doi.org/10.1080/14779757.2021.1938184

Frankel, E. (2005). *Sacred therapy: Jewish spiritual teachings on emotional healing and inner wholeness.* Shambhala Publications.

Frankl, V. E. (2006). *Man's search for meaning*. Beacon Press. (Originally published in 1959).

Frankl, V. E. (1967). *Psychotherapy and existentialism: Selected papers on logotherapy*. Penguin Books.

Frediani, G., Krieckemans, L., Seijnaeve, A., & Vanhooren, S. (2023). Engaging with the client's existential concerns: The impact on therapists and counsellors. *Person-centered & Experiential Psychotherapies, 22(3)*, 283–302. https://doi.org/10.1080/14779757.2022.2133000

Frediani, G., Rober, P. & Vanhooren, S. (2025). Maintaining therapeutic presence and empathy when engaging with a client's existential concerns. *Psychotherapy, 62(3)*, 376–386. https://psycnet.apa.org/doi/10.1037/pst0000588

Fuchs, T. (2013). Existential vulnerability: Toward a psychopathology of limit situations. *Psychopathology, 46*, 301–308. https://doi.org/10.1159/000351838

Fuchs, T. (2019). The life-world of persons with mood disorders. In G. Stanghellini, M. R. Broome, A. V. Fernandez, P. Fusar-Poli, A. Raballo, & R. Rosfort (Eds.), *The Oxford handbook of phenomenological psychopathology* (pp. 617–633). Oxford University Press.

Gardinger, P. (2001). *Kierkegaard*. Lemniscaat.

Geller, S. M., & Greenberg, L. S. (2012). *Therapeutic presence: A mindful approach to effective therapy*. American Psychological Association.

Gendlin, E. T. (1962). *Experiencing and the creation of meaning: A philosophical and psychological approach to the subjective*. Northwestern University Press.

Gendlin, E. T. (1964). A theory of personality change. In P. Worchel & D. Byrne (Eds.), *Personality change* (pp. 100–148). John Wiley & Sons.

Gendlin, E.T. (1970). Existentialism and experiential psychotherapy. In J. T. Hart & T. M. Tomlinson (Eds.), *New directions in client-centered therapy* (pp. 70–94). Houghton Mifflin Company.

Gendlin, E.T. (1973). Experiential psychotherapy. In R. Corsini (Ed.*), Current Psychotherapies* (pp. 317–352). Peacock.

Gendlin, E.T. (1978). *Focusing*. Everest House Publishers.

Gendlin, E.T. (1984). The client's client: The edge of awareness. In R.L. Levant & J.M. Shlien (Eds.), *Client-centered therapy and the person-centered approach. New directions in theory, research and practice* (pp. 76–107). Praeger.

Gendlin, E. T. (1986). *Let your body interpret your dreams*. Chiron publications.

Gendlin, E. T. (1990). The small steps of the therapy process: How they come and how they help them come. In G. Lietaer, J. Rombouts, & R. Van Balen (Eds.), *Client-centered and experiential psychotherapy in the nineties*. Leuven University Press.

Gendlin, E. T. (1996). *Focusing-oriented psychotherapy: A manual of the experiential method*. The Guilford Press.

Gendlin, E. T. (1997). *A process model.* The Focusing Institute.

Georganda, E. T. (2019). Eros, Thanatos, and the awakening of Oistros: Being in love with life and our world. *The Humanistic Psychologist, 48*(2), 133–141. http://dx.doi.org/10.1037/hum0000142

Geuzinge, R. (2015). Concrete zelf-zorg strategieën voor de therapeut: Compassie versus empathy [Concrete self-care strategies for the psychotherapist: Compassion versus empathy]. *Tijdschrift voor Cliëntgerichte Psychotherapie, 53*, 197–212.

Glaw, X., Kable, A., Hazelton, M., & Inder, K. (2017). Meaning in life and meaning of life in mental health care: An integrative literature review. *Issues in Mental Health Nursing, 38*(3), 243-252.

Glück, J., Bluck, S., & Weststrate, N. M. (2019). More on the MORE Life experience model: What we have learned (so far). *The Journal of Value Inquiry, 53*, 349–370. https://doi.org/10.1007/s10790-018-9661-x

Goldman, R. N., Vaz, A., & Rousmaniere, T. (2021). *Deliberate practice in emotion-focused therapy.* American Psychological Association.

Golovchanova, N., Dezutter, J., & Vanhooren, S. (2021). Meaning profiles and the perception of the working alliance at the start of outpatient person-centered, experiential, and existential psychotherapies. *Journal of Clinical Psychology, 77*(3), 770–781. https://doi.org/10.1002/jclp.23057

Gordon, S. (Ed.) (2013). *Neurophenomenology and its applications to psychology.* Springer.

Gordon, A. M., Stellar, J. E., Anderson, C. L., McNeil, G. D., Loew, D., & Keltner, D. (2017). The dark side of the sublime: Distinguishing a threat-based variant of awe. Journal of *Personality and Social Psychology, 113*, 310–328. https://doi.org/10.1037/pspp0000120

Greenberg, L. S., & Pascual-Leone, J. (2001). A dialectical constructivist view on the creation of personal meaning. *Journal of Constructivist Psychology, 14*(3), 165–186. https://doi.org/10.1080/10720530125970

Greenberg, L. S., Rice, L. N., & Elliott, R. (1993). *Facilitating emotional change: The moment-by-moment process.* The Guilford Press.

Greening, T. (1992). Existential challenges and responses. *The humanistic psychologist, 20*(1), 111–115.

Gundrum, M. (2007). Een therapiesessie bekeken door de lens van existentiële verantwoordelijkheid. [A therapy session viewed through the lens of existential responsibility]. *Tijdschrift voor Cliëntgerichte Psychotherapie, 45*(1), 19–32.

Gunst, E., & Vanhooren, S. (2018). The destructive pattern: An experiential and existential theory-building case study. *Person-Centered & Experiential Psychotherapies, 17*(1), 1–18. https://doi.org/10.1080/14779757.2017.1396239

Harrington, S., Pascual-Leone, A., Paivio, S., Edmondstone, C., & Baher, T. (2021). Depth of experiencing and therapeutic alliance: What predicts outcome for whom in emotion-focused therapy for trauma. *Psychology and Psychotherapy: Theory, Research and Practice*. Advance online publication. https://doi.org/10.11111/papt.12342

Heidegger, M. (1999). *Being and time*. Sun Publishing. (Originally published in 1927)

Hertmans, S. (2018). *Oorlog en Terpentijn* [*War and turpentine*]. De Bezige Bij.

Heschel, A. J. (2011a). *Man is not alone: The experience of God's presence*. Altoria. (Originally published in 1951)

Heschel, A. J. (2011b). *God seeks man: A philosophy of Judaism*. Abraxas. (Originally published in 1955)

Hickman, C., Marks, E., Pihkala, P., Clayton, S., Lewandowski, R. E., Mayall, E. E., Wray, B., Mellor, C., & van Susteren, L. (2021). Climate anxiety in children and young people and their beliefs about government responses to climate change: A global survey. *Lancet Planet Health, 5*, 863–873. https://doi.org/10.1016/S2542-5196(21)00278-3

Hill, C. E. (2017). Therapists' perspectives about working with meaning in life in psychotherapy: A survey. *Counseling Psychology Quarterly, 30*(4), 373–391. https://doi.org/10.1080/09515070.2016.1173014

Hill, C. E. (2018). *Meaning in life: A therapist's guide*. American Psychological Association.

Hlava, P., Elfers, J., Bieber, J., Maitra, S., Burge, C., Howard, A., Carbajal, R., Jamieson, M., & Casey, A. (2024). Reorienting through the body: The correlation among self-transcendent emotion experiences and interoceptive awareness. *Journal of Humanistic Psychology*. Advance online publication. https://doi.org/10.1177/00221678241292482

Hoffman, L. (2009). Introduction to existential psychology in a cross-cultural context: An East-West dialogue. In L. Hoffman, M. Yang, F. J., Kaklauskas, & A. Chan (Eds.), *Existential psychology East-West* (pp. 1–67). University of the Rockies Press.

Hoffman, L. (2014). The therapist's use if poetry in therapy: Deepening relationship and understanding through creativity. In M. Heery (Ed.), *Unearthing the moment: Mindful applications of existential-humanistic and transpersonal psychotherapy* (pp. 208–221). Tonglen Press.

Hoffman, L. (2021). Existential–humanistic therapy and disaster response: Lessons from the COVID-19 Pandemic. *Journal of Humanistic Psychology, 61*(1), 33–54.

Hohl, L. (2014). *Bergtocht* [*Mountain trip*]. Leesmagazine.

Holzhey-Kunz, A. (2014). *Daseinsanalysis*. Free Association Books.

Homer (2012). *Ilias & Odyssey*. (M. A. Schwarz, Trans.). Singel Publishers.

Ikemi, A. (2017). The radical impact of experiencing on psychotherapy theory: An examination of two kinds of crossing. *Person-centered & Experiential Psychotherapies, 16*(2), 159-172. https://doi.org/10.1080/14779757.2017.12323668

Ikemi, A., Okamura, S., & Tanaka, H. (2023). The experiencing model: Saying what we mean in the context of focusing in therapy. In E. R. Severson & K.

C. Krycka (Eds.), *The psychology and philosophy of Eugene Gendlin* (pp. 44–62). Routledge.

Iverach, L., Menzies, R. G., & Menzies, R. E. (2014). Death anxiety and its role in psychopathology: Reviewing the status of a transdiagnostic construct. *Clinical Psychology Review, 34*, 580-593. https://doi.org/10.1016/j.cpr.2014.09.002

Janoff-Bulman, R. (1992). *Shattered assumptions: Towards a new psychology of trauma*. The Free Press.

Jaspers, K. (2003). *Way to wisdom: An introduction to philosophy*. Yale University Press. (Originally published in 1951)

Jung, C. G. (1994). Herinneringen, dromen, gedachten [Memories, dreams, reflections]. Lemniscaat. (Originally published in 1961)

Kaufman, S. B. (2020). *Transcend: The new science of self-actualization*. Tarcher Perigee.

Keij, S. (2014). *Levinas in Practice: A guide to the best possible helping, privately and in the concern.* Klement/Pelckmans.

Kesebir, P. (2014). A quiet ego quiets death anxiety: Humility as an existential anxiety buffer. *Journal of Personality and Social Psychology, 106*, 610–623. https://doi.org/10.1037/a0035814

Kierkegaard, S. (2013). *Fear and trembling, and the sickness unto death. Translated and with notes by Walter Lowrie with a new introduction by Gordon Marino.* Princeton University Press. (Originally published in 1843)

Kierkegaard, S. (1978). *Wild geese. Diary notes 1846–1855. Compiled, translated and introductions provided by Drs. W. R. Scholtens.* Ten Have. (Originally published in 1846)

Kjellenberg, E., Nilsson, F., Daukantaitė, D., & Cardeña, E. (2013). Transformative narratives: The impact of working with war and torture survivors. *Psychological Trauma: Theory, Research, Practice, and Policy, 6*(2), 120–128. https://doi.org/10.1037/a0031966

Klein, J. W., Case, T. I., Fitness, J. (2017). Can the positive effects of inspiration be extended to different domains? *Journal of Applied Social Psychology, 48*, 28-34. https://doi.org/10.1111/jasp.12487

Klein, M. H., Mathieu, P. L., Gendlin, E. T., & Kiesler, D. J. (1969). *The experiencing scale: A research and training manual. Volume 1.* Wisconsin Psychiatric Institute.

Kramer, R. (2019). *The birth of relationship therapy: Carl Rogers meets Otto Rank.* Psychosozial-Verlag.

Krebs, P., Norcross, J. C., Nicholson, J. M., Prochaska, J. O. (2018). Stages of change and psychotherapy outcomes: A review and meta-analysis. *Journal of Clinical Psychology, 74*, 1964-1979. https://doi.org/10.1002/jclp.22683

Krycka, K. C., & Ikemi, A. (2016). Focusing-oriented – experiential psychotherapy: From research to practice. In D. J. Cain, K. Keenan, & S. Rubin (Eds.), *Humanistic psychotherapies: Handbook of research and practice, second edition* (pp. 251-282). American Psychological Association. https://doi.org/10.1037/14775-009

Laing, R. D. (1965). *The divided self: An existential study in sanity and madness.* Penguin Books.

Längle, A. (2018). Spirituality in psychotherapy? The relationship of immanence and transcendence in existential analysis. In S. Laengle & C. Wurm (Eds.), *Living your own life: Existential analysis in action* (pp. 35–52). Routlegde.

Lao Tzu (2000). *Tao te ching. Based on the translation by Stephen Mitchell.* Ten Have.

Larson, D. G., Chastain, R. L., Hoyt, W. T., Ayzenberg, R. (2015). Self-concealment: integrative review and working model. *Journal of Social and Clinical Psychology, 34*, 8, 705–774.

Leijssen, M. (1998). Focusing microprocesses. In L. S. Greenberg, J. C. Watson, and G. Lietaer (Eds.), *Handbook of experiential psychotherapy* (pp. 121–154). The Guilford Press.

Leijssen, M. (2007). Making space for the inner guide. *American Journal of Psychotherapy, 61*, 255-270.

Leijssen, M. (2009). Psychotherapy as search and care for the soul. *Person-Centered & Experiential Psychotherapies, 8*(1), 18–32. https://doi.org/10.1080/14779757.2009.9688478

Leijssen, M. (2013). *Living from love: A path to existential well-being.* Lannoo.

Leijssen, M. (2021). Living forward: The challenge of carrying forward Gendlin's legacy. In N. Kypriotakis & J. Moore (Eds.), *Senses of focusing. Volume 2* (pp. 79–94). Eurasia Publications.

Leijssen, M. (2025). Gids voor gesprekstherapie, Jubileum-editie [Guidebook for psychotherapy (Jubilee ed.). Boom.

Li, J., Dou, K. & Liang, Y. (2020). The relationship between presence of meaning, search for meaning, and subjective well-being: A three-level meta-analysis based on the meaning in life questionnaire. *Journal of Happiness Studies.* Advance online publication. https://doi.org/10.1007/s10902-020-00230-y

Lou, N. (2019, November). *Eugene T. Gendlin: My relation to an ultimate.* [Video, YouTube]. https://www.youtube.com/watch?v=NonZSHazpjs.

Lou, N. (2020). *Eugene T. Gendlin: Living is always a fresh forming.* [Video, YouTube]. https://www.youtube.com/watch?v=7e8hUXtX8UA&t=31s

Loveling, V. (2021). *Een revolverschot* [*A gun-shot*]. De Geus. (Originally published in 1911)

Lux., M. (2021). Working factors of person-centeredness from a neuroscience perspective. *Journal of Person-Centered Experiential Psychotherapy, 59*(4), 220–231.

Maddi, S. R. (2013). Hardiness as the existential courage to grow through searching for meaning. In J. A. Hicks & C. Routledge (Eds.), *The experience of meaning in life: Classical perspectives, emerging themes, and controversies* (pp. 227–239). Springer.

Madison, G. (2010). Focusing on existence: Five facets of an experiential-existential model. *Person-centered & Experiential Psychotherapies, 9*, 189–204. https://doi.org/10.1080/14779757.2010.9689066

Madison, G. (2014). Exhilarating pessimism: Focusing-oriented existential psychotherapy. In G. Madison (Ed.), *Theory and practice of focusing-oriented psychotherapy. Beyond the talking cure* (pp. 113–127). Jessica Kingsley Publishers.

Maitland, D. W. M. (2020). Experiential avoidance and fear of intimacy: A contextual behavioral account of loneliness and resulting psychopathology symptoms. *Journal of Contextual Behavioral Science, 18*, 193-200. https://doi.org/10.1016/jcbs.2020.10.002

Marcel, M. (1969). *Om de menselijke waardigheid: Een terugblik op mijn existentiële uitgangspunten* [The existential background of human dignity]. Bijleveld.

Martela, F., & Steger, M. F. (2016). The three meanings of meaning in life: Distinguishing coherence, purpose and significance. *The Journal of Positive Psychology, 11*, 531–545. https://doi.org/10.1080/17439760.2015.1137623

Martínez, M., Arantzamendi, M., Belar, A., Carrasco, J. M., Carvajal, A., Rullán, M., & Centeno, C. (2017). Dignity therapy, a promising intervention in palliative care: A comprehensive systematic literature review. *Palliative Medicine, 31*(6), 492–509.

Maslow, A. H. (1964). *Religions, values, and peak-experiences*. Kappa Delta PI.

May, R. (1975). *The courage to create*. W. W. Norton & Company.

May, R. (1983). *The discovery of being*. W. W. Norton & Company.

May, R. (1991). *The cry for myth*. W. W. Norton & Company.

May, R. (1996). *The meaning of anxiety*. W. W. Norton & Company.

Mearns, D. (2002). Further theoretical propositions in regard to self theory within person-centered therapy. *Peron-centered & Experiential Psychotherapies, 1*(1), 14-27. https://doi.org/10.1080/14779757.2002.9688275

Mearns, D., & Cooper, M. (2005). *Working at relational depth in counselling and psychotherapy*. Sage.

Merleau-Ponty, M. (2002). *Phenomenology of perception*. Routlegde. (Originally published in 1945)

Missiaen, C., & Vanhooren, S. (2021). Facing our existential demons: A focusing-oriented and existential approach. In N. Kypriotakis & J. Moore (Eds.), *Senses of Focusing* (Vol. 1; pp. 317–336). Eurasia Publications.

Moore, J. (2024). Spirituality and transcendence. In G. Di Malta, M. Cooper, M. O'Hara, Y. Gololob, & S. Stephen (Eds.), *The handbook of person-centred psychotherapy and counselling* (3rd ed.; pp. 157–170). Bloomsbury

Morinis, A. (2007). *Everyday holiness: The Jewish spiritual path of mussar*. Trumpeter.

Moustakas, C. (1972). *Love and solitude: Aloneness as a decisive moment of inner growth*. Lemniscaat.

Moustakas, C. (1994). *Existential psychotherapy and the interpretation of dreams.* Jason Aronson.

Moss, R. (1996). *Conscious dreaming: A spiritual path for everyday life.* Three Rivers Press.

Nederlandse Vereniging voor Psychotherapie (2022). *Factsheet person-centered experiential psychotherapies.* https://assets.psychotherapie.nl/p/229378/none/Dvdp2022/NVP_Factsheet%202022%20Persoonsgerichte%20experie%CC%88ntie%CC%88le%20psychotherapie%20bij%20volwassenen%20def.pdf

Norcross, J. C., & Lambert, M. J. (2018). Psychotherapy relationships that work III. *Psychotherapy, 55*(4), 303–315. http://dx.doi.org/10.1037/pst0000193.

Orme, WW., Bowersox, L., Vanwoerden, S., Fonagy, P., & Sharp, C. (2019). The relationship between epistemic trust and borderline pathology in an adolescent inpatient sample. *Borderline Personality Disorder and Emotion Dysregulation, 6* (13), 1–9. https://doi.org/10.1186/s40479-019-0110-7

Pappas, S. (2025). PTSD and trauma: New APA guidelines highlight evidence-based treatments. *APA's Monitor on Psychology, 56(5)*, 44. https://www.apa.org/monitor/2025/07-08/guidelines-treating-ptsd-trauma

Park, C. L. (2010). Making sense of the meaning literature: An integrative review of meaning. making and its effects on adjustment to stressful life events. *Psychological Bulletin, 136*, 257–301. https://doi.org/10.1037/a0018301

Pascual-Leone, A. (2017). How clients "change emotion with emotion": A program of research on emotional processing. *Psychotherapy Research.* Advance online publication. https://doi.org/10.1080/10503307.2017.1349350

Pellens, H. (2025). The existential layers of depression: An exploration of depression as an affective, embodied and relational experience. Unpublished doctoral thesis. KU Leuven.

Pellens, H., Dezutter, J., Luyten, P., & Vanhooren, S. (2025). The anxious body: A cross- cultural quantitative study. *Journal of Humanistic Psychology.* Online first publication. https://doi.org/10.1177/00221678251326138

Peluso, P. R., & Freund, R. R. (2018). Therapist and client emotional expression and psychotherapy outcomes: A meta-analysis. *Psychotherapy, 55*(4), 461–472. http://dx.doi.orh/10.1037/pst0000165

Petitmengin, C. (2017). Enaction as a lived experience: Towards a radical neurophenomenology. *Constructivist Foundations, 12*(2), 139–147.

Pinheiro, P., Gonçalves, M. M., Sousa, I., & Salgado, J. (2021). What is the effect of emotional processing on depression? A longitudinal study. *Psychotherapy Research, 31*(4), 507–519. https://doi.org/10503307.2020.1781951

Pommerenk, A. (2018, Aug. 25). *The right to exist.* https://apommenk.medium.com/i-dont-have-the-right-to-exist-757b76ccb705

Preston, L. (2007). Beyond words: The implicit. Lynn Preston interviews Eugene T. Gendlin. *Relay Therapy Media.* https://www.youtube.com/watch?v=AnJu83ZORaE

Proulx, T. (2013). Meaning maintenance Model: Introducing Soren to existential social psychology. In J. A. Hicks & C. Routledge (Eds.), *The experience of meaning in life: Classical perspectives, emerging themes, and controversions* (pp. 47–59). Springer.

Prouty, G. (1994). *Theoretical evolutions in person-centered experiential therapy: Applications to schizophrenics and retarded psychoses.* Praeger.

Rank, O. (1932). *Art and artist: Creative urge and personality development.* Knopf.

Rank, O. (1936). *Will therapy: An analysis of the therapeutic process in terms of relationship.* Knopf.

Rank, O. (1996). *A psychology of difference: The American lectures.* R. Kramer (Ed.). Princeton University Press.

Rank, O. (2014). *The trauma of birth.* Routledge. (Originally published in 1929)

Renders, K. (2005). Rocco aan de rand: Existentiële thema's in de psychotherapie van een adolescent [Rocco on the edge: Existential themes in adolescent psychotherapy]. *Tijdschrift voor Psychotherapie, 31*(4), 165–175.

Reynaert, P. (2006). *Husserl: Een inleiding [Husserl: An introduction].* Pelckmans/Klement.

Rim, K. L., Hill, C. E., & Kivlighan, D. M. Jr. (2022). Changes in meaning in life, working alliance, and outcome in psychodynamic psychotherapy: What leads to what? *Journal of Counseling Psychology.* Advance online publication. https://doi.org/10.1037/cou0000636

Rogers, C. R. (1942). *Counseling and psychotherapy.* Houghton Mifflin Company.

Rogers, C. R. (1951). *Client-centered therapy.* London, UK: Constable.

Rogers, C. R. (1957). The necessary and sufficient conditions of therapeutic personality change. *Journal of Consulting Psychology, 21,* 59–103.

Rogers, C. R. (1961). *On becoming a person.* Houghton Mifflin Company.

Rogers, C. R. (1980). *A way of being.* Houghton Mifflin Company.

Rowling, J. K. (2007). *Harry Potter en de relieken van de dood [Harry Potter and the relics of death].* Uitgeverij De Harmonie.

Ryff, C. D. (2012). Existential well-being and health. In P. T. P. Wong (Ed.), *The human quest for meaning: Theories, research, and applications* 2nd ed.; pp. 233–247). Routledge.

Safran, J. D., & Muran, J. C. (2003). *Negotiating the therapeutic alliance: A relational treatment guide.* Guilford Publications.

Sartre, J. P. (1980). *Over het existentialisme* [Existentialism is a humanism]. Bruna. (Originally published in 1965)

Sartre, J. P. (2003). *Het zijn en het niets* [Being and nothingness]. Lemniscaat. (Originally published in 1943)

Schneider, K. J. (2009). *Awakening to awe: Personal stories of profound transformation.* Jason Aronson.

Schneider, K. J. (2013). *The polarized mind: Why it's killing us and what we can do about it.* University Professor Press.

Schneider, K. J. (2015). *Existential-integrative psychotherapy: Guideposts to the core of practice.* Routledge.

Schneider, K. J. (2023). *Life-enhancing anxiety: Key to a sane world.* University Professors Press.

Schneider, K. J., & Krug, O. T. (2026). *Existential-humanistic therapy* (3rd ed.). American Psychological Association.

Schneider, K. J., Galvin, J., & Serlin, I. (2009). Rollo May on existential therapy. *Journal of Humanistic Psychology, 49*, 4, 419–434. https://doi.org/10.1177/0022167809340241

Schnell, T. (2010). Existential indifference: Another quality of meaning in life. *Journal of Humanistic Psychology, 50*(3), 351–373. https://doi.org/10.1177/0022167809360259

Shaver, P. R., & Mikulincer, M. (2012). An attachment perspective on coping with existential concerns. In P. R. Shaver, & M. Mikulincer (Eds.) *Meaning, mortality, and choice: The social psychology of existential concerns.* American Psychological Association.

Simopoulou, Z. (2019). *Young children's existential encounters.* Palgrave Macmillan.

Singh, T., Pascual-Leone, A., Morrison, O.P., & Greenberg, L. (2021). Working with emotion predicts sudden gains during experiential therapy for depression. *Psychotherapy Research, 31*(7–8), 895–908. https://doi.org/10.1080/10503307.2020.1866784

Sips, R. (2019). Psychosis as a dialectic of aha- and anti-aha-experiences. *Schizophrenia Bulletin,* 45 (5), 952–955. https://doi.org/10.1093/schbul:sby072

Spinelli, E. (2005). *The interpreted world: An introduction to phenomenological psychology.* Sage.

Spit, L. (2016). *Het smelt* [*It melts*]. Das Mag Uitgeverij.

Stanghellini, G., Broome, M. R., Fernandez, A. V. , Fusar-Poli, P., Raballo, A., & Rosfort, R. (2019). *The Oxford handbook of phenomenological psychopathology.* Oxford University Press.

Steele LeBeau, C., & Webster, E. J. (2022). The embodied experience of vulnerability of first-time parents: An existential-phenomenological study of the shared experiences between first-time couples. *The Humanistic Psychologist, 49*(4), 519–542. https://doi.org/10.1037/hum0000189

Steger, M. F. (2022). Making meaning in life: A thematic review of successful experimental psychological and psychotherapeutic interventions. *Atlantis Highlights in Social Sciences, Education and Humanities, 704*, 5–20. https://doi.org/10.2991/978-94-6463-096-1_2

Stellar, J. E., Gordon, A, Anderson, C. L, Piff, P. K., McNeil, G. D., & Keltner, D. (2018). Awe and humility. *Journal of Personality and Social Psychology, 114*, 258–269. https://doi.org/10.1037/pspi0000109

Stillman, T. F., Baumeister, R. F., Lambert, N. M., Crescioni, A. W., DeWall, C. N., & Fincham, F. D. (2009). Alone and without purpose: Life loses meaning following social exclusion. *Journal of Experimental Social Psychology, 45*, 686–694. https://doi.org/10.1016/j.jesp.2009.03.007

Stinckens, N. (2008). Werken met de innerlijke criticus: Microtheorie van een procestaak [Working with the inner critic: Micro-theory of a process task]. In G. Lietaer, G. Vanaershot, J. A. Snijders, & R. J. Takens (Eds.), *Handboek gesprekstherapie: De persoonsgerichte experiëntiële benadering [Handbook of talk therapy: The person-centered experiential approach]* (pp. 433–456). De Tijdstroom.

Sundström , M., Edberg, A.-K., Rämgård, M., & Blomqvist, K. (2018). Encountering existential loneliness among older people: Perspectives of health care professionals. *International Journal of Qualitative Studies on Health and Well-being, 13*(1). https://doi.org/10.1080/17482631.2018.1474673

Swildens, H. (1997). *Procesgerichte gesprekstherapie [Process-oriented Psychotherapy]*. De Tijdstroom.

Taft, J. (1958). *Otto Rank: A biographical study based on notebooks, letters, collected writings, therapeutic achievements and personal associations.* The Julian Press.

Taft, J. (1962). *The dynamics of therapy in a controlled relationship*. Dover Publications. (Originally published in 1933)

Tedeschi, R.G. & Calhoun, L.G. (2004). Posttraumatic growth: Conceptual foundations and empirical evidence. *Psychological Inquiry, 15,* 1–18.

Tedeschi, R. G., & Calhoun, L. G. (2012). Pathways to personal transformation: Theoretical and empirical developments. In P. T. P. Wong (Ed.), *The human quest for meaning: Theories, research and applications. Second edition* (pp. 559–572). Routledge.

Telzera, E., Fuligni A. J., Lieberman, M. D., & Galván, A. (2014). Neural sensitivity to eudaimonic and hedonic rewards differentially predict adolescent depressive symptoms over time. *Proceedings of the National Academy of Sciences, 111,* 18, 6600–6605. https://doi.org/10.1073/pnas.1323014111

Temple, M., & Gall, T. L. (2018). Working through existential anxiety toward authenticity: A spiritual journey of meaning making. *Journal of Humanistic Psychology, 58*(2), 168–193.

Thrash, T. M., Moldovan, E. G., Oleynick, V. C., & Maruskin, L. A. (2014). The psychology of inspiration. *Social and Personality Psychology Compass, 8/9*, p. 495–510. https://doi.org/10.1111/spc3.12127

Tillich, P. (2000). *The courage to be*. Yale University press. (Originally published in 1952)

Timulak, L., & Creaner, M. (2010). Qualitative meta-analysis of outcomes of person-centered and experiential psychotherapies. In. M. Cooper, J. C. Watson, & D. Hölldampf (Eds.), *Person-centered and experiential therapies work: A review of the research on counseling, psychotherapy, and related practices* (pp. 65–90). PCCS Books.

Timulak, L., & Keogh, D. (2020). Emotion-focused therapy: A transdiagnostic formulation. *Journal of Contemporary Psychotherapy, 50,* 1–13. https://doi.org/10.1007/s10879-019-09426-7

Tsirimokou, A., Kloess, J. A., Dhinse, S. K. (2023). Vicarious post-traumatic growth in professionals exposed to traumatogenic material: A systematic literature review. Trauma, Violence, & Abuse, 24(3), 1848–1866. https:/doi.org/10.1177/15248380221082079

Vaidya, D. (2013). Re-visioning Rogers' second condition: Anxiety as the face of ontological incongruence and basis for the principle of non-directivity. *Person-centered & Experiential Psychotherapies, 12*, 209–222. https://doi.org/10.1080/14779757.2013.836128

Van Assche, L., Luyten, P., Bruffaerts, R., Persoons, P., van de Ven, L., & Vandenbulcke, M. (2013). Attachment in old age: Theoretical assumptions, empirical findings and implications for clinical practice. *Clinical Psychology Review, 33*, 67–81. http://dx.doi.org/10.1016/j.cpr.2012.10.003

Van de Veire, C. (2024). *Liminal space*. Workshop VVCEPC, Leuven, June 2024

van Deurzen, E. (1997). *Everyday mysteries: Existential dimensions of psychotherapy*. Routledge

van Deurzen, E. (2018, Oct. 11). *Finding existential freedom.* [Video, Youtube]. https://www.youtube.com/watch?v=9sXFlRmiSzg

van Heycop ten Ham, B. & van Megen, H. (2014). Perfectionisme, intolerantie voor onzekerheid en dwangmatig gedrag. In B. van Heycop ten Ham, M. Hulsbergen, & E. Bohlmeijer (Eds.), *Transdiagnostische factoren: Theorie en prakijk* (pp. 211–239). Boom.

Vanhooren, S. (1997). *Het gebruik van sprookjes in psychotherapy* [*The use of fairy tales in psychotherapy*]. Unpublished licentiate thesis. Ghent University.

Vanhooren, S. (2010). Contact met de leegte [Contacting the void]. In M. Gundrum & N. Stinckens (Eds.), *De schatkist van de therapeut* [*The treasure chest of the therapist*] (pp. 62–64). Acco.

Vanhooren, S. (2014). De moed of niet te weten, het lef om niet te kunnen [The courage not to know, the courage not to do]. Tijdschrift Cliëntgerichte Psychotherapie, *52*, 100–115.

Vanhooren, S. (2016a). The Daseins-exercise. *EdX MOOC Existential Well-being Counseling: A person-centered experiential approach.* https://www.edx.org/course/existential-well-being-counseling-a-person-centere

Vanhooren, S. (2016b). Door de hel gaan: De innerlijke reis naar posttraumatische groei [Going through hell: The inner journey to posttraumatic growth]. *Tijdschrift Persoonsgerichte Experientiele Psychotherapie, 54*(1), 13–19.

Vanhooren, S. (2017). Een loden rugzak: Leven met schuld op zoek naar vrede [A leaden backpack: Living with guilt in search of peace]. *Handelingen, 2. https://www.handelingen.com/index.php/jaargangen/2017/219-2017-2-gevangen*

Vanhooren, S. (2018). Experiential–existential psychotherapy: Deepening existence, engaging with life. In M. Bazzanu (Ed.), *Re-visioning person-centred therapy: The theory and practice of a radical paradigm* (pp. 151–163). Routledge.

Vanhooren, S. (2019a). Struggling with meaninglessness: A case study from an experiential-existential perspective. *Person-centered & Experiential Psychotherapies, 18*(1), 1–21. https://doi.org/10.1080/14779757.2019.1572029

Vanhooren, S. (2019b). Existentiële empathie: Over experiëntiële en existentiële aanwezigheid [Existential empathy: On experiential and existential presence]. *Tijdschrift Persoonsgerichte Experiëntiële Psychotherapie,* 57, 3–10.

Vanhooren, S. (2019c). Op zoek naar zingeving? Antwoorden uit de positieve en experiëntieel-existentiële psychology [In search of meaning? Answers from the positive and experiential-existential psychology]. In: W. Krikilion, J. Pieper (Eds.), *Positieve psychologie en zingeving: Integratie en toepassingen [Positive psychology and meaning: Integration and applications* (51–66). KSGV

Vanhooren, S. (2022a). Existential empathy: The challenge of "being" in therapy and counseling. *Religions, 13,* 752. https://doi.org/10.3390/rel13080752

Vanhooren, S. (2022b). Existential empathy: A necessary condition for posttraumatic growth and wisdom in clients and therapists. In M. Ferrari & M. Munroe (Eds.), *Post-traumatic growth to psychological well-being: Coping wisely with adversity* (pp. 225–244). Springer.

Vanhooren, S., & Cooper, M. (2024). Existentially-informed person-centred therapy. In Cooper, M. (Ed.), *Tribes of the person-centred nation: An introduction to the schools of therapy related to the person-centred approach, 3rd edition (pp. 183-200)*. PCCS Books.

Vanhooren, S., Conrado Veiga Bosquetti, Y., & Frediani, G. (2022). The development of the Existential Empathy Questionnaire. *Journal of Humanistic Psychology.* Advance online publication. https://doi.org/10.1177/00221678221144599

Vanhooren, S., Grosemans, A., & Breynaert, J. (2022). Focusing, the felt sense, and meaning in life. *Person-centered & Experiential Psychotherapies, 21*(3), 250–268. https://doi.org/10.1080/14779757.2022.2028660

Vanhooren, S., Leijssen, M., & Dezutter, J. (2016). Profiles of meaning and search for meaning among prisoners. *The Journal of Positive Psychology, 11*(6), 622–633. https://doi.org/10.1080/17439760.2015.1137625

Vanhooren S., Leijssen M., & Dezutter J. (2017a). Ten prisoners on a search for meaning: A qualitative study of loss and growth during incarceration. *The Humanistic Psychologist, 45*, 162–178. https://doi.org/10.1037/hum0000055.

Vanhooren, S., Leijssen, M., & Dezutter, J. (2017b). Posttraumatic growth in sex offenders: A pilot study with a mixed-method design. *International Journal of Offender Therapy and Comparative Criminology, 61*(2), 171–190. https://doi.org/10.1177/0306624X15590834

Vanhooren S., Leijssen M., & Dezutter J. (2018). Posttraumatic growth during incarceration: A case study from an experiential-existential perspective. *Journal of Humanistic Psychology, 58*(2), 144–167. https://doi.org/10.1177/0022167815621647.

Vanhooren, S., Missiaen, C., & Renders, K. (2024). Experiential practices: Explicit ways of facilitating therapeutic processes. In G. Di Malta, M. Cooper, M. O'Hara, Y. Gololob, & S. Stephen (Eds.), *The handbook of person-centred psychotherapy and counselling* (3rd ed.; pp. 252–265). Bloomsbury.

Vanhooren, S., & Schneider, K. (2026). Existential and humanistic integrative therapies. In L. Hoffman, L.X. Vallejos, D. Hocoy, P. Tummala-Narra, & E.M. DeRobertis (Eds.), *APA Handbook of Humanistic and Existential Psychology* (Vol. 2): *Clinical and Social Applications* (pp. 351–368). American Psychological Association. https://doi.org/10.1037/0000432-018

Van Veen, A. F., & van der Sijs, N. (1997). *Etymologisch woordenboek: De oorsprong van onze woorden. Tweede editie [Etymological dictionary: The origin of our words* (2nd ed.) Van Dale Lexicographie.

van Wijngaarden, E., van Thiel, G., Hartog, I., van den Berg, V., Zomers, M., Sachs, A., Uiterwaal, C., Leget, C., Buijsen, M., Damoiseaux, R., Mostert, M., & Merzel, M. (2020). *Het perspectiefonderzoek. Perspectieven op de doodswens van ouderen die niet ernstig ziek zijn: De mensen en cijfers. [The Perspective study. Perspectives on the death wishes of the elderly who are not seriously ill: The people and the numbers]*. ZonMw.

Verdegem, S., Dezutter, J., Vandenberghe, J., Debeurme, I., & Vanhooren, S. (2022). Wa kanker mee? Existentiële groepstherapie met mensen met kanker. [What can I do with it? Existential group therapy in people with cancer.] Tijdschrift Klinische Psychologie*, 52*(1), 50–70.

Verdegem, S., Rens, A., Vandenberghe, J., Dezutter, J., Vanhie, T., Bemelmans, L., & Vanhooren, S. (2025). Relating to life and death: A qualitative study of individuals with a long-lasting death wish related to unbearable psychiatric suffering. *International Journal of Qualitative Studies on Health and Well-Being, 20*(1). https://doi.org/10.1080/17482631.2025.2469361

Verhofstadt-Denève, L. (1994). *Self-reflection and person development: A handbook for developmental psychotherapy*. Acco.

Verhofstadt-Denève, L., Vyt, A., & Van Geert, P. (1991). *Handbook of developmental psychology: Foundations and theories* (3rd rev. ed.). Bohn Stafleu Van Loghum

Vos, J. (2022). Meaning in life across cultures and times: An evidence-based overview. In A. C. Chan, M. F. Steger, R. C. Chui, N. Y. Siu, S. C. P. Wong, I. , & B. Y. Lam (Eds.). Proceedings of the Meaning in Life International Conference 2022: Cultivating, promoting, and enhancing meaning in life across cultures and life span (MIL 2022). *AHSSEH, 704*, 21–40. https://doi.org/10.2991/978-94-6463-096-1_3.

Vos, J. (2023). Existential psychological therapies: An overview of empirical research. *Pratiques Psychologiques, 29*, 211–229. https://doi.org/10.1016/j.prps.2023.06.001

Vos, J., & Vitali, D. (2018). The effects of psychological meaning-centered therapies on quality of life and psychological stress: A meta-analysis. *Palliative and Supportive Care, 16*(5), 608–632. https://doi.org/10.1017/S1478951517000931

Wachowski, L., & Wachowski, L. (1999). *The Matrix.* https://en.wikipedia.org/wiki/The_Matrix_(franchise)

Wampold, B. (2015). How important are the common factors in psychotherapy? An update. *World Psychiatry, 14*, 270–277.

Warner, M. S. (2013). Difficult client process. In M. Cooper, M. O'Hara, P.F. Schmid, & A.C. Bohart (Eds.), *The handbook of person-centred psychotherapy & counselling* (2nd ed.; pp. 343–358). Palgrave.

Watson, J. C. (2016). The role of empathy in psychotherapy: Theory, research, and practice. In D.J. Cain, K. Keenan, and S. Rubin (Eds.), *Humanistic psychotherapies: Handbook of research and practice* (2nd ed.; pp. 115–145). American Psychological Association.

Weiser Cornell, A. (2013). *Focusing in clinical practice: The essence of change.* Norton.

Weststrate, N. M., & Glück, J. (2017). Hard-earned wisdom: Exploratory processing of difficult life experience is positively associated with wisdom. *Developmental Psychology, 53*, 800–814. https://doi.org/10.1037/dev0000286

Wille, R. (2014). The shame of existing: An extreme form of shame. *The International Journal of Psychoanalysis, 95*, 695–717. https://doi.org/10.111/1745-8315.12208

Wong, M. L., Cleland, C. E., Arend, D. Jr., Bartlett, S., Cleaves, H. J. II, Demarest, H., Prabhua, A., Lunine, J. I., & Hazena, R. M. (2023). On the roles of function and selection in evolving systems. *PNAS, 120*(3). https://doi.org/10.1073/pnas.2310223120

Yalom, I. (1980). *Existential psychotherapy*. Basic Books.

Yalom, I. (2008). *Facing the sun: Death anxiety and how to overcome it*. Balans Publishers.

Yang, M. C. (Ed.) (2017). *Existential psychology and the way of the Tao: Meditations on the writings of Zhuangzi*. Routledge.

Yu, E. A., Chang, E. C., & Kim, J. H. J. (2016). Asian American culturally relevant values as predictors of meaning in life in Asian and European American college students: Evidence for cultural differences? *Asian American Journal of Psychology, 7*(3), 159–166. http://dx.doi.org/10.1037/aap0000042

Zegers, H. (2021). *Welfare science: Positive psychology in 30 questions*. Kloosterhof Publishing House.

Zegers, H., & Vanhooren, S. (2026). The use of research in humanistic and existential psychotherapy. In L. Hoffman, L.X. Vallejos, D. Hocoy, P. Tummala-Narra, & E.M. DeRobertis (Eds.), *APA Handbook of Humanistic and Existential Psychology* (Vol. 2: *Clinical and Social Applications*, (133–152). American Psychological Association. https://doi.org/10.1037/0000432-007

Zilcha-Mano, S., Mikulincer, M., & Shaver, P. R. (2011). Pet in the therapy room: An attachment perspective on animal-assisted therapy. *Attachment & Human Development, 13* (6), 541-561. https://doi.org/10.1080/14616734.2011.608987

Zock, H. (1990). *A psychology of ultimate concern: Erik. H. Erikson's contribution to the psychology of religion*. Atlanta.

Index

A
Anavah, 93–94, 117, 178–179, 185, 196
Anxiety
Existential anxiety, ii, 8, 47–48, 52, 83, 103
Authenticity, 14, 22, 38, 67, 90, 149–150
Autonomy, 13, 63, 68, 70, 73–74, 120, 143, 154, 168, 170, 191–192
Awareness
Existential awareness, iv, 1–8, 10–14, 16–19, 23, 33, 66, 96–97, 99–100, 104, 155, 182
Awe, i, 35, 52–53, 66, 97, 120, 130, 144, 147, 197

B
Basic trust, 4, 8, 10, 40–42, 109–112, 116–118, 128, 137, 145, 152
Being, i–iii, 4, 6–11, 13–17, 22, 27, 31–32, 45, 87–90, 96–103, 105–106, 109, 113–116, 162–164, 169, 184
Bodily, 8, 10, 12–13, 28, 40, 45–48, 52, 56, 84, 103, 125, 141–142, 163, 171, 175, 185
Body
Embodied, iii, 2–3, 10, 20, 33, 44–47, 50, 78, 83, 92, 99–100, 112, 119–120, 124–125, 146, 163, 171, 187
Buber, v, 20–21, 31, 53, 64, 66–67, 69, 89, 94, 119, 152, 177–179, 188
Bugental, ii–iv, 3, 11–12, 14, 36, 47, 78, 125–126, 128–129, 136–137, 146, 157, 190

C
Carrying forward, iii, 82, 94, 160, 163, 167, 176
Chair
Chair dialogue, 90, 165, 167
Empty chair, 166
Choice, iv, 10, 61, 75–76, 78, 84, 91, 93, 101, 103, 126, 137, 145–146, 159, 169–170, 172, 183
Conditions of worth, 39–40, 51, 57
Congruence, 70–71, 188
Connectedness, 3, 59, 63–64, 68, 92, 101, 103, 142, 144, 152, 170, 184, 188
Cosm
Cosmic, ii, 10–11, 13, 53
Macro-cosm, 52
Micro-cosm, 52
Crossing, iii, 56–57, 174–176

D
Das Ganze, 51–52, 69, 97, 130, 176
Dasein, 64, 105–106, 184
Death
Death anxiety, ii, 27, 29–30, 33, 37–38, 65, 102, 130, 154, 187
Depression, ii, 25, 41–42, 48, 55, 71–73, 77, 79, 83, 87, 90, 102–105, 122, 131–132, 134, 138, 142, 146, 152–154, 171, 186
Despair, 5, 8, 15, 22, 32, 53, 78, 103–104, 106, 130, 137, 142, 162–164, 175, 181
Dreams, 38, 65, 67, 99, 104, 157–159, 167, 180

E
Emotion
Emotion regulation, 114–115, 125, 138
Over-regulation, 82
Under-regulation, 82
Empathy
Existential empathy, v, 15, 54, 155–157, 161, 194
Emptiness, ii, 48, 53, 55, 57, 72–73, 132, 184
Experiencing, ii–iii, 23, 28–31, 35, 37, 42–52, 56–57, 68–71, 85–87, 98–99, 106, 119, 141, 174–176, 194

F
Fear
Fear of life, 37–39, 58, 62, 77, 145
Felt sense, 28–30, 35–36, 47–49, 56–57, 65, 72, 78, 80, 83–84, 90, 92–93, 103, 126, 140, 146, 150, 158, 160, 163, 180, 183–184, 190
Focusing, iii–v, 28–29, 40, 47–49, 52, 57, 67, 72, 83, 90–91, 103, 115–116, 132, 135, 147, 149–150, 152, 160, 162–163, 180, 183
Frankl, 4, 40, 42–43, 53–55, 58, 76, 88, 101, 109–110, 144
Freedom
Experiential freedom, 82, 84, 86, 89, 112, 137, 144, 146, 169, 176, 183

G
Gendlin, iii–iv, 2, 7, 10–12, 19–20, 23, 28, 33–36, 44–45, 47, 49, 53, 78, 81–83, 87, 92, 97–99, 106–107, 127, 150, 158, 162–164, 180, 188
Greening, iv, 22–23, 43, 76, 100–102, 188
Growth, 3, 7, 23, 26, 34, 36–39, 58–59, 62, 68, 70, 98–99, 116–122, 135–139, 157, 172–173, 176–178, 185, 196
Guilt
Existential guilt, 6, 18, 27, 75, 77, 88, 144, 147, 154, 172, 186–187

H
Heidegger, 8–9, 11, 53, 63, 105, 184
Helplessness, 15, 78, 103–104, 137, 144
Heschel, i, 6, 31, 35, 59
Hineini, 184–185
Hope, iii, v, 24, 80, 85, 123, 130, 137, 139, 147, 165
Hopelessness, 5, 55, 103–104, 106, 144, 159

I
Incongruence, 40, 84, 97–98, 119, 171
Inspiration, v, 172–181, 194
Isolation
Existential isolation, ii, 3, 10, 29, 63, 69, 103, 152

J
Jaspers, 8, 53, 104, 112, 164
Jung, 103

K
Kierkegaard, 8, 38, 53, 62–63, 69, 73, 92, 109, 128–129, 164

L
Language, iv, 3, 5, 27, 45, 48–50, 56, 64, 83, 109, 119, 128, 162, 174, 177, 181–183
Life, i, iii–v, 1–19, 21–24, 26–45, 47–60, 62, 65, 68, 72–104, 106, 108–110, 112–135, 137–147, 149, 152–165, 167–172, 175–

176, 178–188, 190–191, 193–196
Living process, 12, 23, 27–29, 33, 39, 69, 73, 81–82, 87–90, 94, 97–98, 110, 112, 124, 136, 145, 160, 163, 172, 177, 180
Loneliness, 6, 10, 15–16, 18–19, 53, 57, 60, 62–65, 72–73, 101, 103, 107, 114, 147

M
Macro-dimension, 12–16, 21, 32–33, 50, 52, 58, 70, 74, 84, 90–91, 97, 103, 106, 108, 114, 120, 134, 141–142, 144, 147, 171–172, 181, 188, 195
May, ii–iii, v, 2, 13–15, 19, 24–26, 31–32, 37–39, 51–52, 54, 60, 63–64, 66, 70, 74, 77–78, 84, 97–98, 110, 115, 125, 128, 140, 146, 148, 156, 181, 196
Meaning
  Loss of meaning, i, 6, 8, 13, 45–46, 50, 107–108, 110
Meaninglessness, 10, 19, 32, 42–46, 51–53, 55, 92, 102, 108, 137, 142, 144–145, 154, 157–164, 172, 185
Meso-dimension, 11–13, 15, 29–30, 50–51, 57, 73, 84–85, 89–91, 101, 106–108, 114–115, 139, 143–144, 146, 151, 164
Micro-dimension, 10–12, 28–30, 32–33, 46, 48, 50, 52, 56–57, 71–73, 82–85, 90, 97, 108, 115, 141–142, 146, 164
Mortality, i, 1–2, 9–10, 16, 24–25, 27–28, 184, 196
Moustakas, 62–63, 158

N
Non-being, i, 4, 10, 22, 27, 31–32, 52–53, 78, 87, 102, 164, 179
Not-knowing, 22, 26, 54, 138, 140, 157

O
Ontic, 9–11, 17, 27, 29–30, 38–39, 44–46, 49, 61, 104–105, 144–145, 147, 155–156
Ontological
Ontological insecurity, iv, 106–109, 113, 117

P
Posttraumatic growth, ii, 14, 16–17, 44, 89, 96, 121, 129–130, 181, 187
Powerlessness, 15–16, 78, 163, 188
Presence, 14–15, 68–70, 72, 83, 85, 105, 112, 125–127, 131–132, 177, 193
Process
  Growth 3, 17, 26, 118-119, 172, 178, 183, 196
  Life/Living 11-12, 20-21, 23, 26-29, 33, 37-38 40, 54, 66, 69, 72-73, 81-82, 87-90, 94. 97-98, 105, 110, 112, 145, 172, 177
  Meaning-making *see process, therapeutic*
  Therapeutic iv-v, 36, 43, 45, 47-49 57, 70, 74, 78-79, 81, 112-113, 115, 118-119, 122, 123-169, 173-180, 187-192, 194-195

R
Rank, i–iv, 10–11, 13, 17, 33, 37–38, 52, 59–62, 66–70, 74, 82, 152, 176–177, 189, 192
Resilience, 14, 34, 120
Right to exist, iv, 4, 40–41, 57, 89, 95, 106, 113–114, 116–117, 119, 151–152, 165, 167, 184, 186
Rogers, i, iii, 2, 11–13, 17, 21, 28, 34, 36, 39–40, 43, 51, 66–68, 70, 77–78, 82–84, 97–99, 114, 119–121, 123–125, 146–147, 151,

155–156, 176–177, 195

S
Sartre, 9, 22, 53–54, 75–76, 89, 92
Schneider, iii–iv, 1, 11, 13, 15, 20, 33, 35, 38, 50, 66, 77, 81, 86, 93, 97, 103, 120
Self
  Self-healing capacity, 36–37, 164
  Self-transcendence, 173
Shattering
Space
  Existential space, iv, 6, 15, 19, 21–22, 43, 138, 154–157, 169, 182–183
Spiritual, 6, 13, 34–35, 61, 66, 93, 96, 104, 143–145, 152–153, 181–182
Spirituality, 17, 31, 120–121, 129, 147, 161, 182
Structure-bound, 50, 54, 98, 104, 106, 133, 137, 141, 145, 151, 161, 165, 171, 175
Symbolization
  Symbolizing, 49, 163, 180

T
Taft, iii, 27, 38, 66, 96, 103, 110, 119, 123, 137
Therapeutic relationship, 10, 59, 67–71, 74, 82, 111–112, 115, 124–126, 135–137, 145–152
Tillich, i, 4, 8–9, 13, 22, 27, 32, 45, 53, 102, 129, 164, 178, 187
Transcendent, 13, 38, 52, 120, 173, 176–177, 188
Transdiagnostic, 102–103
Trauma, ii, 41, 60–61, 96, 111, 115

V
Values, 12, 31, 51–52, 55, 89, 91–92, 122
Van Deurzen, 13, 76, 96

W
Well-being
  Existential well-being, ii, 194
Wisdom, 19, 34, 65, 78, 91–92, 96, 100, 102, 121, 140, 149, 180

Y
Yalom, iv, 9–10, 22–24, 26–27, 31, 43, 53–54, 63, 75, 106

Author Bio

Siebrecht Vanhooren (PhD) is a professor of clinical psychology at the University of Leuven (KU Leuven) in Belgium. He is a licensed clinical psychologist, psychotherapist, and supervisor. Siebrecht teaches counseling skills, psychological interventions, and humanistic, person-centered, experiential, focusing, and existential psychotherapies at the undergraduate, graduate, and postgraduate level at KU Leuven. He is the program director of the psychotherapy programs at the Faculty of Psychology and Educational Sciences, as well as the academic director of the Person-Centered Psychotherapy training programs, the Existential Well-being Counseling program, and the online MOOC Existential Well-Being Counseling program at KU Leuven.

He is a senior staff member of the Faculty of Psychology and Educational Sciences and the Research Group Clinical Psychology, co-director of the Meaning & Existence Research Center, and the Center for Experiential–Existential Psychotherapy at KU Leuven. He is a committee member of The Eugene T. Gendlin Center for Research in Experiential Philosophy and Psychology at The Focusing Institute (New York). His research includes existential concerns, meaning in life, posttraumatic growth, focusing, dreamwork, experiential–existential psychotherapy, and existential empathy.

Siebrecht also works as a person-centered experiential–existential psychotherapist, supervisor, and dream-work facilitator at PraxisP (KU Leuven). Last but not least, he loves spending time with his family and friends, hiking in nature, gardening, stargazing, playing music, and volunteering in his local Jewish community.

Websites

Personal website: https://www.siebrechtvanhooren.com

Personal website at KU Leuven:
https://www.kuleuven.be/wieiswie/en/person/00096809

Meaning and Existence Research: https://ppw.kuleuven.be/meaning-and-existence/eng

Center for Experiential–Existential Psychotherapy—training and research: https://ppw.kuleuven.be/eep/center-for-experiential-existential-psychotherapy

MOOC Existential Well-Being: https://www.edx.org/learn/health-wellness/ku-leuven-existential-well-being-counseling-a-person-centered-experiential-approach

ResearchGate: https://www.researchgate.net/profile/Siebrecht-Vanhooren

LinkedIn: https://www.linkedin.com/in/siebrecht-vanhooren-ph-d-b56bb114/

www.ingramcontent.com/pod-product-compliance
Lightning Source LLC
LaVergne TN
LVHW010651110826
845149LV00014B/3039
* 9 7 8 1 9 5 5 7 3 7 7 2 2 *